P9-BYJ-821

Theatre in crisis?

MANCHESTER
UNIVERSITY PRESS

theory•practice
•performance•

series editors
MARIA M. DELGADO
PETER LICHTENFELS

advisory board
MICHAEL BILLINGTON
SANDRA HEBRON
MARK RAVENHILL
JANELLE REINELT
PETER SELLARS

The series will offer a space for those people who practise theatre to have a dialogue with those who think and write about it.

The series has a flexible format that refocuses the analysis and documentation of performance. It provides, presents, and represents material which is written by those who make or create performance history, and offers access to theatre documents, different methodologies and approaches to the art of making theatre.

The books in the series are aimed at students, scholars, practitioners, and theatre-visiting readers. They encourage reassessments of periods, companies, and figures in twentieth-century and twenty-first-century theatre history, and provoke and take up discussions of cultural strategies and legacies that recognize the heterogeneity of performance studies.

The series editors, with the advisory board, aim to publish innovative, challenging and exploratory texts from practitioners, theorists and critics.

Theatre in crisis?

Performance manifestos
for a new century

edited by **MARIA M. DELGADO**
and **CARIDAD SVICH**

Manchester
University Press
Manchester and New York

distributed exclusively in the USA by Palgrave

Copyright © Manchester University Press 2002

While copyright in the volume as a whole is vested in Manchester University Press,
copyright in individual chapters belongs to their respective authors, and no chapter
may be reproduced wholly or in part without the express permission in writing of
both author and publisher.

Published by Manchester University Press
Oxford Road, Manchester M13 9NR, UK
and Room 400, 175 Fifth Avenue, New York, NY 10010, USA
www.manchesteruniversitypress.co.uk

Distributed exclusively in the USA by
Palgrave, 175 Fifth Avenue, New York, NY 10010, USA

Distributed exclusively in Canada by
UBC Press, University of British Columbia, 2029 West Mall, Vancouver, BC,
Canada V6T 1Z2

British Library Cataloguing-in-Publication Data
A catalogue record for this book is available from the British Library

Library of Congress Cataloging-in-Publication Data applied for

ISBN 0 7190 6290 X *hardback*
     0 7190 6291 8 *paperback*

First published in 2002

10 09 08 07 06 05 04 03 02   10 9 8 7 6 5 4 3 2 1

Typeset by Northern Phototypesetting Co. Ltd, Bolton
Printed in Great Britain
by Bell & Bain Ltd, Glasgow

This is for all those who have yet to enter into the active struggle of a life in the theatre, and for those who have found hope in that struggle over the years, and remain confident of its future

CONTENTS

ILLUSTRATIONS

ACKNOWLEDGEMENTS

We have been aided in the compilation of this volume by the intellectual generosity of all the contributors. Gregor Turbyne, technical director in the School of English and Drama at Queen Mary, University of London, was an invaluable associate in assisting with the opening and printing of transatlantic e-mails. Our thanks are also due to our colleagues in the School of English and Drama, New Dramatists, Joel Anderson, Carles Cano, Olga Celda, David Bradby, and Maribel San Gines. We also extend our gratitude to colleagues who expressed a strong interest in contributing to this volume, but for various reasons could not do so. Their kind words and thoughts are appreciated: Wendy Belden, Albert Boadella, Migdalia Cruz, Mitchell Gossett, David Greig, Frédéric Maurin, Jason Neulander, Juan Carlos Pérez de la Fuente, Mark Ravenhill, Dan Rebellato, Brad Rothbart, Richard Schoch, Octavio Solis, Merce Saumell, Colin Teevan, and Michele Volansky. Many thanks also to the wide range of artists – Paul Bernstein, Sharon Bridgforth, Paula Cizmar, Rickerby Hinds, Leon Martell, Cherríe Moraga, and Diana Raznovich – who took of their time and energy to share their eloquent thoughts on crisis and the state of theatre with us. For a number of reasons, their voices could not be accommodated in this volume, but their contribution remains invaluable to us. We have benefited from the wisdom of Lesley Ferris and Janelle Reinelt, whose astute comments on the manuscript have helped shape it into its current form. Matthew Frost has been an invaluable guide and friend to the volume and we thank him for his guidance and support. Special thanks to Emilio and Aracely Svich for their extraordinary patience and faith in the work, and to Henry Little, who has lived with this book for the past year and a half. His insightful comments mark its final form in ways that transcend our debt of gratitude to him. With a warm embrace of thanks to artist Frederic Amat for his generous spirit and exalting vision.

Theatre in crisis? Performance manifestos for a new century: snapshots of a time

Maria M. Delgado and Caridad Svich

Maria M. Delgado is Reader in Drama and Theatre Arts at Queen Mary, University of London. She is editor of *Valle-Inclán Plays: One* (Methuen, 1993 & 1997), the special edition of *Contemporary Theatre Review* entitled 'Spanish Theatre 1920–95: Strategies in Protest and Imagination'; co-editor of *In Contact with the Gods? Directors Talk Theatre* (Manchester University Press, 1996), *Conducting a Life: Reflections on the Theatre of Maria Irene Fornes* (with Caridad Svich) (Smith & Kraus, 1999) and *The Paris Jigsaw: Internationalism and the City's Stages* (Manchester University Press, 2002). She is the author of numerous articles on contemporary theatre practice and a translator of dramatists including Susana Torres Molina, Mario Benedetti, and Bernard-Marie Koltès. A Fellow of the Royal Society of Arts, she is currently working on a study of twentieth-century Spanish theatre for Manchester University Press.

Caridad Svich is a playwright-songwriter-translator. Credits include her play *Alchemy of Desire/Dead-Man's Blues* at Cincinnati Playhouse in the Park (winner of the Rosenthal New Play Prize), and *Any Place But Here* at Theater for the New City/NY under Maria Irene Fornes' direction. Recent work: *Fugitive Pieces* (a play with songs) at Salvage Vanguard Theatre/TX, and *Iphigenia Crash Land Falls on the Neon Shell That Was Once Her Heart* (a rave fable) work-shopped by Actors Touring Company/UK at the Euripides Festival in Monodendri, Greece under Nick Philippou's direction. Her work has also been seen at theatres in Britain, Belgium and Canada. She has taught playwriting at the Yale School of Drama and Ohio State University. She is co-editor of *Out of the Fringe: Contemporary Latina/o Theatre and Performance* (Theatre Communications Group, 2000), and her translations are collected in *Federico García Lorca: Impossible Theatre* (Smith & Kraus, 2000). *The Booth Variations*, a multimedia collaboration with director Nick Philippou and actor Todd Cerveris is currently in development. She is a member of New Dramatists in New York.

When my crisis was over (and they do end: and a crisis can't go on being a crisis), I saw it was intrinsic and structural. (Martin Amis, *Experience*, London: Jonathan Cape, 2000, p. 63)

Performance as an artistic 'genre' is in a constant state of crisis, and is there-fore an ideal medium for articulating a time of permanent crisis such as ours. (Guillermo Gómez-Peña, *Dangerous Border Crossers*, London: Rout-ledge, 2000, p. 9)

For the future is the stage, that grand canopy that drapes and folds our most unspeakable desires, the stage that promises to dramatize our pasts, to enact them in such a way that we might begin to understand them, to touch them, to know them, to become intimate with them. Those pasts that we have not encountered we label 'ends' so that we might one day reach them. For we know that there is no future that remains untouched by the whispering pass of our many pasts. (Peggy Phelan, 'Introduction: The Ends of Performance', in *The Ends of Performance*, eds. Peggy Phelan and Jill Lane, London & New York: New York University Press, 1998, p. 6)

Is it possible to document a dialogue among artists and scholars, both emerging and established, about the role of theatre in our ever-changing world when it is, of necessity, a dialogue in constant mutation and evolu-tion?

At the end of 1999, we approached a series of artists, academics and critics in the hope of providing some documentation of debates currently raging in contemporary theatre practice around the relationship between theatre, plays and performance, the places where performance is taking place and the kind of issues being played out in the performance arena. A hundred years ago, it seemed to us that the onset of a new century brought with it a series of *fin de siècle* reflections on the role of theatre in troubled times. With the emergence of the figure of the director in the second half of the nineteenth century and the replacement of the picto-rial stage with the facsimile stage, playwrights began to provide oral and written 'manifestos' as to how their work *should* be staged. Strindberg's preface to *Miss Julie* (1888), Ibsen's 'The Task of the Poet' (1874) and Zola's 'Naturalism on the Stage' (1881) all sought to present visions of what a relevant theatre could be and how theatre might participate in the debates of the age.[1] Later André Antoine and Otto Brahm too provided written commentaries on their craft and on the role they envisaged for theatre enveloped in the onslaught of naturalism. Later, in Russia both Konstantin Stanislavsky and Vsevelod Meyerhold were to juggle their careers as directors with the production of a series of written documents which not only justify their own approach to *mise-en-scène* but also pro-

---

1 A collection of writings/lectures on theatre by playwrights are published in Toby Cole, ed., *Playwrights on Playwriting* (New York: Hill and Wang, 1961). For the views of directors see Toby Cole and Helen Krich Chinoy, eds., *Directors on Directing: A Source Book of the Modern Theater* (New York: Macmillan, 1976).

vide polemical opinions on what a 'realist' theatre might be and how the-atre might escape the shackles of literature. Those who have come in their wake, Bertolt Brecht, Antonin Artaud, Jacques Copeau, Erwin Piscator, Jerzy Grotowski and Peter Brook have similarly provided engagements with the theatre of the present to envisage a theatre for the future. More recently, 7.84 director John McGrath's *A Good Night Out*, first published in 1981, and *The Bone Won't Break*, first published in 1990, reworked lec-tures given at the University of Cambridge as an interrogation of popular genuinely working-class forms of theatre, articulating ideas around what a counter-theatre might be and how it might successfully function.

Our admiration of such writings, as well as the bold statements offered in the past couple of years by Forced Entertainment's Tim Etchells and Goat Island's Matthew Goulish, led us to wonder about how current developments in contemporary theatre practice were being debated and documented.[2] Issues of *The Drama Review* published in 1975 and 1983 offered a panoramic view of new experiments in theatre practice by pub-lishing a series of manifestos which presented a 'public declaration of motives and intentions',[3] relating both theory and practice to the cutting edge of developments in avant-garde performance. As such, in the December 1975 issue, essays by Theodore Shank, Arnold Aronson, Kate Davy, and Eugenio Barba, among others, on new performance were jux-taposed alongside contemporary manifestos by Charles Ludham, Richard Foreman, Michael Kirby and Shuji Terayama and historical manifestos which chronicled the influence of Italian futurism in Russia, Eccentrism, and Radlov's theatre of popular comedy. The 100th issue of *The Drama Review* published eight years later sought to revisit the territory but this time asked solely theatre practitioners (as opposed to critics and writers) to provide an indication of their 'dreams, proposals and manifestos for the future'.[4] These included director Anne Bogart whose oppositional body of work within the realist-dominated paradigms of North Ameri-can theatre has provided such a potent example to practitioners emerg-ing in the past ten years, writer-director Daryl Chin, the performance artist Stuart Sherman, and the writer-director Matthew Maguire, then with Creation Production Company. Our remit for this volume involved both asking practitioners who had contributed to that volume, like

---

2 See Tim Etchells, *Certain Fragments: Texts and Writings on Performance* (London and New York: Routledge, 1999) and Matthew Goulish, *39 Microlectures: In Proximity of Performance* (London and New York: Routledge, 2000).

3 Michael Kirby, 'New Performance and Manifestos: An Introduction', *The Drama Review*, 19, No. 4 (December 1975), p. 3.

4 Michael Kirby, 'Dreams, Proposals, Manifestos: An Introduction', *The Drama Review*, 27, No. 4 (Winter 1983), p. 2.

Maguire, to provide manifestos for the future of theatre fifteen years on and engaging with a younger generation of scholar-artists who were currently forging 'alternative' paths within the North American and European performance landscape. As such we hope that this volume offers the opinion of a cross-section of different generations of critics, practitioners and academics who all contemplate the *doing* of performance in interdisciplinary times.

Our own observations of working practices across Europe and North America shaped by the renegotiation of relationships between the commercial and subsidized sector and mainstream and fringe have thrown up key questions around the production and reception of that which has been traditionally understood to be theatre. As the parameters of theatre practice expand into the realms of that which is now known as performance studies we have sought to assemble a collection of fragments, essays, letters and reflections from differing generations of practitioners which comment on the past, present and future of the discipline in which we work and teach.

As artists are forced to respond to the funding limitations which beset contemporary culture, numerous contributors probe the ways in which this is affecting artistic production. The economy is certainly driving new modes of collaboration and creation as witnessed by the work of Lisa D'Amour and Goat Island in the US and Frantic Assembly and Blast Theory in Britain. Alongside the forging of such methodologies comes a performative culture of confessional minimalism which has spilled out from the alternative performance spaces of Greenwich Village and the London Fringe and which, in mutated form, now stalks the outer recesses of prime time television with alarming frequency.

D'Amour writes of 'scavenging' from the resources and creative support offered by 'generous colleagues and organizations' (p. 162) in defining her working process but, as Matthew Maguire and Erik Ehn make clear, the forging of practices based on necessity rather than the display of an opulent budget is producing work with direct links to the communities in which it is being presented. Both Tori Haring-Smith and Alice Tuan single out the work of Cornerstone Theatre in catering for local audiences (pp. 102 and 119). Critic Michael Billington bemoans the dominance of consumerism and celebrity within a mainstream theatre culture where production costs must be clearly displayed for the paying public. In an age of musical spectacles and Disney-generated products like *The Lion King* and *Aida*, should theatre attempt to visually match such productions or should it reject such imitative strategies in favour of more contemplative works which challenge the consumerist impulse of a populace which Roberta Levitow describes as 'obsessed with an insatiable hunger for immediate experiences and acquisitions' (p. 28). Producer Ricardo Szwarcer questions the future of opera, which has become so dependent, in the public's eye, on lavish spectacle and the re-creation of a standard repertoire that its very existence as an art form is in peril. Have the Globe, the Royal Shakespeare Company, and the West End and Broadway turned theatre into what Tori Haring-Smith describes as 'tourist sites' (p. 98)? Have the politics of representation created an unforeseen burden on artists engaging with the society in which they live and work?

Contributors who are all working in the veritable trenches of the theatre of identity politics, which has come to mean, especially in the US, the theatre of African-Americans, Asian-Americans, and Latina/os, offer their passionate views on the difficult place in which they find themselves. Kia Corthron, who works in both the US and the UK, discusses the multivalent textures of African-American theatre and what it is, and can be. The constant debate between the spiritual and the practical, identifying the work as being of 'colour' and not, and the pull between doubt and courage that energizes the vision and the work, are all felt deeply in her piece. Alice Tuan seeks to define what is for her the Asian-American lens, and finds herself caught in its reflecting gaze, as she negotiates her hypertext sensibility with expectations aimed at her both from within and outside her 'culture' which, she is quick to recognize, goes beyond the Asian-American village in which she is often placed because of her name, or her features. Jorge Ignacio Cortiñas in the section 'Some quick thoughts on the theatre and its future' looks to the past for strength and courage, and Oliver Mayer predicts that the best theatrical space is 'one that lets us be most ourselves' (p. 20). Marked by the politics of race and gender, these artists are not only fighting the established culture but their own as well. Caught often in the structures of identity set forth by society, dominant and otherwise, they are articulating their conflicts, negotiating doubt and passion as they try to make a bit of art that will speak to their particular cultures.

These manifestos, however, represent just a tiny fraction of the working practices currently redefining the theatre of North American identity politics. While Suzan-Lovi Parks galvanizes the Broadway stage with *Topdog/Underdog*, and John Leguizamo works across TV, film, and theatre, a new generation of upstarts in the multicultural wars are making their voices heard. Young performance troupes have emerged in the fertile and raucous world of comedy, rock 'n' roll and performance. The Slant Performance Group is a resident company of La Mama in New York City and has gained notice for its provocative and innovative brand of performance art that mocks sexual questions while holding up Asian men to the mirror of American pop culture. Peeling the Banana, also based in

New York, is a collective of writers, performers and directors exploring Asian-American identity, while Ma-Yi is a theatre company dedicated exclusively to the presentation of new Asian theatre voices. In San Francisco, The 18 Mighty Mountain Warriors have taken up where their mentors, the Latino comic theatre troupe Culture Clash, left off, and are forging a new, wild comic voice. Latino/a companies finding their way include CaraMia Theatre in Dallas, and the Latino Theatre Group based in Vancouver, and inspired by the venerable SpiderWoman, Native American voices are making themselves heard from North Carolina's Turtle Vision to Chicago's Red Path Native Theatre. Our groupings of these specific pieces within a larger section on theatre and identity serves to indicate the ways in which the identity of theatre has mutated through the economic, political and cultural circumstances of the past thirty years, and how these changes in circumstance have both offered opportunities to new voices and challenged those same voices to question their position within their respective communities and the world at large.

The construction of self becomes a recurring motif as artists wrestle with crisis as an idea, firebrand and economic reality. Performer-scholar Anna Furse filters crisis through her body, pointing to a time of flux in the arts wherein the reconstruction of the self speaks to the body of the world. Certainly, Jim Carmody in his essay 'The comforts of crisis' situates the strange uplift which any moment of questioning produces in the art and its maker by affirming the inseparable link between crisis and historical time.

With theatre in a particularly precarious state as we find ourselves at the beginning of the twenty-first century, this volume is offered as a marker of a time, a snapshot, if you will, of what working artists and scholars were thinking about theatre's recent past, fractious present, and looming future. The word 'crisis' is used here both provocatively and seriously. It is, after all, an art created under duress, under economic circumstances both trying and not, and within the often combustible environment of a rehearsal hall. It is also an art that has seemed to reach yet another break point in its identity, mode of presentation, and structural efficacy, given the rise of more popular forms of entertainment and instruction like film, television, and the internet. Theatre artists and scholars dedicated to advancing theatrical discourse have been placed in a position of having to struggle for not only the continuing growth and effectiveness of the form, but also its very importance in a society that has made theatre, especially the kind of theatre made by experimental artists, an increasingly elitist form.

This climate has created a crisis of practice. In other words, art which uses the condition of crisis as its essential trope. Not merely rebellious, this is art that contains its struggle within the making and its articulation. It is art that reflects the crises of the past and tries to make active sense of the present. Often created in reaction against the sentimentality of bour-geois art, this work belongs to a well-established tradition of opposition that is part of the theatre's history. The only difference here may be that there are fewer forums for oppositional voices to be heard in a global economy that is eradicating difference in favour of a McSociety built in the celebration of the common dollar – a point made with eloquence by Erik Ehn in his essay 'Bad glamour'.

Indeed the role of oppositional performance within the current cli-mate of rampant consumerism, which sees theatres as business enter-prises funded less and less by government agencies and increasingly by private sponsors, is touched on by a number of contributors. Matthew Maguire debates the ethics of such deals while Max Stafford-Clark prag-matically posits that economics 'affects everything' (p. 85); cuts in fund-ing have radically affected the types of plays being written, as the epic play has largely been abandoned in favour of small cast texts which present fewer challenges on dwindling company budgets. Michael Billington, John London, Peter Lichtenfels and Lynette Hunter all address how this crisis has been played out in British playwriting, offering discordant views on the new generation of English playwrights whose work is seen more and more on North American and Western European stages. Phyllis Nagy bemoans the celebration of a playwriting of 'artful reportage from the front lines' which 'lacks intellectual rigour or curiosity' (p. 77). She argues passionately for the need to gamble and 'to court loss as a necessary com-ponent to winning big' (p. 82).

The relationship between process and product is also a feature of the pieces contributed by DD Kugler, Len Berkman and Goat Island, all of whom present examples of the ways in which process often manifests itself as product. The necessary role of the audience and its re-education, which has become the target for new funding and research in today's theatre, is at the core of much of their discussions, even as they differ as to how the artists should work, train and relate to the imagined audience. Len Berkman examines the notion of 'live-ness' in relationship to the development circuit which has been created for new plays, and finds all sorts of corpses waiting to be rediscovered. In fact, he is heartened where other artists bemoan the development mill as one of the chief factors in the paucity of risk-taking by producers trained to fly safely but with a firm net. DD Kugler's mischievous and passionate plea for education links to Goat Island's practical yet visionary 'letter', as it were, to practi-tioners who must start anew and toss the burden of the past's cynicism aside in order to make work: a notion that will echo and re-echo through this volume, as we point to the unknown, knowing full well that is where all work for the theatre begins in one way or another, and where it points to inevitably.

In this unknown sphere, technology plays a part in the way in which we can think about the creation of new languages for plays, texts, and spectacles that do not follow the lines comfortably within our reach. Mixed media has had an erratic time of it in the US, especially, although some of its most daring practitioners are from the US: Robert Wilson, Laurie Anderson, John Jesurun, The Wooster Group, and Mabou Mines. When the avant-garde experiments with media were appropriated by the commercial theatre, a prime example of this being Des McAnuff's staging of the rock opera *The Who's Tommy*, a significant shift occurred in the manner in which the investigations played themselves out in the established fringe. For a time, use of media elements was disdained and mistrusted by artists perhaps cautious of having their experiments codified too quickly by mainstream culture. Slowly, however, two opposite yet compatible strains of media exploration began to rise again. One was the re-exploration of old media forms to adapt them as a new linguistic or imagistic tool in the theatre. Here we can point to the use of tape, phonographs, daguerreotypes, and other 'lo-fi' artefacts. The other was an explosive interest in opera and music-theatre, which necessitated a 'hi-fi' ingredient in its directly energetic link to club culture, and forums for music fusion like The Knitting Factory in New York, where jazz klezmer, torch-punk music, and other experiments in sound and motion have affected the theatre scene.

The fusion of artistic disciplines which exposes the inadequacy of existing labels and artistic practices in which theatre, dance, and the visual arts appropriate each other's languages has called into question the very nature of performance, fuelling changes in theatrical composition which have in some cases reworked the playwright's role into that of another company collaborator. Authorship has become a contested concept as writers are displaced as a central theatrical force – a point ironically observed by Martin Epstein in 'Poor Tom's A-cold: reflections on the modern theatre in crisis'. Authorship has widened out as the established boundaries between writer, director, performers and designer have broken down, calling for new vocabularies of criticism and engagement.

On 5 January 2000, one of the *Guardian*'s theatre critics, Lyn Gardner, asked whether the Renaissance in British playwriting – commented on by Stafford-Clark and Michael Billington in their contributions to this volume – seen in the 1994/5 Royal Court Theatre season in London, which produced Mark Ravenhill's *Shopping and F***ing*, Sarah Kane's *Blasted* and works by Joe Penhall and Nick Grosso, was at an end.

The success of companies such as Frantic Assembly, Théâtre de Complicité, Forced Entertainment and Improbable Theatre point to the pleasures
experienced by audiences who are challenging critical and commercial
markers in their desire for rawer, more physically challenging performative forms. Tori Haring-Smith writes of the need to celebrate the 'non-
predictability' of theatre (p. 101), listing companies that question
predictable forms in their reinvention of performative languages, and
plunging audiences into the thrill of the unknown. Claire MacDonald
charts the evolution of such performative forms outside the play, addressing the formation of critical discussions around the very liveness of
experiments grounded in the counter-culture of the times.

While geographical centres like New York and London have provided
the landscape for a number of the most exciting trends in oppositional
theatre practice, over the past twenty years increasingly, these geographical sites can no longer be regarded as the exclusive terrain of counter-
culture. The Sheffield-based Forced Entertainment, Austin's Rude
Mechanicals, Seattle's House of Dames, and Swansea's Frantic Assembly
have all built up their reputations on the currency of hard work and innovation, not on the ready limelight of the city as power site. Working off
centre has allowed these companies to flourish and find idiosyncratic
voices to speak to both the margins of culture and the mainstream. Rude
Mechanicals' rough and appropriately brash theatrical take on Greil
Marcus' *Lipstick Traces*, for example, began as an experiment for their
Austin community and has now been seen in a successful run in New
York. An artist like Anne Bogart has been a strong inspiration for many
younger companies working outside press-heavy centres. SITI Company
has become a model not only of a way to work but of actor training, sound
design, and brave entrepreneurial savvy in a climate dominated primarily
by the regional theatre structure. Oppositional voices have now also per-
meated the very structures of academe, where their practices inform the
nurturing of future generations of artists. Anna Furse's own progress
from writer-performer to writer-teacher-performer is chronicled in
'Those who can do, teach' but the presence of Shelley Berc, Ruth Margraff,
Claire MacDonald, Matthew Maguire, Martin Epstein, Matthew Causey,
Mac Wellman, Len Berkman, DD Kugler and Andy Lavender is testament
both to the prising apart of the scholar–artist binarism and to Furse's
observation that whilst subsidy for the arts might have drastically shrunk
over the past thirty years, 'scholarly interest in performance in its widest
sense has grown and opportunities for study and training at tertiary level
along with it' (p. 65). The documentation of the tensions prevalent in such
geographical environments points to a practical exploration of issues
which look to occupy a ever more conspicuous role in contemporary per-

formance studies. How to 'classify' and discuss the work of writers, then, who work on the boundaries without necessarily aligning themselves with either theatre or performance as their primary playing field?

It is not insignificant that a number of contributors posit their own manifestos for alternative or oppositional practices. Shelley Berc's 'Theatre of the mind', Ruth Margraff's 'An evangelical capitalist', Erik Ehn's 'Bad glamour' and Goat Island's 'Letter to a young practitioner' all offer practical solutions to the challenges faced by working artists in the contemporary North American performance landscape.

The *why* of performance determines many of the contributions in this anthology. Claire MacDonald reflects on the purpose of performance while Goat Island posit that they 'perform to remember' and 'memorize to perform' (p. 245) – a concept articulated in different forms by both John London and Dragan Klaic. Tori Haring-Smith, Andy Lavender, Paul Heritage and Michael Billington all comment, in different ways, on the 'liveness' that distinguishes theatre from other artistic forms – although each articulates a differing understanding of what constitutes the act of 'liveness'. Lisa D'Amour argues for 'the unique immediacy of live performance' (p. 163) as its discerning mark and yet draws a distinction between productions like that of The Wooster Group, Dah, and the Japanese No master Akira Matsui and a mainstream theatrical culture that takes that immediacy for granted. A self-conscious articulation of the processes of theatre is present in both Ruth Margraff and Mac Wellman's dissection of a particular brand of realism's stranglehold on American theatre.

Wellman's landmark interrogation of the ideological currents of the well-made play, first published in 1985 in *Performing Arts Journal* (*PAJ*), is still alarmingly resonant. As such, we reprint it with the author's permission, in the hope that its observation that 'what is shown annihilates the showing' (p. 229) will register with further generations of theatre makers working against the dominance of method acting and theatrical forms which appear increasingly redundant. Contributors such as Erik Ehn, Ruth Margraff, Jorge Ignacio Cortiñas, and Lisa D'Amour have all personally expressed the debt they feel they owe to Wellman as a master iconoclast and dramatist of the US stage, and in particular to this essay as being one of the first to ignite their passions to make theatre that challenged ingrained perceptions based on decades of Freudian-constructed dramaturgy. Lynette Hunter and Peter Lichtenfels as well as John London point to the overwhelming reliance of British theatre practice on pseudo-realist forms, a debate which continues across the Atlantic.

While the actor–spectator axis may be posited as constituting the very essence of theatre, the mediation of that role presented by technological interventions presents an increasingly complex understanding of the processes of simulation and fundamentally questions the very 'liveness' or ephemerality which cannot be preserved and which is performance's discerning quality. Digital technologies have far-reaching implications in the making and marketing of theatre. From Patrick Marber's *Closer*, Craig Lucas' *The Dying Gaul*, and Arthur Kopit's *Y2K* to the interactive technology of Els Joglars' *DAAALÍ* and Robert Wilson's *Monsters of Grace*, electronic paradigms are becoming both stage subject and stage object. While Roberta Levitow seeks theatre makers who are 'practitioners of an ancient artisan's craft, anachronistic in a world of mass production and advanced technology' (p. 26), Andy Lavender and Matthew Causey advocate a response to mediatized culture which engages with the technologies that have generated such a culture. Theatre needs to represent the changes being played out in the larger technological worlds. A balance will be determined as texts reconfigure themselves within and around the technological axis, not unlike the manner in which the Futurists reconfigured a theatrical ideology to suit their times. As the growth of internet e-commerce renders it increasingly possible to buy a designated seat from the comfort of the home, we are faced with a theatrical culture in which audiences are being given ever-increasing choices on one level while the range of material contained within the mainstream seems ever more narrow. Technological advancements might perhaps herald a curtailment of the swelling of theatrical managements which have accompanied the production of less and less work. One way this is evident is the forays into online text creation which have eliminated to some degree the dependence on the producer or marketing person to 'sell the show'. While online productions, which vary from silent production to 'live' theatrical broadcasts and encounters are definitely an alternative model to production, the ready access to virtual production frees artists from some of the strangleholds of the mainstream, and stresses the playful, free-flowing nature of art.

Live and spirited, these voices signal through many flames towards a theatre that positions itself off the map, a theatre which responds to the immediate crisis of war, or that seeks its future in the investigation of technology and the demarcations of space. This is a geopolitical theatre that is off the map because it is so rarely discussed on the front pages of our daily newspapers or our populist theatre journals. Off the map, artists like Dragan Klaic and Lluís Pasqual speak to the remembered selves of their culture with forthrightness, compassion and humour, and thus link to the voices struggling within the boundaries of identity and those living with crisis as a signpost for the making of their work.

Living on trade, this theatre seeks life beyond the stranglehold of economics to liberate its passions for a new and hungry audience that will never tire of seeing human tales enacted on a stage, whether they be partly on video, digital film, or a sound machine.

Perhaps as interesting as what has been addressed are the issues which have lain at the peripheries of the discussions presented here. The role of the classics – revived with alarming regularity and exported across the international festival circuit – is mentioned only briefly by Jon Fosse, Peter Lichtenfels and Lynette Hunter. The commonplace laments of writers and critics that we are now invited to the theatre to watch Peter Sellars' *The Merchant of Venice* or Ivo Van Hove's *A Streetcar Named Desire* – the prefix acknowledging the artistic dialogue that characterized the modern western stage throughout the twentieth century – suggests dissension as to the continued ascendancy of the *metteur en scène*. It is a commonly held view that there are few directors – Max Stafford-Clark is here a prominent exception – who have successfully dedicated their career to working largely with contemporary playwrights, and even fewer who have succeeded internationally as a result. The classic text has become and continues to function as a key component of the dialogue as well as the market of theatre across nations, a fact made eloquent by Paul Heritage in his piece 'Stealing kisses', wherein he relates his exploration of Shakespeare's *Romeo and Juliet* with young inmates of a Brazilian prison. In Heritage's case, working with a classic was a way to test the boundaries of language, and cross borders, societal and educational. The actors – the inmates – were asked to inhabit Shakespeare's text and, as such, revelations were made as layers upon layers were brought forth and made fresh for both actors and an audience which functioned as active witnesses to a staging where twelve Romeos met one Juliet and a classic's very 'liveness' in a media-saturated culture was tested.

Part of the fascination with reworking classic texts has to do with how a contemporary writer will bring their voice to bear on an age-old story, which may or may not be familiar to an audience. Education, thus, also plays a part in the reworking model. Mark Ravenhill's *Faust Is Dead*, Jose Rivera's adaptation of Calderón de la Barca's *Life is a Dream* entitled *Sueño*, Chuck Mee's adaptation of Sophocles' *The Suppliant Women* entitled *Big Love*, Naomi Iizuka's adaptation of Büchner's *Woyzeck* entitled *Skin*, and Caridad Svich's rave-set *Iphigenia Crash Land Falls on the Neon Shell That Was Once Her Heart* all signal the reclaiming of a long-held tradition in theatre of reworking stories, reconfabulating them, and reconfiguring them for a new generation. The shift from directors reworking the classics to playwrights is significant in that it places the emphasis on the text rather than the image. The texts in these new plays made up of the old, speaking across centuries, are in a sense new images woven in words and imagined pictures. They are performances that take place both in the spectator's memory of the 'original', and in the space created by the writer who chooses to recontextualize the story in full or adopt a kernel of it for a meditation on where we are now or where we are going.

In fact, performance has moved away increasingly from the theatrical box to streets, churches, train stations, abandoned buildings, and other spaces which will break with the rectangular configuration of the cinema screen, providing new spatial locations for a text to breathe and for an audience to experience them. David Greig's *Candide 2000* played itself out in Glasgow's historic Tramway, Iizuka's *Skin* found a home in an aircraft hangar in Seattle when Printer's Devil Theatre staged the play. Companies are exploring outside or alternative spaces in an effort in part to find a sense of adventure that they feel has been lost by the comforts of the traditional theatre space. It is a sense of adventure they wish to offer an audience. It is also a way in which to explore a text or image's relationship to architecture, and that architecture's memory.

The nature of performance extends far and very wide as this volume seeks visions past, and through many memories, in the hope of articulating the passions and valiant spirits who awaken us to newly created territories. Catalan director Lluís Pasqual and others point us to the useful 'perils' of the word 'crisis' and its multifaceted conditions for being in the realm of making art. These thoughtful, rigorous, open-hearted essays leave us with questions about the necessity of theatre in the modern age, questions that enliven us to articulating possibilities for expression beyond this volume's borders. The volume's differing yet complementary statements of purpose are offered as a call and alarm to artists mired in the making of work, and those yet to find themselves struggling with issues of how their art can/does speak to their culture.

Embracing the complexities that are at the heart of the theatrical experience necessitates that we present aesthetic and political viewpoints which offer less comfortable or easily negotiable prescriptions for a new theatre. While we have intended throughout to foster our own belief in theatre's beauty and power, we have also included in this volume more despairing and negative visions, which speak to the cost of making art of the soul in a perceived soul-less climate. Such darker visions nevertheless illuminate essential problems and crises at the root of making a piece of art. The honesty of the contributors in expressing their stark sentiments is a testament to the passion which drives their engagement in and/or distance from the practice.

Jon Fosse's 'When an angel goes through the stage' offers a message of hope and grace and purity as we look at more utopian visions of theatre-making in our final section. The book is meant to be read as a journey from, through, within and out of crisis (a state which is constant and

is accentuated depending on the nature of the times). Ways of making art
and dealing with the economic pressures governing decisions as applied
to work are directly related in many instances to the struggle between
doubt and passion, which is linked to identity formation. Theatre and
performance which exist off the map reflect back on how crisis is mani-
fest in intimate and global ways through art. The categories in this book
are neither neat nor simple. Arguments made in one section spill over
into those made in another. When artists are reacting against categories,
it is natural that the categories in which one tries to examine their words
be unbound. Thus, this book can be read in a series of different ways. Kia
Corthron and Alice Tuan's essays, while grouped in a section on theatre
and identity, could also function in any number of sections in the book.
Rather than prescribed categories, these are the ideas thrown up to contributors when pieces for this volume were commissioned. One category
that many of the pieces, most especially perhaps those in the final section
('Looking forward, looking back: theatre and the spiritual, messages to a
new world') fall into is performative writing. In her landmark study,
Mourning Sex, New York University professor Peggy Phelan judges performative writing as

> different from personal criticism or autobiographical essay, although it owes
> a lot to both genres. Performative writing is an attempt to find a form for
> 'what philosophy wishes all the same to say.' Rather than describing the per-
> formance event 'in direct signification,' a task I believe to be impossible and
> not terrifically interesting, I want this writing to enact the affective force of
> the performance event again. ...[5]

Fusing both anecdote and critical analysis, the musings and meditations
on the boundaries between theory and practice, poetry and prose, provided by contributors like Epstein, Margraff, Ehn, and Berc rupture
established notions of creative, academic and intellectual work. They are
further indications of how the collapse of boundaries witnessed in theatrical practice over the past thirty years has now further reverberated in
the paradigms of critical writing.

This sense of rupture also affects our bibliography and the choices
made within it. It is by no means intended to be comprehensive, but rather
as a marker of works which have influenced us as editors, and have also
influenced our contributors in their writing and thinking about their
work. Novels sit next to critical studies next to volumes of poetry: we offer
the bibliography as a way of reading and touching on material that is
personally significant to us but also which we think allows for different
kinds of links to be created in the mind. This liberal spirit extends to our

---

5   Peggy Phelan, *Mourning Sex* (London: Routledge, 1997), pp. 11–12.

annotation in the volume. Although we have aimed for a degree of consistency, allowing the individual voices of the contributors has meant ensuring that we respect their ways of annotating sources. While some have wished to annotate in academic ways, others have requested a more informal way of acknowledging sources. We have made every effort to honour and respect the varied individual voices in this volume, voices which reflect differences in sensibility, aesthetic choices, and political ideology. The healthy nature of crisis has informed our decisions. It is in such a spirit that we wish for more constructive debate, honest turbulence and active dreaming about theatre to take place both inside and outside these pages.

Theatre in crisis? Living memory in an unstable time
Caridad Svich

My decision is a mask, behind which there is disorder, *apeiron*. To be honest, I had not decided to come here. Yet here I am. (Raul Ruiz, *Poetics of Cinema*, Paris: Disvoir, 1985, p. 23)

As one century turns and we find ourselves in the midst of another, thoughts turn to crisis. Advances in science, technology, population and belief systems have left us in a panic about where we will go next. If we are indeed going anywhere. The spectre of fascism, rises and our souls tremble at the thought of mistakes repeated, and civilizations lost. Everything is called into question. Doubt hangs in the air. Faith can no longer sustain us. If it ever did.

The once divinely ordained universe has been split many times over, and as citizens of the global village we have become inheritors of a new way of thinking about the essential nature of randomness in our lives. We turn to decadence for a while, and the amoral celebration of pleasure. It is a decadence steeped in nostalgia, infused with pain and the necessity to feel something, anything, at any cost, because feeling reminds us that we are in the present. The immediate touch, blow, pierce through the skin reminds us of our humanity. Decadence soothes and keeps sickness alive. A sensation is better than no sensation at all.

Spiritual malaise intersects with spiritual quest. Morality is our watchdog. We shield ourselves hoping that we will not be found out. Faith is an elusive concept, but we cling to it, because it gives our lives meaning. Evangelical entreaties give us hope in the next and next tomorrow. Even as we witness acts of 'ethnic cleansing', industrial warfare, the proliferation of hate crimes, and mass suicide.

The citizen who is an artist during an unstable time has the weight of responsibility on their shoulders, unless that citizen-artist decides to shrug off responsibility altogether. If the artist does not defend and advance sensibility in an age of violence and concern, then what is the role of the artist? Moreover, what is the artist's responsibility to memory?

Acts of performance are necessarily fleeting. Discussions about those acts are evanescent. This means that each act must carry with it the artist's full measure of experience, passion, pleasure, whimsy, and pain. The artist leaves an imprint, caught by the eye of the witness who is the audience. In the theatre, this witness becomes the living record of the performance, the messenger who will send word, thought, feeling to the next and next generation. Tomorrows are multiplied in the act of witnessing. And the performance exists in society's living memory.

If a society is ruled by violence and decay, the artist must defend with ferocity, with teeth, the preservation of our more compassionate nature. Kindness, generosity, tenderness, and beauty must be held up as reminders to an audience more than ready to let nihilism and its attendant seductive gestures hold sway. A flaccid, easy kindness, however, is not what stays in the mind, and, therefore, is recorded in memory. The responsible artist seeks to illuminate and remind the witness through a presentation of kindness stripped to its core. Tragedy must have its place.

The moral position of the artist is an embattled one in this age because the concept of morality has been disabused by sectors of society who seek only to cast judgment, and obtain or retain political power. An artist's responsibility to culture has been shifted to the margin. Entertainment has become the artist's only province, and often artists are only too willing to let go of their voice in order to suck at the breasts of fame.

Identity politics has splintered artists to such a degree that a certain kind of voicelessness has begun to subsume the role an artist can play in society. It is as if the claiming of identity that was so much a part of the 1980s and early 1990s has left artists exhausted of the further possibilities that its claiming can bring. Establishing a political identity, and therefore, a viable, recognizable economic entity has been the pale reward of the identity politics movement, and while the efforts must be championed, much unfiltered debris has been left in the movement's wake.

The documentation of a feeling, a moment in time, is what theatre offers. It is a public art that comes, often, from private obsessions. This contradiction is what makes the very form of theatre a continually radical one. Artists wrestle in an open forum, exposing their dreams, the petty stuff of their lives, what moves and angers them, trusting that there will be a response of some kind within the social arena where the art is staged. However, as another century turns, the very real, concrete politics of economics hinders the staging of work, and even its creation. Lack of funds, resources, and support for, especially, experimental artists has forced the makers of art to doubt their very 'usefulness' in society. In the US, for example, the emphasis on box-office receipts, entertainment 'value', and 'marketable content' has caused some artists to not only question their life's work, but to stop working altogether.

Doubt is healthy, and does keep artists alert to aspects of their craft, their duty to society, and even to the shape of the work itself. From doubt, new forms have indeed arisen. But the inordinate pressure to bow down to an economic god has distinctly changed the questions artists ask themselves. Limits are placed on the imagination of the artist. These limits are self-imposed before the creation of work begins. An idea, an image, may entrance the artist, and just as soon as it does, and the stirrings of a new piece are felt within the body, questions interfere with the process: 'Will this be a relevant piece? Is there a market for this kind of work? If the play has too many characters, will it ever be staged?' This is not to suggest that economics should be ignored. Beautiful solutions to what were originally economic hazards have created great art, but the culture of consumption, the 'cool society' that wants everything 'hot' right now causes destructive artistic restlessness, and audience impatience. Junk food mentality does not reward meditation, or density in a piece of art. A quick message is sought, and thus, there is a pressure on the artist to deliver work that serves and speaks to every denominator.

Applause is seductive, and artists are easily seduced. We work, after all, in the realm of pleasure. Concessions are made in order for that applause to be sustained over time. Artists begin to repeat themselves and to enjoy the comforts of repetition. An audience is cultivated, expectations are raised, and we live our lives in nagging bliss. The place where we work is a pure, humble space so that our imagination is free to go anywhere. This freedom is our most important asset. To lose it is a high cost indeed.

Discontentment creates furtiveness, as artists eye each other across rooms, keeping their work hidden in drawers, tucked inside their coats. The need for the open exchange of ideas that keeps art alive has been replaced by a selfishness that has nothing to do with protecting the work's integrity, but more about guarding the precious few spaces where the work can be seen. This atmosphere of veiled contempt has been abetted by economic pressures. To steal a spot has become part of the artist's weaponry at this turn of the century. Thievery has made us exclusionary, and has made much of our art petty and thin. By guarding the work, we have lost our ability to be open-hearted and expansive in our thinking.

As with any form in decline, theatre is finding itself at a perilous crossroads. With radio, television, cinema, the internet, and other digital technologies taking precedence in people's lives, theatre in its most traditional sense has stopped speaking to its immediate culture, especially in the US where the consumerist impulse has infected the decision-making in both the profit and non-profit sectors. The energizing post-decadent art signalled by the rise of the UK playwrights dubbed the 'new angry Brits' (significant voices like Mark Ravenhill, the late Sarah Kane, and David Harrower, among others) can be viewed as a phenomenon limited to a culture with a longer tradition of theatre, and therefore, passing through its necessary decadent phase at least a century ahead of the US. The US is barely in its Jacobean age.

Technological advances have not created a utopian mentality in the theatre, but rather a more restrictive one. Nostalgia is rampant, as theatre companies seek out the naturalistic classics of the 1940s and 1950s, in particular, and offer them to audiences who are equally nostalgic. These big-budget theatrical vehicles emphasize spectacular costumes and scenery along with the requisite glittering 'movie' star in the lead. In addition to revivals, which are often staged to accommodate the given star (not necessarily out of true passion to reinvestigate the work), the other kind of work that seems to be encouraged is the work of living writers aping the structures and modes of these plays of the 1940s and 1950s. The nostalgic streak in contemporary theatrical production is evidence of the fear producers, and artists themselves, have of the representations of worlds more akin to our own: freely chaotic, random, and without concrete answers. The desire for an ordered universe is so strong we desperately recreate the past even in present writing to cling to that which is both familiar, and known. Repetition, not renewal, is what we seek.

To combat this debilitating mentality, a generation of artists stirred by the possibilities of technology and the ennobling power of poetry have begun a serious underground revolt. Creating challenging, sometimes obscure pieces often suffused with a neo-Marxist agenda, US playwrights like Erik Ehn and Ruth Margraff are carefully, thoughtfully, passionately and fearlessly breaking down the walls of holy commerce in order to stage their visions. Working firmly in the tradition of the poet-philosopher, this generation of artists is committed to not only making work but also examining it in the midst of making. A spirited, open discourse is slowly emerging in reaction to the increasingly marginalized state of artists and theatre in society.

Why do we write/act/stage? Why is theatre still important? What comes after crisis? Non-Western models of narrative, and scientific models proposed by the computer age are providing some of the answers as artists continue to explore the cultural necessity for theatre. The very notion that theatre is an obsolete form galvanizes artists to reclaim it. We want to excavate the old to create the new, and what is older than theatre? In digging, we imaginatively revive the dumbshow, *commedia* scenarios, ancient myths, and the forgotten art of letter-writing. We steal not to fill our pockets, but to fill our souls. In so doing, we rediscover the alphabet, and speak a language newborn.

Looking back and looking forward, the snapshots of a time click and settle on a blank frame that becomes the theatre of the future, or the theatre of the spiritual. Out of struggle, pain, and dreams, utopian visions rise for a moment flickering in the light, then find themselves in the less media-haunted gaze of a theatre that looks outward and within, that incorporates elements of all its histories to bless both its ancient and nascent soul.

The place where writing begins is a pure one. It is an intense, electric silence where we meditate deep within ourselves, and breathe through the pen or pencil, and leave the circle of our breath on the page. We discover characters through the contact with the page, through the heart to the brain. We discover the environment that contains the characters – the ecology that makes them breathe, the tectonic shifts that give them light. As technology moves our lives forward, influences our ways of shaping text, we are still, in the end, in the theatre, left with the most dangerous, radical subject of all: the human being framed in space and light, governed by time.

> And there is being all alone in the world.
> And a stone heap on the ground,
> A stone heap where one is lying.
> And there is sky and sand,
> And emerald water.
> And arms wide open,
> Standing with arms wide open
> To touch the light.[1]

---

1 Caridad Svich, from *12 Short Prayers for Life When Dying*, unpublished playscript, 1998.

Some quick thoughts on theatre and its future

Oliver Mayer, Jorge Ignacio Cortiñas, Neena Beber and Craig Lucas

Oliver Mayer was born and lives in Los Angeles. He is the author of *Blade to the Heat* along with many other plays. A graduate of Cornell and Columbia Universities, his literary archive can be accessed via the Stanford University Libraries.

Jorge Ignacio Cortiñas' plays include *Maleta Mulata* (Campo Santo Theatre Company, San Francisco) and *Odiseo, could you stop for some bread and eggs on your way home?* (INTAR, New York). His 1999 play, *Sleepwalkers*, completed a two-month run at the Area Stage in Miami and was subsequently presented at the Alliance Theatre in Atlanta. It was awarded a Carbonell Award by the South Florida Critics Circle in the category of Best New Work.

Neena Beber is a playwright. Her plays have been seen at New Georges, Actors Theatre of Louisville, Padua Hills Playwrights' Festival, and the Magic Theatre. Plays include *Tomorrowland*, *Thirst*, and *Failure To Thrive*, among others. She has received MacDowell Colony and Paulette Goddard fellowships.

Craig Lucas is the author of *Stranger*, *The Dying Gaul*, *God's Heart*, *Prelude to a Kiss*, *Blue Window*, *Missing Persons* and the movie *Longtime Companion*. He is married to set designer John McDermott.

OLIVER MAYER Theatre will get better. But we have to own it. Make it ours. I predict that we will.

The best theatrical space is the one that lets us be most ourselves: a place of confluence in the city with a lot of people of colour, preferably with a good bar nearby.

Theatre's best invention is its oldest – the bare stage where writer, actor, director, designer and audience are willing to show and share who they really are.

The writer can only gain from writing and reading and seeing anything and everything, then funnelling it through his/her own particular madness.

The audience begins with us, all of us. We're searching for an image of ourselves.

JORGE IGNACIO CORTIÑAS Theatre will, like cockroaches, always be with us.

The ideal theatrical space is one with a door that actually opens, with access unfretted by rent, cost of admission or other extortion techniques.

As writers we should recognize our responsibilities to our ancestors, to the living, and even to those future generations we invoke but that we will never get to meet. This is not the same as being beholden to or controlled by those parties, only that we bear them important degrees of attention, which can include certain moments of strategic disrespect. However, a writer has no responsibility to anything called a form. Forms, unlike people, can take care of themselves.

NEENA BEBER I predict that, someday, everyone will write at least one play, and will start staging them on each other's rooftops (and e-mailing them to each other, collaborating en masse)!

My ideal theatrical space is intimate and traditional – maybe a high school theatre. I love proscenium stages and slightly shabby red velvet curtains on a pulley.

Theatre's next mutation – I always read about people predicting the use of more technology on stage, more media collage, etc. But I think it might mutate into something very bare bones and raw. If it is not spectacle, it will be very pared down. It will be the antithesis of film and television. It will be very strange and wonderful and private, and more poetic again. The sitcom and TV movie plays will be littering the offices of Hollywood and removed from all theatrical venues.

The audience should be reinvented the way the form is being rein-vented (if it is). Maybe any time a ticket is over sixty bucks, the patron must also purchase six ten-dollar tickets for more risky fare; they must attend or give the tickets to people who wouldn't other-wise have access to them. Maybe if people won't come to the theatre, theatre has to come to them: more school tours, and prison tours, and how about corporate tours where the play comes to your office at lunchtime (and all the office buildings will build theatres and day-care). Or the play comes to your living room after the 6 o'clock news – yes, we make house-calls!

CRAIG LUCAS I predict that theatre will be the primary form of enter-tainment after all the machinery breaks and we're too poor to be able to pay Mel Gibson's salary anymore.

The ideal theatrical space is any place with people sitting side by side, facing in the same direction, not talking.

Theatre will always be about storytelling. Any form will do.

The writer's responsibility is to tell good stories, tell them well, make them live.

The audience is anyone who is sick of TV and mass market paper-backs and studio movies, anybody looking for an authentic experience, eager to be told the truth, any truth.

Crisis as practice: strategies, concepts and working decisions

The comforts of crisis
Jim Carmody

Jim Carmody teaches at the University of California-San Diego, where he is Head of the Ph.D. Programme in Theatre Studies. He is the author of *Rereading Molière: Mise en Scène from Antoine to Vitez* (University of Michigan Press, 1993) and is currently working on a book on Molière in America. He also serves as Editor of *TheatreForum*, an international theatre journal devoted to the documentation and discussion of contemporary theatre.

There is doubtless some small portion of millennial angst lurking in the subtext of any discussion of the contemporary theatre in crisis, but one hardly needs the occasion of the end of the 1900s and the advent of the 2000s to return once again to recognize and to acknowledge the theatre's perennial status quo – crisis. 'Is the theatre really dead?' Simon and Garfunkel asked, somewhat tongue in cheek, a quarter century ago, secure in the knowledge that the theatre industry to which they referred, Broadway, 'the fabulous invalid', was indeed moribund. French theatre critic and scholar Alfred Simon asked a similar question in his 1978 book *Le Théâtre á bout de souffle?* (Is the theatre gasping for breath?), only unlike

Paul Simon and Art Garfunkel, Alfred Simon was deadly serious when he opened his polemic with the proposition that French theatre was in serious danger of dying and that the situation of the theatre in other countries was no less critical. Certainly Alfred Simon recognized that the situation of French commercial theatre was quite similar to that of Broadway; he was concerned, however, with the health of the non-commercial theatre, especially the state-subsidized theatrical institutions that had been created in the provinces of France during the post-war movement toward decentralization, a movement that had its American analogue in the growth of regional theatre that occurred at roughly the same time. In his view, the non-commercial theatre in France and elsewhere was already endangered by the end of the 1970s. At the end of the 1990s and at the very beginning of the 2000s, we are still in crisis, even if the contours of crisis have shifted over time. And, I want to argue, that is precisely the situation in which we are most comfortable.

Sophocles's *Oedipus*, the paradigmatic play of Aristotelian dramaturgy, opens with a city in crisis. That particular crisis is resolved through a process of exploring the impact of the past in the present; the society represented in that play is finally able to move forward only when all of the factors contributing to the crisis have been clarified, blame has been apportioned, and the principal actors have exited the stage. While much of the commentary on the play and on its productions has focused on Sophocles's characters, their actions, feelings, and ideas, the great exemplary impact of the play on the western tradition has been in its elaboration of the dramatic possibilities of the crisis situation itself. From Oedipus flows the tradition of drama as the exploration of a crisis situation, a tradition that includes thousands of plays as diverse as, for example, Racine's *Phèdre*, Chekhov's *The Cherry Orchard*, Williams's *A Streetcar Named Desire*, and Vinaver's *L'ordinaire* (*High places*). In each of these plays, the playwright structures a series of events that gradually unfold for us both the nature of the present crisis and the narratives of significant past experience relative to all of the individuals and locations represented, revealing the overwhelming power and influence of the past over the present.

With all of the time and effort devoted to the reconstruction of the past in all its emotional and symbolic force, it is tempting to conclude that the Aristotelian and neo-Aristotelian dramaturgy of crisis is obsessed with the past. It is important, however, to distinguish between the dramatic technique used to convey information to the spectators and the dramatic situation actually performed on stage. The dramatic situation performed on stage is that of the intolerable present, the present as crisis. While the narrative(s) may range over time and space almost without limit, the locus of crisis itself is fully represented by the stage in the present moment; the scenic space in such plays is always precisely equivalent to the boundaries of the situation – once the principal characters have made their final exit, the crisis is, by definition, past. In the audience, we watch the characters' lives unfold over time, time past superimposed on time present by the dramaturgic skill of the playwright, certain that the moment of crisis will have passed, or rather, that the characters will have discovered how to make their exit, by the time the play comes to an end. We come back to our favourite plays again and again, I suspect, not because we empathize with one character or another, or because we take pleasure in living vicariously in that particular set of narratives, but because we are fascinated with the specific contours of the crisis unique to that play, irresistibly drawn to the precise moment at which a particular present can no longer contain either itself or its past and at which the nature of the characters' future is the all-embracing dramatic question.

A lifetime of watching dramas unfold leaves us with an accumulated store of crisis situations to which we can return at will in our imaginations. I make no distinction with respect to medium, for we encounter drama, even of the Aristotelian sort I have been discussing here, in many different circumstances. For those of us who work at the production of drama in the theatre, or elsewhere, the experience of encountering so many crisis situations is considerably amplified, with the result that the dramatic crisis has become one of the fundamental structures of our imaginations, one of the intellectual and emotional technologies that allow us to perceive and act on reality. We are comfortable in crisis situations because we have been exploring, explicating, imagining, recreating, rehearsing, remembering, performing, and marketing them for much of our lives.

The sense of crisis, of being in crisis, is inseparable from the sense of historical time, of being in a moment filled with foreboding while heading toward a future moment whose contours and textures give rise to a potential gamut of emotional states ranging from apprehension to despair. To be in crisis is to be in a present moment of danger, discomfort, and discontent, searching for a possible, albeit difficult and painful, trajectory toward a less critical future moment. Crisis is inseparable from teleology, and a theatre in crisis is a theatre searching for a set of vectors that will carry it forward to a future moment less fraught with apprehension and foreboding. Ultimately, of course, to move beyond crisis is to move outside history, to exit from the stage.

Some words about the theatre today
Roberta Levitow

Roberta Levitow is a US director. Her directing credits include Marlane Meyer's *Moe's Lucky Seven*, *Miriam's Flowers* by Migdalia Cruz, *Memory Tricks* by Marga Gomez, *Each Day Dies With Sleep* by Jose Rivera, and *Etta Jenks* by Marlane Meyer. Theatres: Playwrights Horizons, Circle Rep, Public Theater, Hartford Stage, Berkeley Rep, Actors Theater of Louisville, and many others. She was awarded an NEA Directing Fellowship with Seattle Rep, and was the recipient of the TCG Alan Schneider Award in 1990. She is a graduate of Stanford University.

These are the musings, questions and rantings that clutter my mind and spirit. I share them as I would share a diary entry. These thoughts are full of my own strivings and disappointments. Perhaps they will strike a chord ...

Crisis number one: the disconnect between the art form and the great disruptions and transformations dominating contemporary life

The question of *Theatre* in Crisis seems petty in the face of *Human Life as We Have Known It* in Crisis. I don't need to list the ways in which we are all careening towards the future – the usurping influence of the American global culture; the dissolution/desperation of unique ethnic and cultural identities in relation to the vast consuming global culture; the transformation of human life from an emphasis on the necessities of survival to the dilemmas of technological mastery and leisure-time expenditure; the widening power and income distribution gap between people with financial resources and the expanding underclass of American and global society; the scientific and social re-imagining of procreation and definitions of familial bonds; the mutation and disappearance of the natural world; pervasive and unending massacres and civil wars in revolving countries and geographical regions; advances in genetic engineering that threaten to redesign notions of human destiny, purpose, character, and identity – to name a few. It is no surprise that artists, like us, can barely begin to comprehend the transformations that dominate our lives. They – we – are overwhelmed.

The history of dramatic literature teaches us that the theatre was the place where human beings gathered to examine, debate, and reveal the nature of their experience. But these societal disruptions that characterize contemporary life are not the subject of most American theatre. They are, however, ad nauseum the subject of television and film. Environmental catastrophy, genetic engineering, virtual realism, cultural hegemony, the ethics of modern medical treatments, terrorism, social-sexual-familial permutations – these are the subjects of major motion pictures, action films, made-for-television movies, even weekly episodics and soap operas.

What comprises the majority of the work presented in the American theatre? Revivals, classics and some new work that generally steers clear of the controversial, politically or socially. The arena that writers feel some safety working within seems to be 'the personal' – family, relationships, and psycho-sexual dilemmas, seldom cast within the larger context or with a larger societal concept. The exception must be work that deals with racialism, of course, but that work finds itself generally marginalized, just as the topic of the racialism of America is marginalized at the edges of public discourse. Ask an American writer what they fear to write about, and many will tell you – race.

We are, in the theatre, out of touch. Going to the theatre, more often than not, is the escapism of a great denial.

Crisis number two: the disconnect between the practitioners of the art form and the tastes and interests of the general public

Working in the American theatre today is like being a cobbler or a glass-blower in a world of e-commerce, virtual realities, political tumult, celebrity culture, illiteracy, digital imaging and cyberspace. We are like practitioners of an ancient artisan craft, anachronistic in a world of mass production and advanced technology. Only the rarest individuals today prefer their shoes handmade or their kitchen glasses hand-blown. We are not the medium for the masses. We are like the monks preserving a library from antiquity – that rare entity, once so prized, of a storyteller and players recounting adventures for those gathered around a sacred campfire.

Most practitioners I know don't go to the theatre much anymore. It's a confession generally saved for private and sober discussions about being burnt-out. Most playwrights I know are concentrating on their screenplays or their TV-movie-of-the-week or getting a TV series. Most directors I know are desperate to get a job teaching or directing television and film. Most actors act for the theatre with their gaze fixed upon landing a better agent and a television series or some juicy film roles. For entertainment, like everyone else in America, we rent a video or DVD.

What is our sacred flame?

At its most primitive – or primal – the theatre is stories around a campfire so that a community can make sense of what has happened, what could happen, what will happen; so that an individual can understand the nature of their unique experience with the enriched perspective of the collective experience. The laughs at things well recognized and the tears at things well recognized. We used to go to the theatre to help make sense of our lives.

At its most primitive – or primal – the theatre is a spiritual church. It is a collective experience greater than the sum of the individual members. In singing, laughing, crying or listening – praying together – the community knows itself for what it is, as a community. And the individual knows that life is partly just that: membership in community. It is a collective experience transcendent of average days and average individuals, infused with that which is greater than ourselves. It celebrates the unique and remarkable holiness of being alive.

At its most primitive – or primal – the theatre is a pagan ritual. It is a collective celebration of the dynamism, energy and sound of life. Music and dancing, the spectacle of lights and costumes, catapult us out of our single life shell into a vortex of multiple life forces. We are uplifted by the sheer fervour and vitality of the collective sound and physicality.

Every kind of theatre expresses a definition of what it means to be human. Griots and Native American storytellers told stories of people living lives interwoven with animals and natural spirit forces, surrounded by living ancestors. The Greeks presented their notion of what it means to be human – creatures with divine aspiration and quality completely subservient to the whims and wiles of fate and the gods. Shakespeare saw humans as flawed but marvellous creatures, independently creating the heaven or hell of their reality. Ibsen and Chekhov captured the evolving notion that human beings were pieces of a larger social fabric which bent and determined their destiny as surely as the psychological influences described by Sigmund Freud. Eastern European Absurdists saw humans trapped inside absurd familial and social power dynamics that turned logic upside down. Brecht saw humans as cogs in the great machinery of economic power struggles. García Lorca portrayed people struggling against familial and community obligations that often proved fatal to body and soul. Modernist playwrights like Beckett envisioned humans as helpless creatures, set in motion on a rock spinning purposelessly through space, waiting for an indifferent world to offer some relief for a desperate loneliness.

This is what we 'monks' are preserving. The storytelling, the church, the pagan ritual. The desire to know what it means to be human. The belief in community. The community of artists. The community of artists and audience. This ideal of what theatre can be resides more in our memories than in reality.

What are our 'profound' reflections worth to a populace that is obsessed with an insatiable hunger for immediate experiences and acquisitions and an impenetrable fear or loathing of contemplation – for a populace addicted to visual excitement and increasingly uninterested in the subtleties of language and the nuances of the human need for meaning beyond self?

What do you see as the most profound questions of our time? I ask you to list them. Do you think that the theatre that you see reflects or explores these questions? Where do you go to make sense of your life, to get a better understanding of the nature of your human experience? To the acupuncturist? To the television? To the psychic? To the latest self-help book? To your best friend? Where do you go to know yourself as a member of a community, to transcend the averageness of your individual life and experience something greater than yourself? To a sporting event? To a restaurant? To church? Where do you go to experience the fervour and vitality of the life force? To a rock concert? To a shopping mall? To the gym?

You see, you don't go to the theatre either.

Crisis number three: the absence of the avant-garde

I started making theatre in the 1960s, when youthful radicalism was given free airing in our theatre. We, the Political and Social Avant-Garde, made plays that our peers attended and cheered. It was like tribal gatherings. Everyone in the audience was young and simpatico. It was like church, the church of the politically and socially impassioned. Or at least that's how I like to remember it.

Then the times, under President Reagan, I remember, oh so clearly, changed. Funding evaporated but we carried on performing. To surprisingly fewer and fewer of our peers. Where had all the young radicals gone? Into business or family maintenance, I'm sure. Meanwhile, our parents stayed the course, at those dull big theatres we abhorred. And those dull big theatres hired us to do our somewhat less radical work for them, since supposedly we would bring our 'younger' audience in tow.

And that's how it was for many years. Then what I like to call the Cultural Avant-Garde took over the reinvention of the American theatre. Cultures that wanted to have their tribal gatherings, to give their radicalism free airing – gay and lesbian theatre, Latino and Hispanic theatre, Black theatre, Asian-American theatre – created plays where everyone in the audience was young and simpatico. The plays changed form into

Performance Art so that the Substance of Unique Experience would be represented in the Form of Unique Experience.

Meanwhile, the ever-ageing parents stayed the course, at those dull big theatres that the new Cultural Avant-Garde abhored. And those dull big theatres hired them to do their somewhat less radical work, since they supposedly would bring their 'younger' audience in tow.

But what is the avant-garde now?

Sometimes it appears that the present avant-garde is the Avant-Garde of Style. Yes, again, a tribal gathering of young simpatico peers who love the dynamism of the visual and aural sensation. But wait ... I'm older now. My time and my taste are no longer of the moment. Am I wrong to fear that the Avant-Garde of Style has forgotten the first two characteristics of theatre – Story and Church? Do we have now predominantly Pagan Ritual? Can we have a theatre that is Style with superficial substance? Is it because we live in a time when our lives have only superficial reality, even to ourselves?

My hope is that in the future, the next avant-garde will be the Avant-Garde of Truth. Theatre artists will run to the theatre because it is the only place that they can tell the truth about what it means to be human. As the world becomes more alienating and more superficial, the Theatre will be the Human Place – the place where we breathe together in one room, where we know ourselves as part of a community, where we experience that transcendence of beauty and meaning that is greater than ourselves, where we remember the fervour and vitality of the life force. And most important of all, where we go to make honest sense of our lives, so that we are improved human beings for having shared the time, the space, and the words together.

Crisis number four: the corporate model has demeaned the making of theatre from art form to consumer product

American theatre is now often an embarrassing regurgitation of simple-minded, superficial, convenient representations of human life. It is dishonest, market-driven, self-censored. How is it that we are so compromised?

We persevere. There are theatres all across America. Many of them have beautiful buildings and regular audiences. Many of them pay wages to a variety of artists – albeit the majority of those artists are managing on abysmally low levels of income without yearly health benefits or any assurance of pensions for precarious old ages. So, why can't we make the kind of theatre that we want to make when we are left alone in our rehearsal rooms eight hours a day?

Those institutions, and their managers, hold artists in esteem and dedicate their lives to serve the creation of art works, often at a considerable loss of salary potential. But these institutions are not artist driven; they are management driven. These rehearsal and performance schedules are a brutal compromise of artistic models in favour of financial realities. These buildings, these timetables, these salary levels, these accommodations, these subscription seasons, these play selections are dominated by corporate bottom lines. Every single decision is mediated by the demands of the marketplace. And the artists are reflecting the same compromises in the microcosmic universe of a rehearsal room. The product is often hurried, slick, and superficial. There's no time, no support, no encouragement to do anything more.

Outside the larger institutions are the small fledgling theatres where everyone works for nothing or the fascination of stability lures even the most adventurous towards their bigger brothers. It becomes the most vicious cycle when the work suffers and the audience grows indifferent. And then, of course, the work suffers.

Which came first – the audience indifference or the mediocrity of our work? Who can say?

Crisis number five: hopelessness and the abandonment of the art form by the artists

Do I sound cynical? I'm beyond cynicism. I'm in mourning. I'm in mourning for the death of my long-lost love which represented my ideals – Humanism, Compassion, Political Consciousness, the Struggle for Moral Insight, the Search for Truth. I am not alone. I know many, many theatre artists who are enthusiastically looking for any other way to spend their lives – artists who have successful careers in most people's terms.

The ageing artist runs towards financial security in teaching or film and television work. Or to the personal control of writing novels or short stories. Or to put paint on canvas.

The truly gifted and ambitious young artists are not driven towards our art form anymore. Film and television drafts the best and the brightest. Who can blame them? Who would be drawn to the theatre as the most expressive art form through which to transform a vision of the world?

It's too hard. It's too unsatisfying. Hundreds of American theatre artists are operating on sheer inertia. We feel impotent. We cannot change the forces that surround us. We are no longer invigorated by the fleeting moments of artistic inspiration. We continue because we can't imagine stopping – not now, after having given so much. And yet, for almost all of us, if there were any other way …

Crisis number six: the demonization of the artist

This today, above all, is the tragedy not just for practitioners, but for the community itself that the work of the artist, which both glorifies and exposes the truth of human life, has been called demonic. Once we were considered the high priests and shamans, because we created magic, beauty, and transcendence out of the nothingness of mundane existence. Once we were glorious messengers from the gods. Once we were wise, gifted, virtuosos of the language arts – capable of spinning a tale that enraptured and transported our audiences – celebrated and held in awe.

Today we are beggars – seen as desperate carriers of sordid tales – accused of, literally, blasphemous acts against the social good. Beggars for money. Beggars for audience. Beggars for attention. Beggars for respect.

Who can say that our spirits have not been broken?

Mine has.

And who can say what it will cost us all if we let the flame die?

Seeing through the national and global stereotypes: British theatre in crisis
Peter Lichtenfels and Lynette Hunter

Peter Lichtenfels, having been Artistic Director at the Traverse Theatre in Edinburgh and Executive Director at the Leicester Haymarket, now focuses on freelance directing in many countries, the editing of Shakespearean texts, and is a teacher of acting at Manchester Metropolitan University.

Lynette Hunter is the Professor of the History of Rhetoric at the University of Leeds. After brief experience as a director and actor, she has engaged with theatre consistently as both critic and audience. Her most recent works are *Critiques of Knowing* (Routledge, 1999) and *Literary Value/Cultural Power* (Manchester University Press, 2001).

Money, sex and politics: British theatre in crisis or simply smothered?

The main question we want to ask is: why is so much current theatre in Britain without challenge or enjoyment? To do so, we will turn to two waves of British theatre over the past thirty years, that of new writing and of classic revivals, to build a background for this and some other questions. The areas we would most like to look at are concerned with political authority, and more and more with the regulation of sexuality. Possibly the only thesis we would like to advance is that increasingly sexuality is being used as the site for examining political authority. To make sense of this we would also like to pay some attention to the growth of artistic conservatism that grew up under the Thatcher government in the 1980s and was extended into the 1990s under Prime Minister John Major, especially alongside the various governments' attempts to rein in the theatre. These developments had an enormous impact on government policy under the Labour Culture Secretary, Chris Smith, and have largely defined British theatre to the year 2000.

If we look back on the 1970s, it's clear that there was an extraordinary amount of immediate, in-your-face political theatre going on. This was the decade of David Hare, David Edgar, Howard Barker, Howard Brenton and Caryl Churchill. Because the repertory companies did not produce new work, and had not begun to organize the studio spaces, many of their shows were initially put on by the Royal Court or by small touring companies such as Foco Novo, Joint Stock, Freehold, 7.84, or David Hare's Portable Theatre. These companies were almost by definition groups of people committed to something political or social or aesthetic – the post-World War II equivalent of the early twentieth-century manifesto movements, although only Barker and Churchill could be said to follow the emphasis of those earlier movements on the questioning of established formal and dramatic structures and their ideological implications. Yet by the early 1980s far less of this work was around, and our first question is 'why'?

Why the dearth of small companies, of touring companies?

One reason concerns the touring groups, which suffered systematic destruction during the 1980s at the hands of local councils squeezed by the new government cuts. Not only did overtly critical political companies such as 7.84 (7 per cent of the population own 84 per cent of the wealth) come to an end during this period, but also companies such as Gay Sweatshop. The demise of the Greater London Council, which had an admirable record of funding small group projects, meant that many London companies and, importantly, London venues for small productions such as the Half Moon Theatre or the Open Space, were forced to close. Not that this is conspiratorial. Local government cuts are easiest to make on what appear to be 'leisure' facilities, but the net effect was that committed individuals lost an important structure within which to work. This outcome may or may not have been predicted.

More interesting, the funding did not disappear entirely. Much of it was reinvested in buildings, central civic monuments to culture, with the civic council committee structure. Theatre boards found themselves becoming much more powerful, as they became responsible for the large capital investment in what were often city-centre buildings and land, and ultimately answerable to a government with a much more hands-on approach to policy implementation that involved five-year inspections and assessments. The recent injections of large amounts of Lottery money have exacerbated the situation. One of the most important conditions of National Lottery money is usually that a 50 per cent matching grant has to be found from elsewhere. When theatres such as the Contact Theatre or the Bolton Octagon could not find that 50 per cent they went bankrupt. The Contact Theatre lost its company and its artistic director. In the latter case the Octagon was bailed out by the local council, but reduced to a touring venue for commercial theatre.

This kind of institutional theatre can work in many different ways, but the primary drive of English theatre boards has been to produce a commercially viable building. Again, this is not necessarily conspiratorial or intended, but with boards of some larger theatres being made up of as many as twenty-seven people, the artistic and fiscal conservatism of policy was almost inevitable: if you control capital-intensive locations, you don't have to worry about controlling the writer, the actor, the director. Indeed, the post of Artistic Director, which usually ran in parallel with an Administrator but with the weighting toward the Artistic Director, in the early 1990s changed into the now common role of an Executive Director appointed by a board, with the Executive Director in turn appointing a director for a season or a production, or indeed working at longer term with them but still remaining the primary contact with the board.

Some of the freedom of the productions in the 1970s resulted from the aura generated from the end to theatre censorship in 1968. But, as the case of Howard Brenton's *The Romans in Britain* testifies, the mood was quite different in the early 1980s. As Richard Boon points out in his excellent study of Brenton's work, the media response to the play was 'verging on the hysterical'.[1] To refresh our memories, Brenton's play uses a scene of explicit homosexual rape as part of its exploration of the brutalities human beings are capable of in the name of greed, power and colonization. Having being tipped off by journalists from the *Daily Mail*, Sir Horace Cutler, conservative leader of the then GLC (Greater London Council) and member of the National Theatre Board, went to attend the last preview of the play. He and colleagues staged a walkout shortly before the first interval, and the following day Cutler sent a telegram to Peter

---

1 Richard Boon, *Brenton the Playwright* (London: Methuen, 1991), p. 173.

Hall calling the play a disgrace to the National Theatre, and threatening the theatre's funding. In the event the GLC did then decide against increasing its grant to the theatre, effectively creating a 15 per cent cut in subsidy.

In the aftermath, the play became a focus for a number of right-wing pressure groups, and, notoriously, the object of Mary Whitehouse's prosecution of the director Michael Bogdanov. A loophole in the 1968 Theatres Act on censorship allowed the prosecution a case, but they unexpectedly withdrew it, leaving the judge having delivered a ruling that is still in place, a ruling as Richard Boon puts it, 'in conflict with the spirit and substance' of the Act.[2] The detail of this case is offered to indicate how effectively the shift toward buildings and away from people, can affect the kind of theatre that occurs in our society, not the least because the theatre building becomes a site for big 'P' politics: Caryl Churchill's *Serious Money* lists a board membership of the National Theatre as a prerequisite to political credibility.[3]

Gender, spectacle and careers

At the same time that smaller companies were going to the wall, and theatres were becoming buildings, many of the high-profile men in the theatre world, actors, directors, writers, were moving into opera, film and television. But 'why'? The theatre is a distinct medium. Opera does not work the same way, and film and television are quite different media. So why do we have this consistent shift sometimes into two-track careers, but certainly away from the theatre alone? Was it because these men were approaching, if not well into, middle age, and looking for a more substantial income, thinking about their pensions (like most theatre professionals, they are self-employed)? Was it because the theatre was gradually losing status? After all, it was also during this period that women began to move into the theatre as directors, writers and designers. This may have been a result of several years of hard-won equal opportunities lobbying from the women's movement, or it may be that women are simply more willing to take poorly paid, unstable and part-time jobs. And we know from many examples in other professions such as computing or medicine, that a sure sign of the downgrading of any profession is the ease with which it will allow women entry.

Perhaps a number of the men shifting their careers saw film and television at least as a way of getting into contact with a much larger audience? It may be significant that much political drama of the 1980s

2 Ibid., p. 177.
3 Caryl Churchill, *Serious Money* in *Plays: 2* (London: Methuen Drama, 1996), p. 286.

happened on television: Alan Bleasdale's *Boys from the Blackstuff* or his *GBH*, the series *A Very British Coup*, or Bob Peck's record of acting in television drama concerned with the anti-nuclear movement, ecology and so on. But apart from Bleasdale's phrase 'Gizza job', the keynote of actor Bernard Hill's desperate attempt to keep his family together, which became for a while a signal criticism of a government that had also just said 'get on yer bike', the television productions of political drama were often double-edged. Yes, they could be immediate, challenging millions of people to reassessments, but at the same time they existed in a medium that was contained inside a box in people's living rooms, could be turned down, turned off, taped, and taped over when the excitement had died away, in other words, it could be controlled.

The one thing that you cannot do with theatre is control its physicality. The actor is there, in front of you, in person, with her/his body mediating all the social, spiritual and sexual crises of the moment. From the earliest records of theatre activity, like the Dionysian movements that inspired the classical Greek theatre, through to the Renaissance with its continual anxieties over the body of the actor – the labourer's body that might impersonate a king, the man's body that might behave like a woman, and then be a woman behaving like a man – the theatre has consistently celebrated the potential of human beings for change, even radical change, by putting the human body in interaction on stage and worrying about and rejoicing in its ambivalence. Television does other important things as a medium, but the audience is in a very different relation to the performances it mediates. What it does allow for is a scope that modern British dramatists do not seem to have been able to imagine for the contemporary stage.

Coincident with the shift in career structure and the change in the approach to theatre funding in the 1980s, came an exponential increase in the production of classic revivals, especially of Shakespearean drama. One of the first theatres to make the breakthrough in the 1970s into large-scale classic drama was the Glasgow Citizen's Theatre, where Philip Prowse, Giles Havergal and Robert David MacDonald began staging a series of mainly Jacobean tragedies. Prowse's radically experimental design was to produce visually spectacular shows, parading frocks, as it has been called. This did not happen overnight, but after a period of disastrous audience attendance. The theatre decided, in response, to see what would happen if Prowse was given a free imaginative hand, and if the tickets were reduced to fifty pence. Audiences began to come, learned to love it, and gradually (and reluctantly) ticket prices were increased to three pounds over an eight-year period. If we think for just a moment of the distinction between the English word 'audience' and the word used in nearly every other European country, 'spectator', it may just be that for the first time a British audience was being asked to think in terms of the visual as the most important conveyor of meaning. By 1981 Théâtre de Complicité had arrived with its combination of mime and words, significantly, coming from training in a European context with Jacques Lecoq, Phillipe Gaulier and Monica Pagnaux. Complicité, along with Cheek by Jowl, Joint Stock and the early Shared Experience, have, arguably, had the most profound influence on new directions in British theatre over the past fifteen to twenty years. Both Complicité and Cheek by Jowl talked seriously of leaving Britain in the late 1990s.

Classic revivals and political allegory: conservative or subversive?

The Citizens' use of the visual drew on religious spectacle, of which there is much, but also on the then recent experience of ten to fifteen years of rock concerts, and slightly longer of television. For those of us who taught through from the 1970s to the 1980s, the sudden sophistication of students in the area of visual narrative, a sophistication that seemed just to 'arrive' in the 1980s, was startling. Of course it was related to the visual education that this generation had received for the previous twenty years in television and film, gained inexorably by watching these media nearly every day of their lives, and often for several hours a day. It may indeed be that actors and directors moved into film and television because they recognized the growing appreciation for their scope and sophistication with the audience. Yet parallel with this intense visual education, the 1980s and early 1990s saw huge cutbacks in the Theatre in Education programme, and many young people were, as a result, learning not how to become theatre spectators, but theatre voyeurs. An informative parallel here would be with theatre in Europe, especially the eastern European countries, where there are extensive theatre companies for young children, children, young teenagers and youths, which instil a habit of going to the theatre, as well as offering an education in a wide variety of theatre techniques and skills. Audience skills are learned, not natural.

But spectacle alone cannot explain the upsurge in classic revivals of the 1980s and 1990s. Classics provide both audience and theatre company with the possibility of exploring cultural traditions at a time when traditions are radically changing and under threat. They offer a clear modernist analogue for the stage, in that they convey a structure that can then be dismantled or deconstructed to whatever extent is desired, yet their relatively stable text always insists on some predictable form. And the 1980s and early 1990s were intensely uncertain times, particularly uncertain economic times, framed by a growing awareness of the global

implications of British interests, and a profoundly authoritarian government. One point made by Maria Delgado is that the production of classics allows the director and others working on a production to work with
no playwright looking over their shoulders.[4] While this can be liberating,
it also removes one of the primary tensions that links a play with immediate social issues, with the result that the production can also move
toward the banal and the making palatable. On the other hand, the large
casts and often large landscapes of classic drama allow for a breadth of
inquiry that contemporary drama, curtailed by finances to very small
casts and short rehearsal periods, does not encourage. The use of classic
drama, implicitly conservative, can become subversive. It permits people
to criticize in oblique ways that cannot immediately be dismissed, and
may even make possible the saying of something that otherwise could not
be spoken. In a sense the classics offer an allegorical ground for sorting
out contemporary problems – allegory always being the genre for
responding to political authoritarianism and control. Writers such as
David Pownall, Caryl Churchill or Claire Luckham tapped directly into
allegory in their new plays, as did writers such as John Byrne with his
curious hyperreality of the surreal domestic drama, a combination of
Beckett and Pinter. These 1980s writers are quite different from the 1970s
realism of, say, Tom McGrath and Jimmy Boyle's play *The Hard Man*,
although they draw immediately from the one dramatist whose work
continues to inform current writing, Edward Bond.

Were there political plays in the 1990s? Are there any for 2000+?

In pragmatic terms, classic revivals were also better suited to the theatre
as a 'building'. They needed larger casts and more money, which could
only be earned by bigger theatres. Furthermore, these large-scale dramas
often covered the extra costs by working through co-productions. For
various reasons co-productions are often more conservative in approach,
and frequently aim to glorify the 'production' rather than the play. But
more immediately, a classic drama is much easier to put before a board:
it is traditionally tried and tested, safe, recognized by the audience. This
was so especially in the case of Shakespearean drama. A number of factors have led to the predominance of Shakespeare productions in Britain,
one being simply the long history of the tradition which has given it an
authority. As Gary Taylor has argued in *Reinventing Shakespeare*, the playwright's work has, over the last four centuries become a repository of

4 Private communication, September 1998.

national pride, and the little-England nationalism of the 1980s could call
on this identification.[5]

After World War II the English education system began the policy of
having a play by Shakespeare in the final years of mandatory education to
the age of sixteen: O level or the current GCSE. This means that since
1950 the one cultural denominator for the entire English population is
Shakespeare; every child in the country has been exposed to the printed
drama of this playwright, even if some of them haven't actually read it. By
the 1980s, the generation that had first been experimented on in this way
was into its thirties, and was well-placed to pay the higher price of tickets
to the larger theatres that were emerging. Shakespeare was now so much
part of English culture that even touring companies could find finance to
exist if they focused on his plays. Of course, once in the programme of a
'building' or a touring company, the actors, directors and designers can
do what they want with it, and many productions from the early 1980s
were radically exciting. Today, for a number of reasons, they are more
often produced for tourism. But whether exciting or not, these productions are implicitly compromised by traditional structure. Just like television or film they are caught in a double-handed rhetoric of conservatism
and exploration.

A key feature of the classic revivals has been the exploration of sexuality. Most of the classic revivals have been taken from the English renaissance, Restoration and eighteenth-century canon, in other words they
come from the 'modern' period, and have some points in common with
our own period and some not. They offer a titillating combination of
something 'other' than ourselves yet part of ourselves: *Les Liaisons dan-
gereuses* would be a case in point, or the substantial discussion about
homosexuality that has been generated by productions of Shakespeare. In
common with a number of new plays from the 1990s, it appears that sexuality has become the new ground of interest for contemporary audiences. Yes, *The Romans in Britain* used a sexual act to metaphorize the
rape and destruction of colonialism, but these plays from the 1990s focus
on the regulation of sexuality itself, from which we may deduce ideas
about political authority. From political plays in which sexuality is a subplot to illuminate or extend the political, the focus has shifted to plays
about sexuality, in which politics is a subplot to illuminate or extend our
understanding of the regulation of sexuality.

Two points: first, the regulation of sexuality is of course political. Yet,
second, the structure of the 1990s' plays implies that the political is a
stable, unchanging set of topoi underlying sexuality. It is not 'natural' but

5   See Gary Taylor, *Reinventing Shakespeare: A Cultural History from the Restoration to
    the Present* (London: Hogarth, 1989).

its rules, conventions, understandings are naturalized, inescapable even if man-made. This structure does not imply the big political question of the early twentieth century – how an individual comes to terms with the state, the anarchy/totalitarianism divide of philosophy, literature, art and politics until well after World War II. Instead, it takes state control and regulation as a given and asks how we can survive, move and possibly change within it. We see a problem with this and would like to take a glancing look at three productions that caused outcry in their time. Edward Bond's *Saved* outraged audiences in the early 1970s because it showed the torture and stoning to death of a baby in a pram. However, it was not the death of the baby that was so appalling about the play, but the lack of individual action. The characters appear to have bound them-selves to a place where they can take no moral action, and Bond's message was clearly that they should not have done so and that we have got a choice to do things differently. During the early 1980s came *The Romans in Britain*, which is a play of enormous despair. The individuals are over-whelmed by actions dictated by convention, and cope by joking about their inability to do anything else. In fact, Bond told Brenton that the out-rage the play caused was due to the jokes. Without them, the play would have offered some tragic catharsis; with them, and the self-consciousness they introduce, there is nothing but a desert of inaction.

One of the plays from the 1990s that has caused similar response is Mark Ravenhill's *Shopping and F***ing* (1996), which disgusted many theatregoers with its depiction of greed and sadomasochistic rape. Yet the underlying politics of *Shopping and F***ing* is directly parallel to Orwell's *Nineteen Eighty-Four*, depicting as it does the games people play to sur-vive within a manipulative and seemingly inescapable set of controls. The play also works with Orwell's tension of 'at a distance' manipulation and its distinction from 'real-life' manipulation, and the moral and ethical questions raised by that difference. The sexual focus of Ravenhill's work, which many other 1990s texts by writers such as Sarah Kane or Kevin Elyot have used, certainly responds to a cultural and social anxiety, and inextricably involves the audience – often in ways that individuals within it do not appreciate. But at least there is involvement. Caryl Churchill's *Serious Money* (1987), which also makes an attack on greed and money, was simply co-opted by the very people it criticized. City traders took their champagne to the Royal Court in order to celebrate this satire on themselves. Similarly, David Hare's early 1990s trilogy, particularly *The Absence of War*, which satirized the Labour Party, has resulted, according to Hare himself, in a knighthood from those at the heart of his analysis.[6]

6   David Hare, 'Why I Knelt to Blair', *Guardian Review*, 4 September 1998.

Audience responses to Ravenhill's work have not been quite so co-opting, but the sexuality topos does permit people to evade the political undercurrents. One theatregoer reported on an audience response to the touring production, in which the play's reputation preceded it, and said that there was a small but vocal part of the audience clearly there only to raucously encourage the sexual violence.

The difference between the political and the sexual as central topics may be that we still expect our politicians to have some connection with truth and pragmatic change, whereas we increasingly view sexuality as a type of social display. We know that how we engage our sexuality is socially constructed, but we like to think of politicians as people who can construct society. So where has the direct political theatre gone?

Perhaps the best way of answering this question is to reverse the questions already asked. Rather than 'why the dearth of small companies?' or 'why the dearth of touring companies?', both of which have brought so much vitality into British theatre, we should ask, 'Why were there so many in the 1970s?' The 1970s saw a flowering of cultural confidence that was ironic, given that it followed the birth of widespread political cynicism after 1968. The decade saw vigorous attempts on cultural traditions, even if in an awareness of the limitations of those attempts. The country itself was engulfed in a sentimental national confidence which, again ironically, encouraged it to allow itself to support the arts quite widely. In parallel with that confidence was the tacit permission for a political landscape in which people felt they could be effective rather than merely observers – the women's movement would be a good example of such activism.

But today, English culture at any rate is indecisive, as if our tentativeness about Europe has placed us betwixt and between. The ridiculous shows of military strength in the 1980s and early 1990s, a toytown version of the 1950s fiascos, harked back, didn't look forward. Devolution in Scotland and Wales has left England grasping after past identities, on the verge of becoming a large national theme park. And art with energy is art that looks forward, has something to say and wants to find expression for it. The art encouraged in the 1980s and 1990s was art for profit, therefore necessarily predictable, a known risk, as if the riskiness of the surrounding social unrest and unease made 'safe art' a necessity. Today there is a growing sense of 'difficulty' in face of an increasingly diverse population. The gradual realization that one group cannot speak for all has had an effect on political theatre, not just on politics. And not only have the public begun to claim more diversity, but those in power have changed: Who are they in the year 2000? Has political theatre disappeared simply because nations are no longer the policy-making power sources they were, but are subject to international and global structures? Have we lost our nerve in the face of such vast structures? Do we know too much about them, so they render us ineffective? Or do we know too little? The new global consciousness seems to have left England at a loss.

Can cross-cultural theatre really survive in Britain?

We would like to look first, at the welcome (or not) given to international theatre that visits Britain, particularly European theatre; second, at the place of theatre from a variety of cultural traditions flourishing in the United Kingdom as a result of immigration in the second half of this century; and third, at the export of British theatre to an international setting.

A welcome for international theatre?

During the 1980s, changes to the funding of British theatre had an impact on distinctive waves of new plays and classic revivals but the changes in the funding situation did not change the fact that most theatres in Britain, before and after the 1980s, are not company-based, in other words the actors and other production members come together for each individual production. There are only one or two ensembles in Britain, and nearly all theatres work with very short rehearsal periods. The shift in funding simply exacerbated these factors by making the primary drive of theatre buildings commercial. And lest there be any doubt: the arts never have been, nor ever will be self-funding. Artistic experiment takes time, experience and conversation, for artists to develop and for audiences to learn to value, and often the appreciation is posthumous. The unique hybridity of commercialism and state support that shapes British theatre is fundamental to understanding the relationship between British and international theatre, and between English and non-English cultural traditions in the theatre, although the same relations are not at work in all those relationships.

To begin with the impact of visiting international theatre: the visit of Bertolt Brecht's Berliner Ensemble in 1955 to the Old Vic had a profound effect on British writers, if not other parts of theatre production, and through the 1950s and 1960s the one consistent encouragement for a world season was at the Aldwych Theatre. From the 1970s onward, though, the international theatre presence in the UK has been confined to sporadic one-offs, the occasional 'international season', with some significant exceptions. The Edinburgh Festival, for example, has an enviable record of welcoming some of the major European companies into its short three-week season. The Riverside Studios in Hammersmith during the late 1970s and early 1980s, under the inspiration of David Gothard, became a mecca for international theatre, as did the Leicester Haymarket under Peter Lichtenfels in the late 1980s. For the past twenty years there has been the biennial London International Festival of Theatre, or LIFT, and the intermittent international festivals at the Barbican such as the current BITE (Barbican International Theatre Events) programme. On the whole, Britain has not encouraged international theatre, but more importantly it has certainly not supported co-operation between British companies and those from elsewhere. As a result, British theatre is losing out.

However, the lack of co-operation is not surprising. To focus on European and English theatre for example: the fundamental difference is again that hybridity of the commercial and the subsidized, for most European theatre is fully subsidized. This difference leads to differences in organization, training and production patterns that make it difficult for practical co-operative work, but more importantly, establish a radical difference in the public's expectation of what the theatre should be doing, why we should go to it. Subsidized theatre in Europe has its own pros and cons. In Spain and Italy the theatres are sharply politicized along the political lines of the subsidizers. A play that wants to tour in Italy has to be careful not to perform in a clearly right-wing city before trying to move on to a left-wing town, it can only go to one of them. At the Institut del Teatre and Resad, both national training centres for theatre in Spain, there is clearly felt tension between those staff members hired under Franco and those hired after his death.

Another example from Spain is that of Lluís Pasqual, who was appointed Artistic Adviser to the National Theatre (Centro Dramático Nacional) in Madrid as one of a three-person team, in the dying months of Felipe González's socialist government. All of them, along with the Artistic Director, were promptly fired when the present conservatives, the PP (Partido Popular), were elected. An actor, designer or director in a European country may well feel more like a civil servant than a self-employed, often temporarily employed, artist. In Germany the town gives the theatre a budget, the theatre does its job by putting on the season of plays, and the town gets the box-office takings. In France, major finance is often based around an individual such as Peter Brook or Ariane Mnouchkine, in a way unheard of in Britain, and only faintly similar to Howard Barker's production company, The Wrestling School. Finance is, in the end, the real difference. For example, the cities of Munich and Hamburg each give more to their civic arts programmes than the Arts Council gives to the whole of theatre in England.

The result of higher and more consistent subsidy is, first, that unlike the three weeks of the typical British rehearsal time, European rehearsals are often three months or longer so that the entire company may learn incrementally from each other during that period; second, that there are many ensemble groups with the opportunity to develop new theatre techniques and structures, and virtually none in the UK; third, that a production may play in the city of its company and then elsewhere for a year or more, in contrast to the normal three- to four-week run for a production in this country. These are just three pragmatic reasons why co-operative productions between Britain and Europe are difficult to achieve.

Another reason may be that the written text is so central to British drama that stagecraft and design take second place. European audiences and actors are trained in different ways. Actors on the Continent frequently train for up to six years, without which training ensemble work is difficult. They then move to consistent work in subsidized theatre, producing a play over a six-month to two-year period. Actors in the UK train for only three years at most, at places like RADA or LAMBDA, where the yearly costs are in excess of £7,000. The only university course for acting in the country is at Manchester Metropolitan University, where over 1,500 students apply for twenty-four places. Despite the scholarships offered by generous ex-trainees at RADA, like Sir Anthony Hopkins, Manchester effectively becomes the only place offering any subsidized theatre training for students whose families cannot afford fees. Practitioners such as Peter Brook, who had to leave this country to find support, could not have survived without an independent income.

Of course these days, in stark contrast with the pre-World War II period of repertory companies in nearly every town and city that fell by the wayside in the face of film, television and video, many actors arrive in the profession with no training at all – often from the Oxbridge connection, which has in a sense filled the gap with intelligent and usually relatively well-off graduates. One example might be the group of young people from Cambridge who ended up at the Traverse in 1983–5: after Jenny Killick had gone to the Traverse as a trainee director, she was followed in networking style by Paul Unwin, Simon Russell Beale and Tilda Swinton, all of whom, like others such as Rowan Atkinson, have produced some exceptional work and have gone on to successful careers. In the public's mind in the UK, and fostered by the Oxford and Cambridge situation, there is still a sense of a direct connection between the amateur and the professional stage, which has its own pros and cons. But the general lack of training may be indicative of a larger problem that many other actors have, of limited range, especially when faced with theatre from other cultures and places. Furthermore, the middle-class (and often middle-aged) dominance in the theatre must have an effect on the range of class issues addressed, the kind of material produced, whose life it speaks about and to, which audience it develops. A case in point might be the highly successful Kathy Burke, a no-holds-barred working-class actor who has opened up new material and yet has been treated until recently as an exotic anomaly.

Audiences need training too. One of the striking statistics of the Edinburgh Festival is that the majority of the audience for the main events is from the city itself and nearby environs. This audience has been exposed to so many foreign language productions that they expect and easily deal with the overhead translation boards which dispose of the language barrier that is the most obvious hindrance to international cultural exchange. More subtle and more important, audiences have to learn how to understand different stage techniques, different production structures, particularly the intensely visual and physical theatre of contemporary European traditions. Nothing about drama is 'hardwired' into our nervous system, we have to experience and learn a vocabulary for cultural difference whether it is social, ethnic, or religious, before we can respond to it enough to value it.

All this said, the best of European theatre is often better than British theatre for clear reasons, but bad directors, hired alongside actors with long-term job security, as happens with a fully state-subsidized theatre, are a recipe for disaster. The best may be better, but the bad is worse. Indeed, the very lack of training in acting does, in some cases, give British actors an edge, it makes them willing to try anything. Certainly, good British actors are much beloved by European directors, who seem to want the ensemble conditions and longer rehearsal periods along with the nervous hunger of the actor as artist. A difficult balance.

International theatre traditions resident in Britain

The 1976 report by Naseem Khan, *The Arts Britain Ignores*, was the first considered report on the diversity of British culture and its funding although it did not include work from Italian, Polish, or Jewish communities, for example, but focused on African and Asian cultures. As an equally important 1989 report from the Arts Council, *Towards Cultural Diversity*, pointed out, the 1976 report put a wide variety of issues on the agenda, but also instituted the term 'Ethnic Minority Arts', which became a damaging category over the following years. Significantly the 1989 report also criticized the idea that 'Ethnic Minority Arts' were 'community based' and 'an appendix' to national culture. In its turn, the 1989 report attempted to address the western/Eurocentric national consciousness that relegated 'Ethnic Minority Arts' to the periphery, noting in particular the lack of permanent buildings for, say, Black arts:

> Of the thirty new theatres created since the war, not one belongs to a black company, neither do any of the ten new art and photography galleries which the Arts Council has helped to create belong to a black organisation.[7]

In addition it points out the lack of 'black qualified personnel at the top end of administration', and the uneven funding base. The report then goes on to list the achievements of the late 1980s, in redressing some of these problems, while acknowledging that many are still there.

The central focus for the 1989 report was to devise arts policy that would dismantle the notion that culturally diverse traditions are 'Ethnic Minority' based, and only an appendix to 'national' culture. Yet there is a curious division in the resulting projects, with groups that attempt cross-cultural work such as Tara Arts, or the National Theatre Studio initiative on African/Black Theatre, being put forward as central examples of success, at the same time as the marketing and research projects are still firmly based in communities – supposedly one of the areas that was under criticism. In fact, it is impossible to get away from communities, especially where theatre is concerned. Theatre is a clearly social event that is generated by groups of people and performed for groups of people. The energy that makes it possible for the actors, writers and directors to produce a play has to come from some common ground no matter how diverse they are as individuals, and that common ground will define them as a community. Just so, members of an audience, unless they are simply absorbing something they already know, have to find the energy to involve themselves and learn from the experience. Their commitment to this participation has to be a result of social issues, including the aesthetic and the political, that have had an impact on them. It is impossible to divorce oneself from community of some kind.

Although the report may have been a response to the Arts Council reluctance to support 'community arts' more generally, it was also underwriting a line of aesthetic snobbery that suggests that community-rooted arts are ill-thought-out, poorly rendered, and 'amateurish', in order to protect culturally diverse arts from the criticism of being unskilled or without craft, even less 'civilized'. However, all theatre has to be rooted in community. And theatre, like other arts, provides clear indication of whether or not that community is exploring its potential or simply fulfilling its own clichés. A subsequent report, *Going Black Under the Skin*, from the London Arts Board (1995) gives a unique insight into that

---

7 Arts Council of Great Britain, *Towards Cultural Diversity*, 1989, p. 3.

necessity. Doubtless spurred on by the underfunding of writing, as compared to the other arts, from immigrant communities, the report speaks
plainly of the discrimination against Black writers, from the difficulty of
finding an agent, to the cultural perception of language experiment, and
dramatic technique and structure in Black writing, which may be put
down to 'naivety' rather than a different vision. What the report makes
quite clear is that there are definite community links for the writers,
immediate issues that they are addressing. By implication, people who do
not understand those issues, or perhaps do not even see them as issues,
are not part of the community, nor do they accept that this community is
part of their lives.

Writers from the different societies that have emigrated to Britain
have, however, had some success: individuals such as Hanif Kureshi of
Pakistani background, Marcella Evaristi of Italian descent, Caryl Phillips
from a Caribbean family, or Jyoti Patel from India via Uganda. Looking
further back we could take the writing career of Mustafa Matura from
Trinidad as an almost textbook example of how the theatre in Britain has
responded to an incoming theatre presence:

As Time Goes By	Traverse Theatre	1971
Play Mas	Royal Court	1974
Rum an Coca Cola	Royal Court	1976
Another Tuesday	Black Theatre Cooperative	1978
More, More	Black Theatre Cooperative	1978
Independence	Bush Theatre	1979
Welcome Home, Jacko	The Factory/Riverside	1979
A Dying Business	Riverside	1980
One Rule	Riverside	1981
Meetings	Hampstead	1982
Party at the Palace	Channel 4	1983
There's Something Wrong in Paradise	Granada Television	1984
Trinidad Sisters	Tricycle	1988
The Coup	Royal National Theatre	1991

Matura starts out with the theatres dedicated to new writing, not
surprisingly the Traverse, the rather less well-recognized (for no good
reason) theatre in Scotland, and only then the Royal Court. After a few
years with a touring company that he co-founds, the Black Theatre Coop-
erative, he moves to smaller theatres in London like the Bush, and is taken
up into Riverside during its international years. His work then makes the
transition to television, while the stage plays from the late 1980s go into

the Tricycle, dedicated to the development of Black and Irish theatre, and to the National, the pinnacle of theatre canonicity (but at the Cottesloe, the smallest auditorium).

The history is caught up into a major decision by the Arts Council in the late 1980s, which was to put 4 per cent of its budget into new communities so that they could develop their own voice. Results can be seen not only in the Tricycle, but also Stratford East with its policy on developing Asian theatre, or in Tara Arts or Talawa. Certainly this policy decision has integrated actors who might otherwise have been excluded from the stage and has helped constitute the 'rainbow' casts that are often now found on the main stages of London, Birmingham and Manchester. The theatre in Britain is arguably more integrated and less racist than many European countries. What is significant though are the companies that have disappeared like Temba, L'Overture, or Carib. Since 1984 the number of theatre companies across the board in the UK has declined, but because of the smaller base of the Black Arts sector and the sector representing incoming residents more generally such as the Irish, the loss has been proportionally higher. This is partly because the impetus for growth in this sector has not necessarily focused on building-based theatre, which lies at the heart of current arts policy. Those companies that have survived have a record of distinctly cross-cultural work which reflects the cross-cultural lives of their members. For example, the Talawa theatre company's mission statement reflects a self-conscious positioning of black theatre in Britain:

- to use black culture and experience to further enrich British theatre.
- to provide high-quality productions that reflect the significant creative role that black theatre plays within the national and international arena.
- to enlarge theatre audiences from the black community.[8]

If the initial productions worked from Caribbean tradition, it did not take long for Talawa to add productions of work by Wilde and Shakespeare.

Tara Arts has a similar history, one that is informed by Jatinder Verma's characterization of its first production in 1976/7 as one that 'linked Race to Communalism, as being part of the same spectrum of Oppression … to be opposed to the one is, necessarily to be opposed to the other … without the one, the sensibility that is Black slides into xenophobia; and without the other, we are unable to locate our own inadequacies within a larger context'.[9] Tara Arts has an long-running history of

8 Talawa Information sheet. Telephone 44 (0) 20 7251 6644.
9 Jatinder Verma, 'Transformation in Culture: The Asian in Britain', Royal Society for the Arts, November 1989, p. 772. For information on Tara Arts, telephone 44 (0) 20 8333 4457.

productions of European classics, which it has reinterpreted in a startling variety of ways, including the employment of an Indian film actor to play in *Cyrano* at the National Theatre. The actor came, notes Jatinder Verma in an interview, from a tradition 'which had a particular attitude to England as the repository of the greatness of theatre'[10] to work with people who were part of English theatre and had continued to change it. In the same interview it was pointed out that Tara Arts, unlike Talawa, had not operated as a forum for new writing until the 1990s. Verma responded,

> the obvious analogy would be, 'How can you contribute to others when you're not sure of yourself?' By now we are sure of the kind of territory we inhabit, the kind of things that we want to do, the ways in which we want to do them. Therefore there's a clarity for new writers.[11]

Yet despite all the difficulties, some would say that Talawa and Tara Arts, for example, have bedded down, have become the token alternative cultural theatre for a particular ethnic group that makes it difficult for new communities to argue the value of their own voices. At the same time there are the highly successful actors like Josette Bushell-Mingo, of Caribbean origin, who worked with Talawa and, subsequently, the Royal Shakespeare Company. She says that although she is vitally interested in, say, dialect, and how it functions as a performance device, she does not think of herself as a Caribbean actor. Profoundly cross-cultural, she brings the traditions she knows together in generative ways. And several communities have not yet integrated, nor perhaps will ever want to integrate their cultural traditions with those here in Britain.

But this is all to tell a story from the position of the positive effects of the cultural tradition that has found itself resident in this country. If we look at the mainstream theatre it's a different story. Theatre traditions different to those in Britain have been extraordinarily difficult to set up, to keep going, and again, the bottom line is that there is such pressure on the box office that developing a voice is often too expensive and time-consuming. It is rare to find drama from non-British cultures on the main stage of regional theatres. The West Yorkshire Playhouse had two highly innovative seasons of Black theatre in the autumns of 1996 and 1997, yet for various reasons, but especially in the face of very low audience attendance, the season did not continue. Is it reasonable to expect an audience to learn how to respond to different theatre techniques in just two short seasons? Is it reasonable to expect such learning in the board

---

10 Jatinder Verma, an interview with Graham Ley, 'Theatre of Migration and the Search for a Multicultural Aesthetic', *New Theatre Quarterly*, no. 52 (1997), p. 361.
11 Ibid., p. 364.

members of a theatre? It may well be that in Leeds, with the lack of many small theatre companies to encourage people in the community to think in terms of acting and the theatre, there is simply no imagination for it – in contrast to dance, say, which in Leeds has a strong community base and is well supported on the main stage. The sheer hugeness of London, and diversity of its cultural communities, may make it a special case in Britain.

A recent Arts Council report, *The Cultural Diversity Action Plan*, is the basis of current policy. It begins in a typically late 1990s manner, with the statements that:

> Ethnic minorities comprise 5.5% of the total population, nearly half of whom were born in the UK and 80% of which are below the age of 25. They spend, in all, £10 billion a year. (*Marketing Business*, 1997)

And:

> 95% of new business start-ups involve ethnic minority entrepreneurs. (Barclays Bank Report, 1997)

The new plan of action is summarized as the development of diversity through advocacy and access. What is interesting about this plan is the word 'advocacy'. Advocacy has come to be used in some circles of political theory as a 'good word', to distinguish 'representation', or a person who 'stands for' a group of others and expresses their wishes in his/her own words (like our parliamentary system), from 'advocacy', or a person who is asked by a group not to represent them but to advocate their cause. In other words the advocate must at all times recognize difference as well as similarity. Under 'Advocacy' the new report does not seem to be at all aware of this distinction, and offers no guidance whatsoever as to strategies for ensuring that the 'promotion', 'participation', 'approach', 'establishment', 'stimulation', 'support', 'development', and 'set up' that they promise to do on behalf of cultural diversity will in fact be advocative rather than representative.

One immediate aspect that one might want to pursue, especially in terms of studies of diverse societies and cultures elsewhere in the world, is that the word 'black' is the focus for the diverse elements that need advocacy. This country, like others, will need to take on board the multiplicity of other cultures that are becoming more mobile, often enforcedly so, around the globe at the moment. How, for example, are refugees classified? The Birmingham-based Asian storyteller, Vayu Naidu, shows an unusual awareness of this multiplicity in her collaborations, which led in 1997 to the 'Shape Shifting Stories' season by Brumhalata in Birmingham. The season looked at the stories, music and movements from Indian,

African and Irish traditions, as three of the primary migrations into the UK in recent years. Her work explicitly draws on traditional cultural styles, moving them firmly into the needs of a contemporary audience.[12]

The Cultural Diversity Action Plan report is positive and encouraging, yet, as it stands, strong on intentions rather than detail, so it is difficult to assess its potential impact. In contrast *The Landscape of Fact* report, a 1997 consultative Green Paper on 'Cultural Diversity for the English Funding System: African, Caribbean, Asian and Chinese Arts', provides rather more substance. It also attempts to think through the issues of audience, referring to Jenni Francis' *Attitudes Among Britain's Black Community Towards Attendance at Arts, Cultural and Entertainment Events* (1990), which drew on Rex Nettleford's analysis of the existence of three broad categories – ancestral/traditional, classical and contemporary. The terms allow the report to discuss the differences between theatre that provides a first-generation migrant group with a sense of cultural continuity, and theatre that 'crosses art forms', and uses 'a number of frames of reference' to be 'part of an aesthetic that needs an informed response' through which second and third generations may negotiate integration and difference.

Policy-making that recognizes that similar divisions also occur within audiences as a whole throughout the UK could radically change the face of mainstream theatre. What is troubling, is that both these recent reports underwrite the assessment of the mainstream British audience as markedly conservative. The response to Ian McKellan's decision to work in Leeds for the 1998–99 season, rather than London, was indicative. McKellan apparently found the London audiences 'monochrome', as opposed to the 'diverse mix of ages, classes and backgrounds' that Michael Billington sees in regional theatres.[13] We are less sanguine that there is a difference.[14] Billington also cites Ken Campbell's description of the middle-class, mailing-list audience as 'brochure theatre', which might well describe the audiences of many regional theatres. Despite welcoming the Arts Council initiative of 'New Audiences', Billington attributes this kind of brochure theatre to the 'whole system of expensive advance booking', which limits the audience for both culture and sport in Britain. In the face of a growing self-consciousness in international traditions of the way audiences can participate in theatre, in this country there is still resolute sticking to the idea of producer and consumer, with no interaction

12 For information on Brumhalata, telephone 44 (0) 121 429 7927.
13 Michael Billington, 'We Need To Stop Favouring the Middle Class's "Brochure Theatre"', *Guardian*, 24 September 1998.
14 See, for example, Fiachra Gibbons, '"Class Chasm" Excludes Young from Arts', *Guardian*, 14 December 1999.

between the two, which typifies the commercial theatre that has come to dominate the theatre world.

Exports of British theatre

One of the ways that British theatre is exported to the world is through the British Council. Since the Council is part of the Foreign Office there are political dimensions to this trade, for example, the strong policy of increasing Indo-Asian interchange. Yet the finances are not substantial and the programme is limited. Few productions, if any, move out from Britain to other places in the world in entirety unless they come from companies already geared to travel. The Royal Shakespeare Company, for example, might visit the United States in order to hold workshops, but rarely to put on a full production, although it has undertaken seasons in New York and Washington. It is highly unusual for a British production initiated by a regional theatre company to tour internationally: part of this must be the difficulty of obtaining finance, but part must be attributed to a lack of interest from other parts of the world. The Leicester Haymarket production of the Russian director Lubymov's *Hamlet,* which toured in 1989/90 to Rome, Berlin, Amsterdam, Warsaw, Taiwan, Cracow and Japan, was a remarkable exception. However, from the 1980s, transfers of the commercially successful productions of musicals have become more and more frequent.

A transitional production was Trevor Nunn and John Caird's *Nicholas Nickleby* at the end of the 1970s. Drawing on the way Joint Stock produced plays and Shared Experience developed narrative, they constructed a substantial and imaginative international hit. The musical straddles the older style of *My Fair Lady* and *Oliver,* and the new Cameron Macintosh style of *Cats, Phantom of the Opera, Les Misérables* or *Starlight Express.* During the 1980s both British and American producers began to start musicals off in London and then transfer them to the United States and further afield. The procedure was desirable partly because of the weak pound against the dollar at that time, but also because in London there is nothing resembling the all-powerful presence of a theatre critic who can kill a production with one bad review. London productions minimized the risk, and the sheer amount of transatlantic travel allowed for the building of demand by word of mouth. However, this style of production led to an extraordinary, and some would say ridiculous control over the product: it had to be replicated exactly in all its performance venues. So, for example, the first production of *Les Misérables* was by the Royal Shakespeare Company and directed by Trevor Nunn and John Caird. When the show went to New York, it was directed by the same directors, with exactly the same choreography, and in exactly the same style. Just so in Japan. As the show moved further afield, it could be directed by Trevor Nunn or John Caird, and eventually they would train directors to take over from them, and those new assistant directors would be replicating the London production – as far as possible. While the change has partly come about in response to the competition from film and television, which are replicable and train audiences to expect replication, in other ways the MacDonaldization of theatre has resulted in a bizarre situation. One incident: an actress on *Anne of Green Gables* was given a video of her part in a previous show and told, 'That's your part …' The success of the replication of musicals has led Disney into transferring *Beauty and the Beast* and *The Lion King* from cartoon onto the stage.

This kind of replication, although it may be commercially successful because the product is so dependable, changes the nature of audiences. Until mid-century, if not until the 1980s, theatregoing could be relatively cheap. With more expensive productions the tickets become more expensive, hence the paying audience wants to know that the production will be good, or at least, slick. The expense of the production also means that fewer things happen on stage, risks are not taken, and miracles do not happen. Audience expectation has come to demand consistency not only in production, but also in cultural representation. A large percentage of the audience for musicals comes from visiting tourists, arriving from all over the world. Rather like the large boards of theatre buildings, to satisfy such a diverse audience many productions focus on the clichés of globally recognizable culture mediated by Hollywood and advertising. If musicals led the way for the shift, main-stage productions of contemporary classics or classic revivals, especially in London, have followed.

An obvious victim of the shift is British comedy. England in particular has had a strong tradition of comic drama, from Oscar Wilde, through J.B. Priestley and Noel Coward, to Michael Frayn, Mike Stott or Tom Stoppard. Yet although there are several top-quality comedy festivals, which offer a showcase for the burgeoning comic talent that is clearly all around Britain, most of that comedy, despite Alan Ayckbourn, remains stand-up, individual rather than company-based. There seems to be an insatiable need for stand-up comics on television, and since television pays much better, they don't often remain in the theatre. They develop specific personae and they have no need to write plays. There are of course people for whom this is the appropriate medium, but despite the examples of Rik Mayall or Ben Elton, there are many others who would once have made the transition yet have not done so. Central to this choice must be the very specificity of humour. Comedy needs location and place, it needs immediate issues and social relevance, it needs to challenge and take risks, none of which it can do in an effete global superficiality that offers only a reinforcement of stereotypes that we could look beyond.

The irony is that the musical has become a venture that is built rather like the subsidized theatre in Europe, to run for a long time until there is no more demand. While it may therefore pick up many of the drawbacks of that kind of construction, the commercial imperative wipes out virtually all artistic development, and this new form is left with the worst of both worlds. Not only that, it is left providing a template for other theatre, which then becomes completely divorced from the needs of the communities in which it plays: it operates rather like an unself-conscious postmodernism that has no social responsibility and likes to pretend that it is a free-floating cultural signifier. This has come about because the medium is not adequately valued, and therefore not adequately supported. However, the result is that it can produce nothing of any value to the individuals in this society, certainly nothing of the intensity of value that would lead people energetically to try to persuade politicians to change government policy toward the arts. Perhaps this is one reason that performance art is becoming so popular.

Where is the theatre community in the UK in 2002?

Britain's mainstream theatre pales into banality beside international theatre traditions either within this country or from elsewhere. It is brought to life only occasionally by miraculous acting or splendid writing. Perhaps, as Jatinder Verma suggests for Asian theatre, there must be a sense both of communality and oppression: white British people are as involved in these issues as much as non-white.[15] Without a sense of oppression, or politically immediate issues which we tacitly if not actively endorse, we will lose the sense of what needs to be done, what changes are necessary. Without a sense of communality, we slide into the banal, conventional and self-reinforcing cocoon of national sentimentalism. England, at least, seems to have little sense of communality, perhaps because of the media dominance of the United States, perhaps because it has gone too late into Europe, perhaps because it's in a time of fundamental change that is so confusing that strong leaders who claim a moral imperative are welcomed with open arms, whether they be on the right or the left. And without communality, a sense of oppression may just be too terrifying to deal with. Perhaps this is why some younger writers today fill their plays with mutilation: the classic response to disempowerment.

---

15   Jatinder Verma, 'An Asian Agenda for Public Policy', St Catherine's Conference, Windsor, 1997.

The state of reviewing today

Michael Billington

Michael Billington has been drama critic of the *Guardian* since 1971 and of *Country Life* since 1987. He is also the author of several books including studies of the work of playwrights Alan Ayckbourn and Tom Stoppard and the authorized biography of Dame Peggy Ashcroft. Most recently he has written the first full-scale biography of playwright Harold Pinter. He has written for a number of American publications including the *New York Times* and *Vanity Fair* and teaches two courses with undergraduate students in London: one with the University of Pennsylvania, the other with Boston University. He broadcasts regularly on the arts on radio and television. This article first appeared in the *Royal Society for the Arts (RSA) Journal* in Spring 1999 and is republished with the author's permission.

The job of the theatre critic is obviously different in kind from that of the film, television or visual arts critic. The theatre critic is dealing with a fluctuating and variable art form: one that depends on the peculiar chemistry of the occasion. 'No play', wrote Max Beerbohm, 'is ever quite as good or quite as bad as it appears on its First Night'; and, especially if one is writing straight after curtain-fall, one has to guard against excessive praise or condemnation. Given the circumstances, it is not always easy. I recall a recent occasion after the first night of Tom Stoppard's *The Invention of Love* at the Cottesloe Theatre. The play was of immense complexity. It ran for over three hours. Most of the daily critics had to write their notices in about forty-five minutes in the National Theatre's offices. I shared a lift up to the offices with colleagues from the *Telegraph* and the *Mail*: I remember we all stared at each other in silence and raised our eyes to heaven as if to say 'What on earth are we doing?' Theatre reviews are subject both to pressures of time and the peculiar nature of the occasion: sometimes a play takes off, sometimes it remains obstinately grounded. Theatre critics also know, though they rarely admit it, that reviews can have a measurable impact at the box office. Whenever we are asked about our power, we modestly shuffle our feet and deny it; and it is perfectly true that none of us, thankfully, has the Papal authority bestowed on the critic of the *New York Times* by that paper's monopoly of the serious daily market. But the blunt truth is that reviews do make a difference. Musicals, I suspect, remain largely immune to our paper bullets: the mixed press received by *Les Misérables* has not stopped it being the most popular musical in theatrical history. But plays, particularly in the commercial theatre, are vulnerable objects and depend increasingly on a favourable tide of critical opinion.

What fascinates me, however, is the way theatre criticism has changed since I first came into the business in 1965. For a start, much less is covered. I began as a freelance critic on *The Times* when, under the benign editorship of John Lawrence, there was only a single broadsheet page every day for the arts. Yet as a young critic I was sent off to review not only regional theatre but also Oxford University Drama Society (OUDS) and Marlowe Society productions at Oxford and Cambridge, shows at amateur theatres like the Tower and the Questors, even on occasion, shows at Westminster School. Today, although *The Times* has more space and three theatre critics, it doesn't cover the same amount of ground. When I moved to the *Guardian* in 1971 I found – often to my frustration – that there was a network of regional critics covering the Midlands, the North, the West Country, Scotland and so forth. Today all that has changed. I am now free to go wherever I wish, which I welcome. But the coverage of regional theatre, as with most other papers, is far more selective: it tends to focus on what you might call the Premier League theatres. The status of theatre reviewing has also changed over the years: it no longer enjoys the primacy it once did. The reasons for this are numerous. One is that the medium of theatre itself is under constant threat. Virtually all newspapers over the last few years have carried pieces attacking theatre as elitist, old-fashioned, marginal and irrelevant: one such by Bryan Appleyard in the *Sunday Times* argued that theatre is only taken seriously in Britain because Shakespeare happened to write plays. Naturally, I disagree with this; but I would concede that theatre has contributed to its own marginalization by its gradual withdrawal from plays on public issues. It is fascinating to note that in 1999 when The Tricycle Theatre staged its edited version of the Stephen Lawrence enquiry, the event commanded a large amount of space: precisely because the theatre was engaging directly with a topical, public event.

But there is a more profound reason for theatre's, and by extension theatre reviewing's, loss of status; and that is to do with the Thatcherite social revolution of the 1980s with the effects of which we are still coming to terms. Profitability in the 1980s became a test of worth: popularity an index of quality. Inevitably, if you start to play the numbers game, theatre is vulnerable: it cannot easily compete with the mass-audiences commanded by film, television, popular music. No one, to my knowledge, has done a precise study of the co-relation between politics and art in the 1980s. But it is surely no accident that it was an extremely thin decade for new British drama. The one theatrical form that really did prosper was the musical: one that provided exactly the mixture of spiritual reassurance and economic prosperity that chimed in with the prevailing political philosophy; indeed when Sir Peter Hall, as Director of the National

Theatre, was invited to dinner at 10 Downing Street, he found himself being asked by Mrs Thatcher why he couldn't make money for Britain like Andrew Lloyd Webber. No use pointing out, of course, that the National in its own way did just that. It may seem bizarre to link Mrs Thatcher with the decline in theatre reviewing. What I am suggesting is that there was a crucial cultural shift in the 1980s which has had its knock-on effect in the 1990s. So-called 'high art' is now suspect. Reithian principles have been totally jettisoned by the BBC. Opera has become the dirtiest five-letter word in the language. Politicians have lost their nerve: Tony Blair, a constant playgoer by the way, recently admitted to the director Nicholas Hytner that the money needed to permit the arts to flourish was a drop in the ocean but that he couldn't sell that idea to the tabloids. Arts subsidy, like the Euro, clearly doesn't play well with the big proprietors. My point is that, in the current climate, theatre has to struggle to make itself heard. We live increasingly in a culture dominated by the two big Cs: consumerism and celebrity. Theatre becomes big news when it reflects one or other of those: the first night, for instance, of a big musical or the appearance of a major movie star in a fringe theatre. And critics all too willingly play the game: fascinating to note how many end-of-the-year reviews in 1998 gave more space to Nicole Kidman's appearance in an indifferent David Hare play at the Donmar than to Hare's own performance in his magnificent one-man play about the Israeli-Palestinian conflict, *Via Dolorosa.*

One other factor, very much part of our consumerist culture, helps to explain the precariousness not just of theatre reviewing but of criticism in general: the rise and rise of public relations. Many years ago Alan Brien wrote a piece in the *Spectator* entitled 'So you want to be a press agent'. He invented a mythical figure called Hugo Puffball: a theatre press agent characterized by his complete ignorance of the play and its author, by his unawareness of the cast's previous work and by a genial clubbability that consisted largely of serving warm gin to critics in the interval. Hugo Puffballs did once exist. But no longer. Theatre PR is now a highly sophisticated business dominated by one or two key firms brilliantly adept at farming out interviews: before a major new show, interviews and profiles with the stars, the author, the director, the designer will be judiciously allocated to the broadsheets and the tabloids. Arts journalism today is often, to vary Dr Johnson's remark about a second marriage, the triumph of hype over experience. And the better the PR, the more criticism itself is marginalized. I sound like a Jeremiah; and since I came into this strange business I feel that the status of criticism has radically changed. Thirty years ago I would never have guessed that even the most serious papers would be assessing the value of works of art by visual symbols or star-ratings. But I am not entirely without hope. For a start, I genuinely believe that theatre in Britain in the last three years has begun to fight back and reassert its cultural importance. Significantly, the big musicals have started to dry up. What has happened is that a new generation of dramatists of the calibre of Patrick Marber, Conor McPherson, Martin McDonagh, Mark Ravenhill and Sarah Kane has emerged and has galvanized the theatrical scene: what is more their work is spreading like a bushfire – or perhaps a Royal Court fire – throughout Europe and is being endlessly celebrated. British theatre suddenly seems dangerously alive; and that fact is being reflected in arts pages.

I also – and I hope I am not being falsely optimistic – see a growing resistance to the sterile populism that has for too long dominated the arts agenda: it is, for instance, a small but significant step for mankind that the restaurant-column which for too long dominated the arts pages of the *Observer* has lately been put in its proper place. As for theatre critics, I believe the onus is on us to make the case for our art form. Our first obligation is to write better: one reason I haven't even mentioned for our possible marginalization is that we lack the voluptuous style and moral passion of such legendary predecessors as Kenneth Tynan or Harold Hobson. But I also believe theatre critics have a duty to question prevailing values: to resist the lure of the puff-interview, to suggest that a new play in Bolton might be of more interest than a piece of tired West End hackery or that a rare Jacobean revival may be of greater cultural import than yet another Trevor Nunn musical. It is up to us, in consultation with our arts editors, not just to set the agenda but radically to change it: to re-establish that theatre is not just central to our culture but, at its best, a source of opposition to the crude materialism of the age. We have too long been complicit in our own demise. If the minor art-form we practise is to survive, we ourselves need to be nothing if not critical.

Critical path
Claire MacDonald

Claire MacDonald is a freelance writer and critic living in Washington, DC. She is joint-editor of the journal *Performance Research*, was a Senior Lecturer and Research Fellow in Theatre at De Montfort University, Leicester, UK from 1994–98, has been a theatre maker for two decades and has held teaching positions and artistic fellowships in Britain, the USA and Europe. Her theatre texts have been performed in Britain, Europe, the USA and Australia. Her writing on visual art, performance and fiction has appeared in journals including *Performing Arts Journal*, *Performance Research*, and *Women and Performance* and she has contributed to several books on theatre, including the *Cambridge Companion to British Women Playwrights* (Cambridge University Press, 2000).

Theatre is in a state of crisis; a crisis not only to do with the prevailing climate of hostility towards the subsidized arts but with deeper challenges to its significance within the culture. This has, of course, been going on for a long time – the function of theatre as a place for the mediation and representation of social issues through fiction has been undergoing a process of displacement by film and TV since the advent of those technologies. And then 'theatre' is not a monolithic entity, it is a fluid and diverse plurality of practices. But while that plurality of practices within theatre is what keeps it alive, the lack of any serious discourse which can address them may be the death of it. In the end what remains of this illusory and ephemeral art form is what is written about it and if this is to contribute with any significance to the larger life of ideas then it must be engaged by a serious, intelligent critical discourse. This is particularly true of the areas of theatrical experiment outside the play, the absence of a discourse means the absence of continuity. Experimental theatre is engaged in a continual disappearing act, present only as discreet events whose value is often seen in terms of their newness. (Claire MacDonald, 'The Future of an Illusion', *New Socialist*, March 1987)

In the spring of 1987 I sensed the passing of time. I had worked as a performer and theatre maker for eight years non-stop, founding a company and making visual theatre in Britain and Europe and my life was now changing. I was thirty-two, the single parent of a small daughter who had just started school, and I had recently begun a year-long artistic fellowship at Cambridge University; but as I moved into writing plays, and teaching contemporary theatre practice, I found myself fighting a tiring rearguard action against a conservative dismissal of avant-garde theatre that seemed to me to be counter-productive. Academic criticism seemed almost wilfully to neglect innovation, and to seek to confine theatre to a very tight corner of British culture – the history of drama, good productions of modern classics, and Shakespeare. When I began writing journalism I suddenly found myself writing polemical pieces addressed to the absence of intelligent critical discussion about new kinds of theatre making. I realized that if the work I was seeing was to be included in a larger life of ideas, it had to be written about, talked about, taught and referenced. Moreover, I sensed that the very liveness of new work, its resistance to documentation and its fast turnover, meant that it was vulnerable. Conservative times and funding cuts meant the barely lamented disappearance of experiment. How to foster that work – and how to find a critical context for it – perplexed me.

The theatre I had made during the 1980s with Impact Theatre was outside the frame of reference of the well-made play – it was visually based, with words and music as part of the score and, like much cross-art-form performance, it didn't result in a published script. We had been influenced by the kind of work which combined passion and visual inventiveness with intellectual edge – Pina Bausch and Robert Wilson might be the best-known 1980s examples – but there were many groups in Europe, the Americas and Britain whose hybrid, ensemble practice echoed our own. Amongst the people I knew, visual artists and theatre makers worked on joint projects. Installation and live art, photography, film, new music and dance created a context for the cross-fertilization of ideas; but while a lot of energy went into making new work, little went into recording it or addressing it critically. Moreover, the prevailing ethos of my generation of theatre makers was always to look forward and never back – seeing the work as part of a continuously forward-moving process of live engagement. Suddenly, in 1987 when I stopped performing, I saw the possibility that this continuous process would one day become history and nothing would remain of it. It would fall away into darkness, forgotten as quickly as it had been made.

Looking back, I think this awareness of time passing was an inevitable stage of my own life, but I also think that the worlds of public intellectual life and academia, the established theatre and the 'fringe', and the practices of avant-garde theatre making and playwriting were much further apart then than they now are; lines of demarcation were more nervously policed, and the more fluid and lateral kind of collaboration I now see across the arts was less in evidence. What I see now at the beginning of 2002 is different. For good or bad, old institutions and institutionalized behaviours have been radically shaken up. Today's hybridities exist on significantly different levels. One change is to do with the collaboration between the live and the virtual which has created so many new possibilities. Another concerns the relationship between artist and critic. What I want to reflect here, is how ways of making, thinking and writing about theatre have changed over the past decade, and how those changes are linked to shifts in the wider cultural scene. I believe they have changed, and in ways which I could not have foreseen when, in my polemic of 1987, I looked with pessimism at the culture of criticism.

In 1986/87 the public face of Britain was still one of establishment and opposition. The arts-funding culture was under threat, but the clear division between those who had the power to shape public policy and funding and those who did not, on any large scale, was still in place. There were many signs that things were changing – not only through the work of imaginative artistic directors who showed international and experimental work, but also because a generation of theatre makers was beginning to teach in universities, and to research and document contemporary work.[1]

The quotation at the top of this chapter is from a piece I wrote for *New Socialist* about the reception and discussion of new work. Ostensibly focused on a season of new British theatre at the Institute of Contemporary Arts (ICA) in London, the article explored a wider issue, and one which, I felt, lay behind the Arts Council of Great Britain's then recent report on the arts, called – amazingly it now seems to me – 'The Glory of the Garden'. I said then that the use of the garden metaphor was part and parcel of a concept of heritage England, that green and sceptred isle of country houses and gardens. Images of the flowering of culture, and of the fringe as a seedbed of research, were scattered throughout the pages of the report in an extended metaphor suggestive of a set of under-gardeners happily tending seedbeds for the owners of the big house. I found it illuminating. Reading through that report and my article today, I am struck by how clearly the traditional hierarchies of class – us and them, urban and rural, establishment and opposition – were still being played out. I was addressing the establishment from the urban left, arguing that the real work of theatre – the critical, leading, sharp edge – was being silenced and erased and that only a serious critical discourse could place it on the record. The funding establishment's response to the extraordinary inventiveness and persistence of the 'fringe' was to assign it a mute underclass (and underfunded) role, toiling away in the border.

The way in which the establishment, as I then saw it, framed its discourse was, I think, largely unconscious. Now that I live in the USA I am acutely aware of the depth of telling metaphor behind the English

1 This change is the one which my generation – who went to university in the mid-1970s – has been an important part of. The position, and the influence, of artists as university teachers is a subject for much longer consideration – and one in which a transatlantic view could be very illuminating – but one of the issues to consider in thinking about cultural change in Britain is the way in which a whole generation of theatre makers began to teach what I like to call 'informed practice' rather than 'practical work' in theatre. The concept of teaching practice informed by theory arose largely in Britain through the art school tradition, and especially the radicalization of art schools by feminism, conceptual art and critical theory during the 1970s. Many theatre makers, and in particular feminists, found themselves involved in theories of representation, narrative and performance theory through their contact with the visual arts, and brought into the universities not only new practice, but ideas about visual and textual representation which connected theatre to a larger world of critical ideas. The tensions around artists and artistic practice in higher education have been many, but the presence of informed artists has also led to some very productive questions about the nature of research in the arts, and ultimately to rethinking what 'research' itself might be.

predilection for wordplay. The metaphor of the garden is a subject worthy of much more lengthy consideration than I can go into here, but suffice it to say that the way in which it is used in English (as opposed to Welsh or Scottish) culture, and by whom, often relates to more complex issues. In this case I felt that it very neatly reminded all the players in the arts of their place. And it did so at a time of substantial threat. The Thatcher years were ones of draconian funding cuts, combined with an ideology that moved scarce resources from the many to the few – and the few were rarely the new shoots.

Things changed over the next ten years, and things never quite work out in the way you imagine they will. Interesting and often unlikely creative alliances have emerged from the shake-up of institutions which, combined with rapid technological and demographic change, have had a profound effect on the relationship of practice, theory and research in the arts. In 2000 it is now much less clear who controls the discourse and in whose hands is the power to shape imagination.

One of the unlikely alliances that springs to mind is between the vast 'alternative' culture that flowered in the pre-Thatcher 1970s, and the later free-market capitalism of the 1980s. What interested me in 1978, when I co-founded Impact Theatre co-operative in Leeds, was the desire to live a life largely based in alternative networks which had a degree of independence from conventional institutions. That life, as some of you will remember, grew out of a heady mix of romantic bohemianism and hard-headed radical politics in which we lived in big, old shared houses and founded food co-ops and bands, theatre companies, arts centres and radical magazines. It was a life which valued co-operation, and which grew networks based on long-term social and economic relationships and alliances outside the nuclear family. It was, essentially, project-based and left-aligned. It also relied on the organized welfare-state culture of post-war Britain, in which it was possible to live cheaply, and on a liberal climate of opinion which fostered dissent.

The 1980s were different. Margaret Thatcher successfully dismantled almost every foundation stone of the welfare state, the old left disappeared and the arts-funding culture dried to a trickle. But the booms and busts of that decade also shifted economic power dramatically, cutting across old class lines and favouring the entrepreneurial. While Thatcherism preached economic laissez-faire and strict family values, Britain – particularly ethnically and culturally mixed urban Britain – continued to move away from traditional social structures. The dismantling of industries and the shaking up of educational institutions created a bizarre culture of instability and short-termism, but also a project-based, risk-taking culture – the kind of environment which requires the kind of strategic thinking with which people in the small-scale, alternative arts have always worked.

If one aspect of the contradictory nature of late twentieth-century life was the partial convergence of the free market and the free-floating entrepreneurial arts culture, what has happened in academic life – and to the critical discourse which frames discussion of theatre – is also interesting. At the same time as universities have struggled with structural changes and funding cuts, they have also been forced to open up old patterns of professional life and advancement and to create new alliances with arts organizations, publishers and artists, often in ways which have actually fostered serious intellectual discourse in the arts and given visibility to unusual, even avant-garde kinds of art making. New disciplines and new sites for research have emerged. Performance studies, which has taken much of its driving energy from the counter-culture, has fostered critical tools for considering theatre within a broad remit, looking laterally rather than hierarchically at contexts for performance and the sites in which they operate and are located. What is written and taught about theatre is becoming less to do with validation by the old hierarchies – text and author driven, highly specialized and discipline specific, and wary of practices outside accepted conventions – and much more to do with webbing in (as they now say) to emerging arts practices and trying to make sense of them in relation to history and culture.

In the UK, the British Academy (the organization which channelled public money to academic research, largely on an individual basis) has been replaced by the Arts and Humanities Research Board, which now accepts arts practice as research, and encourages applications from individuals and institutions who want to cross the theory–practice divide and set up collaborative projects. On the one hand, a market-driven need to boost excellence in research, and consequent marketability, has produced painful competitiveness amongst universities for small pots of money; on the other hand, the notion of what constitutes research has been increasingly influenced by the wider changes in the culture which I have indicated above. The panels assessing research funding are now likely to be composed not only of scholar experts, but also of people seen as 'stakeholders' in the culture, able to assess the value of research in diverse terms. In the arts, as new rounds of funding assessments come up, there will be equal emphasis on individually generated research and collaborative projects, and some of the people sitting on these panels are the very people who in the 1970s and 1980s were behind the founding of arts centres, theatre companies and radical publications.

The part that technology has played in supporting this change is crucial. Far from directly threatening live performance, it seems as if the biggest change that inexpensive communication technologies have generated is likely to be, once again, in altering the hierarchies of previous systems. If new publishing technologies have allowed ingénues into the market places of design and new writing, and music technologies have changed the culture of popular music, then what has changed in theatre is the means to document and to distribute critical and documentary material, which is now in the hands of the artists to a much larger degree than ever before. In the past ten years the samizdat culture of creative improvisation, which has always been the province of the experimental arts and technologies, has been fostered by technology to such an extent that alternative centres of intellectual life exist to perhaps a greater extent than they ever did.

There are of course no certainties, but if there is one projection I could make about the future it is that art making in its widest sense will have an increasingly important place, not only because we need entertainment and pleasure, but also because the arts provide the kinds of strategic means to work creatively with information, and to foster communication and dialogue among people. The ability to work creatively and independently, to seize opportunities, and to see one's working life as a series of projects is now the model to which many, if not most, people aspire. Printed on the bottom of my Visa bill is this statement: 'According to research carried out by the Future Foundation around 40% of working men and women would like to go freelance.' The dreams of my generation – to live by our wits, to make our own worlds and our own work – have come home to roost. This is now what we all want. Early twenty-first-century capitalism contains the space for making do at a high level of creativity – making and reshaping the culture. The means to imagine has spread far beyond what we expected and is in the hands of far more people.

Whatever theatre is, and whatever one feels and thinks it is, depends on who does the looking. All of the changes I have traced above are very partial, and I am aware of the large element of 'spin' in what I am saying. I am deliberately glossing over the gaps and ignoring the debris from the turbulent technological and political changes of the late twentieth century because I want to put forward an alternative position, one that sees the possibilities of creative alliances as a response to crisis. One that embraces change and sees theatre and the arts as central – not as content but as form.

Theatre remains for me a space of praxis – a place where mind and body come together informed by theory and practice; a space where things are made sense of, where the known world is reorganized into the unknown and tried for size. My own career has continued to move between criticism and creative practice. In 1995 I co-founded a journal, *Performance Research*, which is committed to promoting 'a dynamic interchange between scholarship and practice', and is now in its seventh year of publication. It gives me an interesting position from which to view and to participate in the way in which performance is made and written about. I see it as another site of enquiry, a way of exploring the relationship between doing and reflecting. My engagement with the long-term questions that passionately engaged me at thirty-two has changed. At forty-eight I feel less of a sense of struggle and more a sense of time and space to move. My own intellectual home, I have realized – sometimes euphorically, often painfully – is always going to be in the in-between, continuing to cross the borders of theory and practice. But in a sense the long view allows me to accept and celebrate the piecemeal, samizdat, interventionist nature of things. To imagine continuing to engage with the arts in the twenty-first century is to imagine myself continuing as a critical traveller, and it feels, all things considered, very good.

Those who can do teach

Anna Furse

Anna Furse is an award-winning theatre director of over forty touring productions, and a commissioned playwright. Recent works include *Ultraviolet* (DooCot), *Kaspar* (Cankarjev Dom, Slovenia) and *Gorgeous* (TheatreCentre). Her artistic directorships include Bloodgroup and the new writing company Paines Plough. Having worked internationally for twenty years, she was appointed Lecturer in Performing Arts at the University of North London in 1997 and then to the Department of Drama at Goldsmith's College, University of London, in 2002. She is Visiting Professor at Princeton University, USA.

In 1973 as an undergraduate drama student in the first university in the UK to include the study of theatre at degree level (Bristol), I was set an essay entitled 'Theatre is dead. Discuss'. Almost thirty years later, I'm still exploring whether we are truly facing bereavement or whether resuscitation is on the cards. The years have passed and TV, Hollywood, and new technology, not to mention Thatcherism, the fall of communism, a sexual revolution and now Blairism (to name but a few factors), have all contributed to a total transformation of society and the theatre which reflects it. All of us working in the field have found our own strategies for negotiating change, for responding to crisis, for adapting to survive. My own one as a theatre-making professional since 1979 who has always dipped in and out of teaching is now to work in a full-time university post. In writing about theatre in crisis today, I shall address how I perceive this crisis functioning as a particular set of contradictions and paradoxes, focusing on the fact that whilst subsidy for the arts has been radically cut since I wrote my own essay nearly thirty years ago, conversely scholarly interest in performance in its widest sense has grown and opportunities for study and training at tertiary level along with it.

Theatre/performance (including dance) as distinct from dramatic literature occupies a field of its own and is being taught as a laboratory subject with a praxis-based curriculum all over the UK. Whilst now part of and contributing to such a pedagogic movement, her perspective remains that of a biased practitioner who doesn't want her observations to be interpreted as biting-the-hand-that-feeds but rather as (hopefully) an indication of the healthy tensions that can exist between scholar and artist, especially since that tension is in my case embodied in the same individual.

I want to talk first about making theatre before and since the 1980s explosion of critical theory into the study of theatre in university. And I want to examine some of the issues that can thicken the plot for a practitioner negotiating this new academia from the inside. For, whilst passing on knowledge and skills via teaching is an obvious choice at certain stages in an artistic career, there are distinct preoccupations for the artist and the academic. Sometimes our concerns do overlap into some fabulously holistic praxis. But often we experience instead a profound and sometimes uncomfortable difference between making and teaching, between thinking creatively and thinking as scholars. One of the most obvious differences is that the academic looks back, while the practitioner looks in the present. Academia functions from the benefit of hindsight, gathering the random and the chaotic and giving it shape and order, scrutinizing it, cataloguing it, defining it. The art of theatre, once the ground is prepared by research, is to work in the immediate. This is true both in its preparation and in its delivery before an audience. In making theatre you commit yourself entirely to the now, and build this nowness into a future of built-in obsolescence. Academia is about preservation and accuracy. It values reflection, objectivity and complex discourse even to the point of communicating in a language which excludes the lay reader. Theatre is hell-bent on communicating as viscerally and accessibly as possible, even if in order to do so it overlooks factual detail and makes impressionistic and subjective rather than scientifically accurate statements. Academia permits no poetic licence. Theatre explores it. And so on. The two disciplines are therefore quite different, even though they might feed each other and could well benefit from more interfacing (currently specific science and art partnerships are state-of-the-art recipients of subsidy in the UK – a sign of a need and tendency for quite segregated disciplines to seek to commingle). It is on the fault line between them, the very relationship between theory and practice, teaching and creating, that I now (since the birth of my child constrained my financial and geographical freedom) spend most of my energy. And it is here in academia that I have incidentally happened on a black hole into which all my pre-play-text-based work has fallen. So let me here look back, briefly, by way of talking about a relationship between performance and its analysis, impermanence and permanence, doing and telling, as an orientation. And from this perspective I would like to suggest some of the issues and conundrums practitioners might face when plunging headlong into the classroom, studio and lecture hall.

I'm one of many pre-cyber performance fish who escaped the net of academic textuality because I was too blind or too busy at the time to see the writing on the wall. Publish or vanish. Record or be silenced. Archive or die. Now, as I teach the theatre history of the period in which I emerged, I am forced for example to refer to an era of diverse women's performance with only a handful of play texts to cite. The uninscribed work, the fleeting poetry-of-theatre work remains mostly forgotten (we have to remember that the first feminist project in theatre in the UK to be recognized as such was playwriting – and the two camps of performance and plays tended to view each other with suspicion – so that early feminist critiques tend to cluster around plays and not performance makers). This sense of exclusion and omission I now feel about those years, this wobbly, disorientating sensation of so much work having slipped off the edge, of having gone so liminal as to enter obscurity, is surely a generational thing. We were on the cusp of I.T. and videos, CD-ROMS and all the technological paraphernalia that now makes live performance one of several simultaneous durable media in which most artists produce ephemera. We were *live*. We might have occasionally cluttered our stages with the odd bank of videos, but our work was mostly focused on stretching the boundaries of narrative, light, utterance, the body, structure, theatre magic, rather than the giddying possibilities of multimedia techno-fests on hand today. It's not that we were Luddite, its just that we happened to be born a few decades ago and educated way before the computer ever entered the classroom. I think we just assumed that our little streams would dissolve into the rivers of time. We wanted to make an impact there and then, not in some academic module about the good old days when the Arts Council and touring venues supported a diverse community of professional experimentalists. Now we are older and can perhaps view our own work more objectively we have to accept, however galling it might be, the dialectical relationship between the radical and the mainstream which converts what was once daring and new and different sooner or later into an appropriated version by richer and less bolshie production agencies. Ideas are free – even if it is an artist's natural impulse to wish to claim their own inventions. But we cannot copyright impulses, images, atmospheres or even our manifestos to make action speak louder than words in our desperate bid to revivify theatre's uniqueness when pitted against celluloid drama. A video-maker advised me in 1983 to begin thinking of recording absolutely everything I did, for the future. I didn't quite get it at the time. It seemed, well, academic. The only future I could even begin to envisage was a kind of dream in which global efforts would melt the might of men, transform the world into a better place. Together with my collaborators we allied our work in studio and on stage to passive resistance, hands linked round the perimeter fence. Our political analysis saw connections between absolutely everything. And patriarchy could be blamed for every ill in the world, every detail that was out of balance. Culture was a territory that belonged to them, the men, and into which we had to trespass, bushwhack, and like our hardy Greenham sisters, pitch audacious makeshift camps. It felt exciting and dangerous and new and deliberately unclassifiable. So somehow bothering to ensure our place in any future canon of experimental theatre was irrelevant. Frankly, I am not even sure we ever imagined there might be one. Our actions were in the present tense. And so was our art. You made work, you didn't catalogue it.

Back then making art was one thread in the dream coat of alternative society. Politics was what you did every day in how you lived and worked. And to work artistically for and about the larger project of the left was a be-all and end-all in itself. It didn't require justification. It was quite simply bigger than us and we gladly submerged ourselves into the greater cause. In short, being there was enough, in a kind of eternal present, with no career-plan, no strategy for success, only a burning need to lend a hand in the struggle anywhichway. My own search was for an authentic women's performance language, for putting difficult, painful and even politically incorrect material on stage beyond the framework of psychologically-driven plays. In this search I have been cruel to myself in the name of Artaud and tried feverishly to immolate myself in the name of Grotowski who said the actor was akin to the priest. I scoured strip-joints, literature, popular culture and my own and my collaborators' fantasy and dream-lives in this research and stood literally naked on stage. We were feminist rule-breakers who refused to be categorized politically or aesthetically and for a while we were high on our quest. But even though we made an impact everywhere we went, had an international audience and a kind of art-house cult-following, we never planned to become Big. As women artists at the time we couldn't possibly have envisaged that our ideas would ever enter the mainstream of academia because we assumed a position on the outside of the (patriarchal) institutions. We were pariahs. We defined ourselves by our anti-establishmentarianism. We sharpened our minds on the stolid stubbornness of a phallic society. Being accepted into its fold would have implied bourgeois respectability, a softening of our punches, buying-in. We considered our job was to oppose, to disrupt, to question, not to knock politely and enter to become a subject for analytical scrutiny. I started so I'll finish: we painted ourselves into a corner. It wasn't just towards poor theatre, more like stuck in it. More fool us? Perhaps. For haven't many of my generation of women witnessed the next one hurtle full of confidence into positions of mainstream power? How come we wrote ourselves out of the plot with our ephemera, our collectivism, our reluctance to lead, our squeamishness at thrusting individualistic ambition? It's a conundrum middle-aged women confide to each other at kitchen tables. Today we reinvent ourselves because we must. But we carry our history around like the secret contents of our handbags. We know its precious details, its functions, talismans, keys though we somehow suspect they are too personal to be of real use to anyone else. The personal was political, then. Now, hardly anyone seems that interested. Even duchesses have high-flying careers they won't relinquish after marriage. Sorted.

But suddenly now, teaching a generation we might have mothered, it seems urgent to keep our history as artists and as women alive. Even if only to explain some of the complexity of sexual political culture and the fact that there were always many voices, aesthetics, languages and sexualities arguing away onstage and off. But how can we even begin to test out a hypothesis which suggests that our cultural research in performative feminisms as practitioners is perceived only as distant history by this new generation if the very work we are talking about was transient, written-on-our-bodies, unpublishable *on purpose*?

> The hysteric, whose body is transformed into a theatre of forgotten scenes, relives the past, bearing witness to a lost childhood that survives in suffering. … For the hysteric does not write, does not produce, does nothing – nothing other than making things circulate without inscribing them. The result: the clandestine sorceress was burned by thousands; the deceitful and triumphant hysteric has disappeared. But the master is there. He is the one who stays on permanently. He publishes writings.[1]

1 Hélène Cixous, *The Newly Born Woman* (Manchester: Manchester University Press, 1987), p. 37.

What an irony that Cixous' copious writing on, among other things, hysteria, should be urging us to print ourselves in permanent ink when feminist performance artists were trying to negotiate the patriarchy precisely by working away from the written word and into images, temporality. Aren't the names we remember, the ones students today write their essays and theses about, those of playwrights? (and there's hardly a clutch of female household names here). How do you teach a class full of eighteen-year-olds about a particular era of non-play-text-based feminist theatre without a sexy array of supporting visual aids and academic textbooks?

> Recent scholarly focus on the body grows out of anthropological and historical interest in non-documented human endeavors and from the complementary interest within literary studies towards non-written texts. It equally results from the feminist problematization of gender.[2]

Fine. Great. But where are the theoreticians going to get their material *from*? Where is the evidence of 1970s and 1980s performance culture? How can they reconstruct shows which have been and gone, unpublished, undocumented? In academia this is a hot topic (enter: I.T.). Well, one way these lost fragments of 'performance' culture can live on is in those who made it. Us artists. And in this way we practitioners who work in academia are a kind of walking race-memory. We can operate as live storytellers, translating academe into lived experience, the jargon of critical theory into that of the rehearsal room. I encourage my students to become bilingual here and am always careful to demonstrate the usefulness of a theoretical toolbag to analyse with and a technical one to make theatre with. As artists we can offer a (fallible) human perspective which deconstructs the tendency of academia to see a body of work in logical arcs where we more often than not work from chance and intuition. For the truth is as artists we stumble upon things, our decision making being as prone to the forces of accident, time, money and touring pressures as anything else. For who hasn't known a whole new phase of work to emerge from a proverbial phone call, a chance meeting, a dream or a simple need to pay an electricity bill? I suppose what I am trying to talk about is that the theory looks at the work itself but rarely the conditions that surrounded the making of it. This is after all the project of post-modernism. We as authors, our lives, our budgets, our obsessions, our rows, all of which inform the on-stage product, are completely overridden so that the 'text' can be unpicked. Discourse about experimental productions, where any are available, remains a far smoother, seamless plot than the realities of producing them. It is as if academic writing about performance somehow over-endows the work with coherence. It dignifies

---

2 Susan Leigh Foster, ed., *Corporealities* (London: Routledge, 1996), p. xii.

our often necessarily and even induced chaos by suggesting a kind of pre-
meditated order. It delivers meanings where we perhaps never knew they
existed, and all this with the benefit of hindsight.

Here we hit another conundrum of the art/academia relationship.
We may well have complained of marginalization, of not being understood by critics when we worked at the cutting edge of performance (for
even if we wished to remain outside the institution we certainly didn't
want to be dismissed and patronized by it), but we perhaps didn't foresee
that our small band of followers in academia were eventually going to
enshrine ephemeral experiments in lofty discourses. Nor that this small
band would grow and gradually assert itself as a 'hard' subject (even
though, clearly, theatre academics feel compelled to strive for peer-group
respect within the broader field of academia). If theatre is the one art
form that is by its very nature biodegradable and if its unique temporality is what we seek to affirm and celebrate as we make performances in a
technological age, preserving it in theoretical language can seem a contradiction in terms. Post-modern theories promote the death-of-the-
author/birth-of-the-reader POV on live performance, opening up the
formerly narrow definition of text to the totality of *mise en scène* and the
all-seeingness of reception theory. Theatre is liberated from its previous
domination by its durable by-products: the literature of published
play texts. Whilst this suggests a wide-open embrace of post-Artaudian
illiteracy, paradoxically theatre academia is now striving to archive and
analyse – and thereby elevate – the ephemera of it all with deeply probing
written research. So much so, that verbiage *about* performance far exceeds
the verbiage within it. Whilst academic research is gradually building
itself up as a respectable field of enquiry all of its own – distinct from its
roots in literary studies – the tendency of the work itself it to move away
from the word-driven and towards the interdisciplinary in that slippery-
sliding search for asserting performance as an authentic product of its
makers.

As the published theoretical work now piles up, another paradox
emerges: there is less and less funding for performance makers themselves
and next to no professional full-time experimental theatre in the UK. Yet
simultaneously an academic training industry burgeons. Less and less
theatre; more and more reading and writing about it. I find the irony of
this imbalance painfully acute. What am I educating and training our students *for*? There is a constant supply of school leavers seeking university
places in the performing arts, so that entry is competitive. This is good for
business and for positioning the subject within the academy. But it surely
speaks of a number of issues in which the actual making of professional
subsidized new theatre will remain relatively minimal. By the time our

applicants come to us they have already become enthusiastic wannabes via a grounding in A level or BTEC theatre studies. Thus the greater the provision of performance-related subjects in secondary school and at school-leaving age, the larger the potential undergraduate population.

In a Blunkett-Blairite climate of education-for-jobs, enrolments in many humanities subjects dwindle as non-career options. But ironically performance studies, feeding an industry in which there is a ninety per cent unemployment rate, keeps drawing applicants as if by some magnetic force. Whether this is due to a stars-in-their-eyes syndrome or is a reflection of the profound impact the study of theatre can have on alienated young people, enabling them to integrate a wide variety of social, communicative, intellectual and creative skills (or is a combination of both), doesn't change the fact that there is an ever-increasing supply of eighteen-year-olds wanting to study performance and a number of higher education institutions expanding their provision as a result. Performing Arts is a cash-cow in a university culture which is increasingly struggling to make ends meet. Theatre itself may be in crisis as it enters the new millennium starved of subsidy, striving to resist mediatization, labouring to find the next generation of audiences, but education and training? – a growth industry. And as this particular sector of performance activity grows, inevitably, artists, unable to sustain a decent living or regular lifestyle as freelancers, are becoming enfolded into it. Indeed, looking around me in the UK, I have noticed how many of the more radical theatre-makers of my generation have been persuaded into academic posts in the past few years. It isn't just that we are older, have mortgages and families to feed (many don't). It is surely because it's preferable to enter higher education and hope to inspire others as well as preserve one's own values than to renounce all these in order to become more commercially viable 'out there' in the market place. To retrain or to starve? The choice is pretty stark. It's not a question of those-who-can-do-those-who-can't-teach any more. Whilst some of the most innovative theatre-makers are to be found in these welcome academic posts, still struggling against a huge workload to sustain making professional work on the side, 'the biz' tends to regard them/us as having retired in some way, of having quit the rat race into something cushier, a regular job, security, *not the real thing anymore*. But this is a misunderstanding of what we are struggling to achieve. We may happen to love teaching (I do) and, yes, we may need the stability and income (I do). But there is also something key here to understand in the current landscape of funding for the arts and the artist's role in education. Being practitioner-academic, we are benefiting from a subtle redistribution of wealth. Since our practice is now recognized as legitimate research by research boards, we are in a position of mutual back-scratching. Universities need our names on their prospectuses. Our professional experience endorses the vocational aspects of the degrees we teach on. Conversely, we use the support and security of the universities to help us produce our own work. This seems utterly sensible and mutually beneficial. In the USA the drastic elimination of public funding for the independent artist means that such posts may represent the only means of survival. And we in the UK are not far off.

So what does it mean to be an artist-academic? And how do we negotiate the two disciplines? Thinking about theatre and creating theatre are not the same. They can be negotiated by the same individuals (as I do) but they will be consciously moving between two states of mind and body in doing so. Many artists remain chary of the academy for its apparent ossification of living ideas. We don't need it to do our work, but it needs us to do its. It's easy to be churlish. Theatre artists who enter academia today can discover a critical literature that has in more recent years come to be a parallel industry alongside our own: a theoretical institution that is sometimes sparklingly illuminating and liberating and at others bogged down in deadly dull discourse. Critical-theoretical writing which is now the sine qua non of every theatre student's bibliography produces copious ruminations on the very issues we artists have been negotiating in the past twenty or more years of experimenting. This is no coincidence. My own theoretical roots for instance are Marxism, psychoanalysis, feminism and surrealism. They seeped in like mother's milk, and came with the territory of growing up in the 1960s and studying in the 1970s. But they were maps, not the journey itself. The journey was muddy, bloody, messy, complicated, sweaty and full of human error. Even though grounded in research, it certainly wasn't driven by front-brain intelligence, indeed in my case the work was deliberately seeking to deregulate the senses, knock the rational stuffing out of us, drive towards a poetry of dreams and unutterable truths. Doubt was a tool, but useless in action. As Grotowski said to me in 1976 when I met him to discuss working in his 'paratheatre' project, 'doubt before, doubt after, but never doubt during'. When practitioners take up university posts they find themselves in an environment which is founded on doubt and reason – as well as an enormous burden of bureaucracy and paperwork these days – which require us to function in the exact opposite way to the improvisational spontaneous state of mind and alert responsive reflexes we train ourselves to release when creating work. Academia is a Tower of Babel. And we have to learn its languages, codes and rituals. Its not that the subjects being taught aren't vividly contemporary, but that the linguistic apparatus by which they are being explored is the language of post-modern academia, not post-modern artists.

Languages are heightened to include all manner of sensitivities to distinction, at the same time as the subjects of that language become less and less able to enter the debate themselves, or gain entry into the academy where the debate is taking place.[3]

Well here I am, having gained privileged entry into the academy. I am entering the debate, sleeves rolled up. Or at least trying to. But each day that I work with students to get them to question, to have fresh responses, to thirst for being all-rounders, intelligent, skilled and critical theatre makers, I am appalled by the realities facing them in the market place. Then I remind myself that if theatre is in crisis today in some sense 'twas ever thus, even if far more acutely so since the rapid rise of mediatization. This albeit depressing idea – that we might be working in a field in which potential creators are threatening eventually to outnumber potential audience, perversely keeps my spirit up for the job. It's the challenge. A bit like trying to keep a cult alive by repeating its sermons. Only in the cult of live theatre you can trigger enthusiasm by quite simply making it live in the body of a student. I reckon it is part of my job to refer to my own past and bring to life some of that dormant, unrecorded past. And it is my job to inspire the next generation of independent movers and shakers. So I want to be able to turn the theory into evidence, I want to make jargon sing. I want to share my experiences without sounding like some old has-been luvvie idealist spinning a yarn about the time-I-was-touring-with dot dot dot. I want to be able to bring this sliver of practice into the arena, vivify this history. I want to be able to say: you know this theory here? Well it is at least partly about what I have done with my life and my work. The ultimate irony of it all is that the best and only way I can do this now, I have discovered, is through sharing the practice itself via my own body, via training. And then, aside from the text of my own living flesh – because I no longer want to write only on my body and because I admit to a terror of making things circulate – I speak, I write, I publish. Because somehow, despite everything, I must …

3   Alan Read, *Theatre and Everyday Life: The Ethics of Performance* (London: Routledge, 1993), p. 116.

Hold your nerve: notes for a young playwright

Phyllis Nagy

Phyllis Nagy's plays include *Weldon Rising, Disappeared, The Strip, Never Land* (all premiered at the Royal Court Theatre, London); and *Butterfly Kiss* (Almeida Theatre, London). She is currently under commission to the Royal National Theatre, the Royal Court Theatre, and the Royal Shakespeare Company. Her plays are published in the United Kingdom by Methuen and by Samuel French Ltd. This essay was previously published in David Edgar, ed., *State of Play* (Faber & Faber, 1999) and is reprinted with Ms Nagy's permission.

The contemporary theatre is decadent because it has lost the feeling on the one hand for seriousness and on the other hand for laughter; because it has broken away from gravity, from effects that are immediate and painful – in a word, from Danger. (Antonin Artaud, *c.* 1938)

Be brave. This is harder than it sounds. Because for one thing, we have been led to believe that the act of putting pen to paper is bravery enough. It is not. The decision to write a play is simply the start of a complex moral process which never ends, not even with the production or publication of our plays.

And although most of us write alone, we do not write in isolation. We write with the knowledge – sometimes comforting, at other times terrifying – of the tens of thousands of plays which have preceded ours and the many more to follow. What we write and how we write it are informed directly by the social and political shifts of the societies we inhabit, by the images and aural landscapes of our popular culture. As long as we draw breath, our writing evolves only by the process of engagement with the 'other': other people, other cultures, other political systems, other religious beliefs.

So we do not, must not, write in isolation. Because with isolation comes insularity and narcissism, which in turn lead to a collapse of bravery. Once that happens, the possibility for danger in our work is replaced with cynicism. And once that happens, decadence sets in. Bravery in playwriting starts with recognizing the necessity for the dangerous.

Bravery is also difficult because cultural pundits constantly tell us what our work is really concerned with. Apparently, the abiding preoccupation of plays and playwrights in the 1990s is the crisis of masculinity. Men, we are told, have lost their identities in the home, in the workplace – and by logical extension, in the theatre – and playwrights have begun to reclaim a male identity which was presumably lost without us noticing. The implication being that this was going on whilst women made stealthy but steady gains in the home, in the workplace – and by logical extension, in the theatre. But this analysis seems, at least as far as the theatre is concerned, more like a slightly hysterical response to the gains of a very few women by the ever-robust theatrical disposition of a whole lot of men. It is interesting that because batches of plays in the 1990s have, on their surface, concerned themselves with the pursuits (primarily social and sexual) of young men, media commentary chooses to define the themes or preoccupations of these plays solely by means of their literal components.

The real subject of much serious drama written in this decade is not the crisis of masculinity – no more so than the crisis of feminism, say, might have been regarded by some as the preoccupying concern of late 1970s through mid-1980s drama. Rather, our concern, now as then, as always, is the collapse of our collective bravery, our daring and our imagination – regardless of individual narratives or what cultural commentators interpret as the literal concerns of this work. When Artaud spoke of theatrical danger and decadence in the 1930s, he may as well have been speaking to us from Birmingham in the 1990s, pre-Christian Athens or from any place where plays were written at any time in history we might care to choose.

The literal workings of the world and its minutiae have never been, and must never become, anything other than the tools we use to construct lateral work, which communicates metaphor. Without metaphor, art does not exist. And literalism is the enemy of metaphor. Literalism is attractive because it is immediately satisfying: we are presented with a set of events, behaviours or ideas which do not represent or suggest other related events, behaviours or ideas – but which instead seek to tell us nothing more or less about those events, behaviours or ideas than the fact that these things exist in our world. Because we already know these things to exist, we can remain comfortable in their presence. Reason tells us that it is only when we are comfortable with information that we can understand the information. And understanding something makes us feel smart. In this way, the flat-line of literalism is tremendously seductive. Who doesn't want to be understood? Who doesn't want to feel smart?

But somewhere along the line, we have forgotten that truly dangerous art never seeks to be merely understood. It seeks to communicate, with all the mystery and danger that word implies. The literal, though sometimes dangerous, is rarely mysterious, by definition. This is why we rely on and, indeed, implicitly trust serious journalism to report on the major events of our times: what the journalists tell us about ourselves and our political leaders may be unpleasant or even repellent, but we don't reject the information because it is both literally 'true' and lacks 'mystery'. We therefore comfortably accept, digest and understand the news. And crucially, the news is understood by us in the moment we take it in. We do not need to ponder over it in order to grasp its meaning on a literal level. This is what makes the experience essentially comfortable.

However, plays are not journalism. We do need to ponder over the meaning of good plays beyond the moment in which we watch them. This is the essence of resonance. Thus, plays can never be satisfying on the literal level of reportage. They are not merely the sum of their events. Being what it is, journalism (and therefore journalistic theatre criticism) necessarily seeks to remove the mystery from plays (and therefore their danger), as critics report on them as if they can be reduced to their literal, factual components for the benefit of any potential audience. And when it is impossible to attain either an instant understanding of plays or an instant sense of how to describe them for others, the natural tendency of commentary is to reject such work as being incoherent or incomprehensible.

But it is impossible to convey a sense of the lateral through the literal and so, with all the best intentions, journalistic criticism does not communicate to its audience any sense of the complexity of metaphor or emotion our plays might carry with them. This is how and why the question of what our plays are 'about' has come to be confused with what our 'themes' are. Plots, no matter how fractured or fragmented, can be conveyed literally and very nearly objectively. Of course, conveying plots and concluding that that's pretty much the sum total of what a play is 'about' is ever so much more satisfying than attempting to engage subjectively with a deeper, more fluid meaning of plays – with the *subtext* of meaning. Because bravery also involves engaging with the subjective, and therefore uncontrollable or unpredictable, elements of our work.

Engaging with the 'other' does not mean agreeing with it. In fact, true engagement comes only when we embrace and empathize with ideas, attitudes and systems of belief we disagree with or fear. Empathy is stimulated in equal measure by both fear and fearlessness of those traits we recognize in humanity but do not necessarily comprehend. Recognition is not enough. On its own, recognition merely simulates an empathetic response: recognition reminds us of the trait, but does not communicate the trait itself. Recognition with comprehension – engagement – involves what might be called the higher intellect and therefore, by necessity, true emotion as opposed to sentimentality. And it is a very brave playwright indeed who sees that there is no courage without fear, no fear without fearlessness.

But our fears as writers must not mirror the fears of the literal world, even as the pressure to deliver the literal 'goods' is at its most urgent. It is no use at all to write plays in which we simply affirm the usual, proper fear and horror of war, poverty, political unrest and social indifference. Again, this reduces the power of communication – of communication with an audience – to its basest, most literal arguments. Most importantly, the blind affirmation of thesis, the comfortable reiteration of what we already know to be fact, offers nothing but a vast hopelessness. Because developing just one side of an argument rejects the very duality which makes us humane, the blanket rejection of the 'other' encourages shallow and cynical thought. This may be attractive for sound-bite analysis, but it is the antithesis of provocative analysis. Provocation, because it stimulates thought, offers us a way forward. It puts us on the road to hope. Only metaphor offers hope. And metaphor is definitely lateral.

It is ironic that much of what is currently valued in contemporary playwriting as being politically or morally incisive is really just artful reportage from the front lines, as it were, of popular culture or politics. That this reportage lacks intellectual rigour or even curiosity should alarm us. But the celebration of this kind of playwriting sends us, and our audiences, an urgent and terrifying message: that it is absolutely fine, in fact preferable, to lack any intellectual curiosity, which is increasingly seen as the enemy of popular culture. Though, in fact, intellectual curiosity is popular culture's necessary partner – its life support system, if you will.

Our failure to realize that a lack of intellectual curiosity leads to a lack of emotional empathy is the real tragedy of contemporary theatre. We live in an age of feeling, the media tells us. Of getting 'back in touch' with our emotions. And this, in our work, translates into a return to 'subject-driven' (i.e. emotional) plays and a rejection of 'form-obsessed' (i.e. intellectual) plays. Even those who run our theatres, sometimes especially those who run our theatres, speak the most ridiculously and reductively on this topic. It is sheer nonsense. Emotion does not occur without intellect; the intellect is stimulated only by strong emotion. It is a mistake to believe that there is such a thing as a theatre of 'feeling' as opposed to a theatre of 'thought'. One does not occur without the other, ever, in plays that resonate. But it can be difficult to distinguish between sentiment and sentimentality, between rigorous intellectual pursuit and intellectual sleight-of-hand.

Plays without form are meaningless. To suggest that it is possible, even preferable, to have plays in which content is more important than form is ridiculous. Any single word has content. But an exchange of dialogue has a form. If it does not, we grow bored. No matter how compelling the subject of a play, if the manner in which it is conveyed to us does not shape its content, we will forget the play the moment it ends. It is the way most stories are told, not the stories themselves, which creates emotional intensity. Those who fear form 'overwhelming' content in plays mistakenly overlook this.

Perhaps we can most easily recognize the way form shapes emotional response through television journalism. The same breaking story about an airline crash viewed from the perspectives of several networks illustrates the principle well. The plot of the crash is fixed. What changes is the particular emphasis placed on the details of the narrative by individual reports. Depending on the selection of detail, we may experience – and therefore respond emotionally to – the story in different ways: a panorama of scattered plane parts seeks to depersonalize the tragedy; interviews with survivors seek to highlight the retention rather than the loss of life; rows of body bags in fields or marshes seek to remind us of the shocking and sudden brutality of death; and so on. The way in which our emotions engage with a story while we watch it unfold – in other words, while the story is being communicated to us in the moment – depends entirely on how a writer chooses to relate its events.

The example of television journalism is also useful as it reminds us that what we see now carries more weight that what we hear. This is because, through television and film, the way we learn to receive and process information has changed. Before television and film were widely accessible, the word was our primary source of communication – spoken or written. Photographs, especially in the context of print journalism, engaged our imaginations rather than rendered them useless, because of the literal inertia of photographs. Only a single moment of a narrative is contained in a photograph – but it is nonetheless a narrative moment. We must imagine what happens in the time before and after that photograph is taken in order to complete or extend the narrative. In that way, photography, like good playwriting, invites active participation from its audience. The very moment the photographer chooses to show us in his picture necessarily dictates the narrative we will then attempt to construct around the image.

When we tell people about the plays or films we have seen, our language becomes almost entirely visual. But we translate the visual through the use of the word. Perhaps without realizing it, what we do when we talk about the experience of seeing plays is exactly what we must do in order to write them well. We do not relate narrative detail through dialogue, but rather through image structure, which is built not simply from a literal series of images, but from the collision of word and image. And though a

single image tends to be more potent than a single word, they are interdependent for the purposes of creating metaphor. One without the other
serves only to remind us of thoughts or feelings we already have. But sep-
arately, they do not create thought or feeling. Together, they do. And
together, they define form.

It is only after a story is told, when we no longer actively participate in its
telling, that we may begin to analyse our response to it. Excellent plays
demand that audiences participate in the unfolding of their narratives by
requiring them to simply watch and listen. These are not passive actions.
Communication involves active parties. But the moment a play allows its
audience to analyse its intentions while it is being performed, the audience becomes passive, and thus the experience of the play is passive. An
audience ceases to participate in the unfolding of a play because analysis
during the event itself prohibits communication – by nature a lateral,
associative experience. When we can connect the dots while we watch the
play, that play becomes nothing more than the literal sum of its parts.

However, the temptation to consciously connect the dots in our work
is great for a number of reasons. In the first instance, when we discuss our
plays with dramaturges they insist upon answers – but the questions they
ask are almost always of a literal nature. Such as 'why' people behave in a
certain manner in a certain play. What they fail to realize is that the behaviour of characters in the context of the event is the answer. Also, there is
never a single satisfactory answer to a complex question. This is not to
imply that we should not be able to rigorously discuss the motivations of
behaviour in our work. If we can't, then our plays are incoherent. But if
we are able to definitively answer questions about why our plays exist or
what they mean, then our plays do not allow for active communication
with an audience. But sometimes our plays are programmed because they
can and do definitely answer such questions to the satisfaction of mis-
guided dramaturgy.

It is also nearly impossible to overcome the preconceptions our audiences necessarily bring to the theatre about the way stories ought to be
told. This is not, as condescending media and theatre practitioners alike
would have us believe, because audiences are dumb. It is because television and film have radically altered the form in which we receive most
stories. When we speak generally about the degenerating effect television
and film have had on the theatre, we make the mistake of attributing the
degeneration to their content – to the quality and quantity of the ideas
they present us with. But it is the passivity and mental laziness their forms
promote that cause trouble. If theatre is a truly active form of communication, then the passivity of any potential audience will kill us.

Finally, theatre criticism itself encourages and congratulates passivity because most theatre critics seem to believe that it is desirable to analyse a play while they watch it. That instead of taking an active responsibility for answering the questions plays raise, audiences should not have to 'work too hard'. If this is true, then there is nothing moral – and therefore spiritually, emotionally or intellectually illuminating – about the experience of watching a play. Some of the key components of morality (responsibility, activity, participation) are actually replaced with some of the key components of decadence (indifference, passivity, inertia).

The danger in our current theatrical climate is that instead of fighting the death-knell of passivity, we have adopted a self-congratulatory 'if-you-can't-beat-'em-join-'em' attitude to our work as playwrights. We convince ourselves that by utilizing film and television techniques in our plays, by answering more questions than we raise, by doing nothing other than presenting a self-evident thesis to our audiences, we are actually communing with them. We second-guess the expectations of 'young' audiences and speak excitedly about the 'numbers' of people flocking back to the theatre. We assume they are 'coming back' because we have hit upon a new way to speak to them. What we have really done is to give them the same information they get from television and film – because we necessarily all tell the same stories over and over again – in exactly the same *form* these media already provide. If experimentation with form in art, in concert with content, enables us to challenge or explore our behaviour in order that we might move forward, then what is the possible use of celebrating or encouraging the blurring of formal distinction in the various artistic media?

This tendency towards a theatrical passivity also accounts for a proliferation of topical drama, which purports to be 'hard-hitting' or 'cutting-edge' examinations of life as it is but that is all it is. Such work simply confirms what we already think we know to be truth. Consequently, such work is cynical and narcissistic because it plays on this knowledge and allows us to remain at a safe distance from the events portrayed. We are never provoked by safety. So from the safety of perspective, we confuse the topical with the radical. Most plays which deal with violent sexual practices, drug-taking and general nihilism by utilizing film and television techniques in an effort to engage their audiences actually alienate them. And while they are certainly topical, they are almost never radical.

The suspicion, bordering on contempt, with which rigorous intellectual and ideological pursuit is regarded in the current theatrical climate has led to a laziness in the pursuit of our craft. The confusion of a static, episodic, essentially televisual structure with a pure theatrical structure fusing metaphor with narrative is evident in much of this decade's work. Plays which shift locale from Timbuktu to London may be episodic but not necessarily theatrical, whereas plays which keep their characters firmly rooted to a sofa may be deeply and thrillingly theatrical. But we learn to tell the difference only by maintaining a continual connection to plays other than our own. We must read them, see them, talk about them. Constantly. And not only the plays of the past, but especially the plays of the present.

And we must not forget that popular culture is our greatest resource. We are led to believe that theatre – like opera – is a culture discrete unto itself, having little or no connection to other, more popular art forms like television and film, even though we increasingly try, however misguidedly, to ape the forms such media take in an effort to be as 'popular' as they are. But it is a mistake to equate popularity in the context of culture with numerousness. Rather, it is more useful to begin to equate popularity with commonality (as opposed to the commonplace), in the sense that popular culture is what we, all of us, truly hold in common as a singular point of reference. As a springboard from which we make our leaps into imagination. Popular culture is not just television, film or pop music. It is politics, sports, fashion, religion – in short, those things which shape and affect our opinions or emotions. And the manner in which these things present themselves to us is equally important. Culture, like plays, is never merely the sum of its content.

In an age where theatrical form is ambiguous, it can be very hard to hold one's nerve. Every other day, somebody else tells us that writing has either lost its primacy in the theatre, or that in fact such primacy never existed. That we writers are churlish when we seek to maintain the integrity of a single, abiding vision that yearns to communicate itself to willing audiences. Some have even gone as far as to suggest that in reality, texts are not 'authored' by writers, but are created by collaboration with other theatre practitioners. That the very notion of 'text' implies a stasis we must somehow overcome if theatre is to remain vital.

We must resist this kind of thinking with every fibre of our beings. Plays are *written*. They are usually written by a single person in possession of an idiosyncratic style and point of view. Collaboration is necessary in order that a play exists in three dimensions for an audience on a particular evening. Collaboration is necessary in the creation of theatre, but not in the creation of text. A single, intelligent, evocative and compelling point of view which is interpreted by collaboration creates theatrical excitement. When point of view is muddied or unfocused by the textual contributions of many people, such excitement is usually diluted and dulled.

Text is present in every piece of theatre, even in theatre without dialogue or in improvisational theatre. Because the moment one person performs a single action on a stage, the moment a person decides (and it is a decision, a choice) to speak a particular word, or to utter a particular sound, there is a narrative placed within a specific context. And such narrative is authored whether or not we choose to acknowledge it. Like it or not, it is for this very reason that text, and therefore plays, have and always will have primacy in our theatre. Because without texts, our collaborators have nothing to do.

While this is comforting, it is also terrifying. Because the ultimate responsibility for ensuring engagement with and vibrancy in our art rests firmly with us. If we do not safeguard the traditions and integrity of playwriting, if we allow our spirit and craft to decay, if we sanction a further erosion of form, then theatre really must die. Unless we gamble that in maintaining our nerve as writers (as opposed to thinking of ourselves as people who simply work in the theatre) we will preserve what is extraordinary in theatre, there is no reason to continue. It's as simple and exasperating as that. Like all good gamblers, we must understand that in order to hit the jackpot, we have to not only recognize but court loss as a necessary component to winning big. All gamblers intuitively know that losing and being right are two different things. And however reckless or irrational such a position might seem to be, it also manages to encompass the moral duality that all great art aspires to. So let's roll the dice one more time. We have everything to play for. Be brave.

Against pessimism
Max Stafford-Clark

Max Stafford-Clark was educated at Trinity College, Dublin. He founded the Joint Stock Theatre group in 1974 following his Artistic Directorship of the Traverse Theatre, Edinburgh. From 1979 to 1993 he was Artistic Director of the Royal Court Theatre. In 1993 he founded Out of Joint. His work as a director has been overwhelmingly with new writing, and he has commissioned and directed first productions by many of the country's leading writers. This piece draws from an interview with Max Stafford-Clark conducted by Caridad Svich at the Out of Joint Theatre offices in London on 16 March 2000.

I think there is a desire on the part of journalists and academics to contrast and compare today and yesterday, and, if you're a practitioner dedicated to putting on new work, as I am with Out of Joint, you're really focused on the next thing, what you are practically doing, and interim assessments sometimes distract you.

Theatre is a reflective medium. It reflects the society we're in. And in Britain we're in post-euphoric disappointment with the first socialist government in seventeen years, and theatre is going to reflect that. For example, the play *Some Explicit Polaroids*, by Mark Ravenhill, does that by taking the Rip Van Winkle device of a socialist who has been preserved perfectly because he has been in prison for fifteen years, and contrasts him with kids today, who don't have any particular political beliefs, but are into personal improvement. I suppose that through the 1980s in Britain, what bound people together was a common desire to be rid of Mrs Thatcher. Whether you were a socialist feminist like Caryl Churchill, a Marxist like Howard Brenton and Edward Bond, a nihilist like Howard Barker, or simply a liberal humanist like David Hare, nonetheless what united everybody was the common understanding that Mrs Thatcher was a V.B.T.: a very bad thing.

Once she departed, and at the same time Eastern Europe collapsed, a lot of the common assumptions held by playwrights, directors and people anywhere left of centre began to be requestioned. There was a period in early 1992 or 1993 of unjustified gloom on the part of commentators who felt that theatre was falling apart. This was followed by a period of unjustified optimism, when a new bunch of young writers, including Mark Ravenhill and a number of writers from the Royal Court Theatre, surfaced. Their responses to society were personal rather than collective political ones. This has been followed now this year by another reaction of what seems to me unjustified pessimism. Because the Royal Court Theatre has been suspended for a year, and there's been no great new play that critics can point to, a certain critical gloom has set in.

But these tremors on the seismic graph don't seem to me to significant. What we're in, after all, is a post-war situation. Theatre in Britain since 1956 and *Look Back in Anger* has become a serious medium of social examination, whereas in the nineteenth century it was the novel. I don't see any signs of that changing, so I don't share the elegant pessimism voiced by others.

Theatre is in a constant state of evolution. One thing you could say very clearly is that the five-act form used by Shakespeare and the Restoration playwrights went into a four-act form with Ibsen and Chekhov, moving into a three-act form at the beginning of this century and into the two-act form post-war and is now shifting into a long one-act form with plays like *Some Explicit Polaroids* and Simon Bennett's *Drummers*. A number of plays have recently tended to be an hour and forty minutes without an interval. That is a response to something in society. It is a way of keeping the audience's attention without allowing them to go away for an interval to get a drink. The design and shape of plays are responding to techno- logical advances. Yet, theatre is also very different. It's a much more per- sonal encounter between actor and audience, which means that in a way it's a relief to be free of technology. I think it's a source of stimulation rather than a feeling that theatre is being left behind. We don't have to compete with e-mail or the astonishing technological advances that have been made.

In the 1980s we tended to be isolated as a country. The very debate regard- ing Mrs Thatcher was rather parochial. I don't think it engaged Europe very much. For example, the tradition in Eastern Europe is totally differ- ent from the one in Britain. They are used to commenting obliquely on political matters so that in a production of *Hamlet* in Romania, for instance, Claudius was identified as a Ceauşescu-like figure. That was the nearest they could come as a way to comment on their specific political situation. Thus, their writing involved a whole set of different skills.

There are some places where theatre is not a major part of the cul- ture. In Portugal, under the dictators, the theatre was permitted and you had a lot of scatological student revues. Theatre to some extent became a discredited medium, so young people turned to poetry, music, and film as vocations rather than wanting to become theatre practitioners. How- ever, in Russia, theatre is a huge part of their culture. Recently, in this country, writers suddenly found themselves Euro-fashionable, because in a sense Europe woke up to Britain.

One of the great achievements of this country has consistently been its writers, and, intermittently in literary history, its playwrights. Since the 1950s, our writers have had a vigorous assumption that they are playing a part in the social debate, a tradition not necessarily shared by other countries. Recently the British Council have given Out of Joint and other companies the opportunity to go abroad and the reception has been very enthusiastic. But it's also fashion. Five years ago, Europe discovered British playwrights. Next they could be discovering Catalan flame- throwers. In a sense, as an artist, you are constantly responding to or resisting the vagaries of fashion.

When presenting work in other countries, there is always some cul- tural slippage. It depends on the play. A play like *The Steward of Christen- dom* by Sebastian Barry, which is a lyrical piece about a particular moment in Irish history, had enormous resonance in other ex-Commonwealth countries like Canada, Australia, and New Zealand, because their relationship with England, the mother country, has affinities to that of Ireland. But the same play has a different resonance in countries like Germany and France. A play like *Shopping and F***ing*, or indeed *Some Explicit Polaroids*, which has been in Portugal and is now going to France, speaks to young people everywhere. My observation is that audiences tend to react, given the reservation I have just expressed, to a play in the same way. The major differences are in architecture rather than nationality. If you're playing in a big theatre, then it makes certain demands on the actors that are different from those of playing in an intimate theatre. That's the biggest difference between one performance and the next, rather than in which country we're in. The laughs, as they say, tend to be in the same place. A play like Timberlake Wertenbaker's *Our Country's Good* had a huge response in Israel. In retrospect you can see why. Because it is a country full of people who are displaced, and the debate on the play about nationality and identity had an extraordinary resonance. But Russian audiences who are hugely sophisticated theatrically responded immediately to a structurally demanding and surreal play like Caryl Churchill's *Blue Heart*.

Economics, however, affects everything. I think an English liberal education brings you up to despise economics, but when you run a theatre you realize it determines all. I think I took three or four goes to pass Maths at O level, but now I work out budgets quicker than an accountant because that is my job. Through the 1980s we had to cope with less and less funding, so anyone running a theatre was managing a retreat. I suppose the triumph of the 1980s is that we retreated in orderly fashion. We preserved theatre in some sort of order even though funding was diminishing on a yearly basis.

Lottery funding in Britain meant that expectations went into reverse and suddenly large sums of money were available. When you've been in a culture where you have to cope with less and less, the nature of plays changes. Caryl Churchill's *Top Girls* was written for a cast of sixteen, and played with a cast of eight because we doubled and tripled the parts. Then those lessons were absorbed when I worked with Timberlake on *Our Country's Good*, which was a play that was written not for the twenty-four actors it needed but for a cast of ten. There was no expectation we could have twenty-four actors because the monies weren't available. With lottery funding, somebody turned on the tap and you suddenly had to think in terms of expansion. The lottery-funded redesign of the Royal Court Theatre is a triumph of such expansive thinking.

But although this window of opportunity has been of benefit, there are also repertory theatres all over Britain that are facing huge deficits and that need to be bailed out. Still, it has to be said that even though there is a prevailing feeling of disappointment with the Tony Blair government, the funding situation is better than it was. Much better. And even though this government have wasted a huge amount of money on the Millennium Dome, nevertheless, things are better. Funding for the arts is available. And in the last year Out of Joint's funding has been increased by fifty per cent. That kind of uplift is generous, given the years of attrition through the 1980s during the time of the Thatcher government. You can say the Tories believed in art, but didn't believe in funding, whereas the Labour government believes in funding, but doesn't believe in art. They really believe theatre ought to be mouthing politically correct and supportive statements. They find it hard to approve a medium that is often a voice of dissent.

Out of Joint revived *Our Country's Good* a year ago and, in retrospect, that was an incredibly smart decision because we got an audience full of young people for whom the play was a set text. They had a great time and in the autumn of 1999 came and saw *Drummers*, a play by a completely unknown burglar that was both violent and difficult. It was incredibly heartening to build an audience so tangibly.

As an artist, you have to renew yourself and that is difficult. When you start your career you learn from mentors – Bill Gaskill was a mighty figure from whom I learned a great deal. But then there comes a humiliating point where you start learning from people younger than yourself. And you have to say 'Stephen Daldry has a great deal to teach me about the physical presentation of a play'. Or, 'Katie Mitchell's obsession with research leads to some very fine work.' Particularly if you're involved with new writing – when you start in the theatre, the writers you work with tend to be older than you – while now, of course, the writers I work with are younger than me. You have to learn how to absorb somebody else's obsessions, and to understand the difference between a generation that was overtly political and one that isn't, and to respect those differences.

Out of Joint is a writer's company. I very much relish and want continuity both with writers and with actors. The ensemble is a desired state that constantly recedes before us. It's impossible to achieve the continuity you long for because of economics. Indeed, when you meet companies from Bulgaria, Russia, or Poland who have been working together all their lives, it is enviable. You do the best you can. So, in *Some Explicit Polaroids*, for example, I have three actors with whom I have worked with before, and three actors with whom I have never worked, and that mix is pretty typical. Ideally, you want two new actors and four or five people with whom you have worked with before. Because you do want continuity, and you do want ensemble and you do want a sense that people know your working methods.

What I find frustrating in the US, and more specifically New York, is a certain lack of commitment on the part of actors to the concept of company or ensemble. Things are better here. There's an actor in *Some Explicit Polaroids*, for example, who is in his late forties and who has a family and small child. I believe he sees what he is doing as artistically fulfilling, that he is expressing himself with Out of Joint in a way he cannot do on television or film given the range of parts he is usually offered, but also he can just about survive on the salary he is making with Out of Joint. It is somewhat of a sacrifice, but not an impossible one. However, in New York what is debilitating is that actors always have one eye on the next thing: one eye on Hollywood. Or they may be simply doing something with you not because they want to do it, but in order to facilitate something better that's going to happen. So, if you do a play and put your energy and time into it and it is successful in New York, you can return six weeks later to check it out and find there are two actors in the play whom you have never met before and who have been directed by the stage manager. This is the kind of Victorian working condition that would be inconceivable in this country. I have limited experience, but it seems to me that the economics of US theatre actually militate against real fulfilment.

My own working conditions have changed enormously since I left the Royal Court. Out of Joint is a touring company, and when you tour, you get a more interesting cross-section of the public than playing in London. In London if you're at the Royal Court and it's a gay play, you get a gay audience. If you do the same play in Bury St Edmunds, which is a small town, you certainly get the twenty gay people in that town, but you also get the regular theatregoers, and you get young people, and you also get people who have come just to see a good play without necessarily taking on board the issues that the play is addressing. That sometimes makes for a more interesting audience. In the five years Out of Joint has been going, we have formed relationships with a number of regional theatres. It's been an intriguing and heartening response to a diversity of work. Thus, what continues to sustain me in theatre as a working artist is that I still believe that theatre is an important medium in this country, and that it does reflect the social debate. There was a time quite recently when a lot of right-wing commentators here in Britain were attacking theatre for being old-fashioned and uncomfortable. I found it heartening that they felt threatened enough to attack it. And certainly there was a period in the 1980s when the unions had been demolished and the

Labour party was in a state of enfeeblement, when the theatre was the most articulate voice of opposition in this country. So, I continue to be a proud member of the theatre community.

I think day-to-day all you can do is assess how many people you played to last night, what you can do to improve the marketing, how you are going to get an audience in Edinburgh, what you are going to be doing next in the autumn: practical questions that deserve practical answers. But when you get an invitation like this, an invitation to step out of the trench and see where theatre is, I have to say that I believe theatre is in a powerful position in this country.

Theatre and identity: negotiating doubt and passion

More enterprise in walking naked
Len Berkman

Len Berkman holds the Anne Hesseltine Hoyt Professorship of Theatre at Smith College, where he has taught playwriting and the dramatic literatures of numerous cultures since 1969. Playwright, essayist, and new play development dramaturge, he has worked with the Sundance Institute, Mark Taper Forum, Voice and Vision, WordBridge, South Coast Rep's Hispanic Playwrights Project, New York Stage & Film Co., and other theatre groups across the US. His plays include *Voila! Rape in Technicolor*, *I Won't Go See a Play Called 'A Parent's Worst Nightmare'*, *Excuse Me for Even Daring To Open My Mouth*, *I'm Not the Star of My Own Life*, and *Quits*.

'Live' theatre, our perpetually rediscovered corpse, has (of course) survived crisis upon crisis throughout centuries of its multiple guises: victim of houndings and shutdowns, desperate beggar, eager fawn, contortionist extraordinaire, star of courage, bravado, genius, and compromise. Does our mixedly noble profession now face one millennial dilemma above all urgent others? I think it does. The tugs against theatre doing what it uniquely can achieve have never been as widespread, the lures amongst us to yield to those tugs never so divine. An art form keyed for ages to the shared breaths of audience, cast, and crew, to the electric interact of performance/response, spontaneity/plan, our theatre now increasingly resorts to keypads, switches, screens … the inanimate and costly high-tech of multimedia, razzle-dazzle, 'state of the art' (whose art?), the body electric reduced to electricity.

Needless to say, this thrust is hardly new to the decade just past; it's basically indebted to western Europe's nineteenth-century set design marvels and early twentieth-century stylistic/visual experiment, when such Aristotelian 'advances' had not to compete with TV and film. What Thomas Edison's light-bulb-strewn fashion gowns and the working escalator for David Belasco's New York stage restaurant brought to US entertainment palaces more than and nearly a century ago awes us still, even as such flaunted show(man)ship also stirs impatience and giggles. The 'spectacle' thrust becomes altar to a facet of theatre we alternately downplay or drape with all that shines: artistic dependence on privilege and wealth. No wonder the seats of ultimate power in theatre today support the rumps of producers, boards of directors, angels, and landlords alike.

Is all that glitters, then, yet another corpse? I happen not to care. When in the company of children (or adults still children) as they race toward the dazzle, I find I, at times, enjoy their surprise and delight. My personal delight points, though, elsewhere. Be prepared: what I will argue here affirms as an end what often, at best, receives acclaim as a means.

As my forty-plus active years in theatre range from playwright, professor, and essayist, to new play development dramaturge, it's my last-mentioned role that arouses curiosity in the highest: 'creation' itself is mystery enough; how does anyone facilitate another's creative steps? The presentation modes for new scripts or projects spur a parallel question: How do readings, workshop performances, and 'modest scale' 'no tech/low tech' productions serve our theatrical ideal? At times in near apology, we stress 'work in progress' and 'latest draft'. We offer our audience the chance and honour to be 'in' on our 'process'. Today the reading, tomorrow the world. But watch out, warn some: a play can be 'workshopped to death'. (Theatre corpses come in every which assortment.) Presumably – à la Wordsworth's 'dissect', I guess – we murder to develop.

Do, in fact, 'incomplete production values' constitute an actual absence? Is a play that actors read in a living room, is a project staged in a rehearsal hall or 'lab' with observer space, less truly 'theatre'? (I see numbers of you grinning 'Yes!') Consider this: in an era where 'non-profit', and 'academic' no less than 'commercial' theatre prioritize financial constraints, what modes of presentation remain freer of these constraints than readings and workshops? What modes are freest to embrace risky, adventurous, old as well as new work? What modes are freest to address the passions and concerns shared by few? (How ironic the negative connotation that democracies attach to 'few'.) What modes, indeed, come closest to embodying what once distinguished theatre and literature from purported TV/film damage to viewer imagination: we insisted theatre audiences be actively engaged, not passive recipients of show.

My conclusion goes beyond logic; it conveys my recurrent excited experience: namely, that readings and workshops (and unencumbered 'small budget' productions, 'leaving much to the imagination' whether or not money falls within reach), *are at the forefront* of our fight to keep theatre poised within the magic of live actors/live stagehands/live spectators. ('Spectators' yes, for in readings, too, there's an enormity to *see*, and thereby – with so much space opened – to imagine.) Where other than in readings, workshops, and select productions, do we find no intended rival for focus on the improvisatory feature of each performed moment – no matter how tied that moment may be to script – when each participant (actor/actor, actor/audience, actor/stagehand/stage-directions reader, and all the combos thereof) can impact upon, and alter, the choices and behaviours of the rest? (Film and television drama are also at their keenest for me when there's room in the filming or taping for in-the-moment shift and jolt ... as abounded in 'live' television drama of the 1950s.)

A cluster of instances, performer focused for now, from an array of play-reading riches:

In a rehearsal room with large skylight, Didi Conn and Ethan (Johnny) Phillips play a couple about to discover their baby dead in its crib. They choose as their crib the bright rectangle of sunlight emblazoned on the floor across from where they have 'entered'. Didi moves to the rectangle and kneels, suffused with love, at its edge. Johnny joins her to watch their seemingly sleeping infant from over her shoulder. Abruptly, the sun pouring through the skylight mutes to half, then fades. Didi, numb, reaches toward where the rectangle had been, but the floor is now simply a floor.

Later in this play (Monte Merrick's *Pride and Joy* at the Sundance Institute, 1985), Didi and Johnny invite to a seance at their home a second couple recently met, played by Margo Martindale and Cotter Smith, who uncomfortably agree to attend. Didi's pain is evident to her guests, who themselves face an unwanted imminent parenthood they have found no way to escape. As the seance begins and the participants in silence await reply from the great beyond, a compassionate but sceptical Cotter shifts in his chair, his slight casual movement unnoticed by his hosts. An utterly natural result: his foot taps the play-reading's nearest table leg. Cotter sees the desperate mother react to his inadvertent sound, but he can only sit there, aghast.

Such moments defy calm response even among veteran theatre practitioners. I will not forget the gasp of the actress, Florence Stanley, from her seat in front of mine as she heard the tap and caught Cotter's awareness of his helpless complicity. A whispered outburst came as helplessly from the riveted actress's lips: 'His face!' The audience was as galvanized as when our sunlight chose its incredible time to vanish. I had worked with *Pride and Joy* for three weeks prior to its presentation, and I was no less chilled to the bone.

My most prized experiences in theatre hold their own next to major production display. Despite Ellen McLaughlin's great power as the amply winged logo creature in Tony Kushner's *Angels in America*, I keep an equally potent vision of Didi Conn as that selfsame creature, wingless and on her tiptoes atop a seminar table in Utah, from where she hovered above Daniel Jenkins' stricken and prostrate Prior Walter. Nor can I shake the thrill of Shannon Holt's careening vocal suave as the challengingly unbalanced Rocky in a Mark Taper Forum read-through of Bob Glaudini's *The Poison Tree*. I'm haunted by Robert Sean Leonard's discovery of a Lucky who thinks his phenomenal Beckettian tirade actually communicates and who presses through his agony with a series of 'bright ideas' (this in a reading of *Waiting for Godot* with Ethan Hawke, Austin Pendleton, and fellow members of Malaparte.)

Then there's Marcia Gay Harden, as directed by Peter Gallagher in a New York Stage and Film Company reading of Terri Minsky's *Amazing Frogs and Toads*. The insecurities and emotional swings of her character led Marcia Gay to perform Abby as though inventing on the spot the words right on the page in front of her. Still other actors, even in readings of plays by my son Zachary and myself, have excited us with interpretive surprise many assume reserved for full-scale stagings. Justin Kirk in Zachary Berkman's *Rust* (opposite Marcia Gay Harden, Isabella Gillies, and Peter Frechette) linked the difficult desires his Avery must confront to that troubled youngster's urge (not specified in the script) to fall asleep. Nadia Dajani, opposite David Strathairn in my *I Won't Go See a Play Called 'A Parents' Worst Nightmare'*, had her Susannah believe, as I had not thought to, that her husband hated her: the result magnificently overturned our view of how two presumably intelligent professors deal with their family crisis and re-angled the scale of the wife's dilemma. I think, too, of Kathleen Chalfant's mesmerizing performance in our Sundance reading of Don DeLillo's *The Day Room*. At one point, the author leaned toward me to remark, 'Once you've seen her act, you want to watch her for ever'. This over a decade before Kathleen's heralded Vivian Bearing, PhD, in Margaret Edson's *Wit* (and her extraordinary performances in between).

One last example among so many that beg for telling: Kathy Bates' abandoned wife in Keith Curran's *Dalton's Back*, a woman disturbed enough to scald her son with a pot straight from the stove. As Kathy slumps at her 'kitchen' table, her head buried within her arms against its surface, her son, his childhood form played by Michael Alvarez and directed by Gloria Muzio, tries repeatedly to rouse her attention. All of us who know the play wait for Kathy to look up and order him for ever out of her sight. But when she finally does lift her head to speak these lines, she is bathed in tears. As her attack words come, we know the fullness of her son's wrenched attachment. In the rehearsal where Kathy first unearthed this link between rage and anguish, her face was more than Michael could bear; he fled the room howling.

No critic recorded any of the events I describe above. No season's yearbook that I know of includes photographs of these performances, nor do I wish they would. (It is worth considering how two odd bedfellows, publicity and historical document, became mandatory for art – including 'poor theatre' – to matter.) As we approached our year 2000, we let sheer economics determine whether an event be reading, workshop, or 'fully mounted' production. When we settled for less, we viewed less *as* less, yearning for backers to arrive. I ask instead that we grant readings and workshops – alongside productions of whatever desired scope – the status of full and clear aesthetic preference. The art that backers back may have its place (for as long as any of us wish money to rule); but theatre retains an option that intrinsically technical and costly art forms lack. Shakespeare and Yeats (among others) knew how minimal is that option, that essence. Go beyond a platform and a passion or two and what we have may well pale, however glorified, however 'hyped', beside that 'paltry thing, / a tattered coat upon a stick', Yeats' aged human being in need of a soul to 'clap its hands and sing, and louder sing / For every tatter in its mortal dress'. If what drives deepest in our theatre is its closeness to the ephemera of creation itself, drawing a world from the air and then sending the world into the air again, play-readings are theatre's epitome. The cast, the stage-directions reader, arrive, read, depart, without fanfare or wake. Now you see it and, some say by divine design, now you don't.

Educating the audience:
sharing the process
DD Kugler

DD Kugler is a freelance director/dramaturge working in new play development across Canada. As a baseline gig, he is an Associate Professor in the Theatre Area, School for the Contemporary Arts, Simon Fraser University, Vancouver, Canada. Kugler is currently serving a two-year term as President of LMDA (Literary Managers and Dramaturgs of the Americas).

When theatre practitioners get together, if the chat isn't about money (the lack of it), then it's usually about audience (the lack of it). Most of the discussion seems to be about what's wrong with the audience – they're not sophisticated enough, or not adventurous, or … whatever, you fill in the blank.

Often there's talk about 'educating the audience'. That usually implies a patronizing succession of shows/seasons that incrementally ratchet up the audience's sophistication, or appetite for theatrical adventure.

I gag on the phrase 'educating the audience' because I've long held that the fault lies not with the audience, but with the theatre. Recently I've thought of an educative strategy that fully accepts our responsibility for the failures of theatre. I'm not talking about cosmetic changes in the flavour (musical to drama), the kind (comedy to tragedy), or the brand (Broadway/London pedigree to new work) of theatre. I'm talking about a transformation in the very structure of the transaction between the theatre and the audience – an education that alters the audience relationship to the process (rehearsal) and the product (performance) of theatre.

It's a rare theatre artist who doesn't profess a commitment to process over product. We readily acknowledge that some of the most interesting theatrical moments happen in the rehearsal hall. We talk almost reflexively about theatre as a live performance event, usually to set us apart from film and television.

But theatre isn't just 'live', it is alive, dynamic, variable – a nightly process of re-creation in communion with the audience. If we find the audience an inadequate participant in that live re-creation, then I fear it's because we haven't trained the audience how to enter that process with us. In fact, we exclude them from our central process – the rehearsal – and we stridently promote the public performance as if it were product, rather than an extension and fulfilment of a collaborative process.

The rehearsal process

A high school teacher once asked if he could bring his cast to observe our rehearsal. I agreed immediately. He confided that his young actors could not conceive that there was more to the rehearsal process than learning the lines. I arranged our schedule so that his class observed a three-hour rehearsal of a precise, physically demanding fifteen-second textless sequence. I doubted they'd stay the full time, but they did. The teacher later told me they were fascinated by the hard work of the professional actors – their repeated failure, their unflagging determination, the rigour they brought to a moment that was almost invisible in the performance they later witnessed. They understood that the performance wasn't just learning the lines, but very hard, very repetitive, and very fragile work.

I don't think most audiences are much more sophisticated about the theatrical process than those students. How often are actors damned with the faint praise of 'how did you remember all those lines?' The process from rehearsal through performance, for us, is continuous: table work, early physical exploration, scene work, on-book runs, addition of production elements, scene work, off-book runs, a shift from rehearsal hall to stage, cue to cue, tech runs, previews, and opening through closing performances. The moment at which we allow the audience access to that continuous process – previews – seems more or less arbitrary, and largely unexamined.

Can we not examine, company by company, show by show, the appropriate moment to include the audience in our long-term process? Much like the visiting high school students, the audience will only see and feel the process of performance once we allow them inside the process of rehearsal.

I know the dangers.

Rehearsal is often intimate and private, but so is much that occurs on stage. An awareness of the audience can be unproductive in rehearsal, but that's also true of an audience in performance. There's a difference between actors, who have an audience relationship, and the other participants in the rehearsal process, who don't. I find that actors have the ability to include, or exclude, the audience at different moments in the process – both on, and off stage. In my experience of directing open rehearsals, the actors and I began to accept the audience's presence – much as we accept the comings and goings of administrators, designers, and many others in the rehearsal hall.

A rehearsal hall that includes the audience is a different rehearsal environment, granted. But not all the difference is disadvantageous. For those really concerned about communion with an audience, access to rehearsal may be the most appropriate education you can offer your audience.

The performance process

Theatre promotes the magic of the performance event – the product. We cultivate the mumbo-jumbo, the mystification. It sets us apart, even elevates us. You can't come in until we say so. And when you come in, we will be behind this fourth wall. This side is magic, that side is mundane. We are artists, and you have jobs.

Yes, there's spectacle and magic in the theatre. But we pay a price for elevating the theatrical event. What are we promoting – the closed magical event, or theatre workers creating in communion with an audience?

To really allow the audience into theatre is to admit (confess even) that performance is not product, but process. Perhaps that feels messy, incomplete, and somehow inadequate. But I'm less interested in the illusion of a finished product, than in exposing the audience to the highly skilled collaborative working process that weaves the fragile fabric of performance.

Many productions are product – sufficient unto themselves – and I've felt that my presence in the audience wasn't required. I think that's why script readings, especially staged readings, are so popular. The audience sees the actors working, they contribute their imaginations and, in concert with the actors, create the performance event. Now that's magic.

Radical proposition

Please take my musings about audience and process as speculation about a possible direction. Even if theatres embraced an open-rehearsal policy, few audience members would take advantage of it – our working hours often conflict with theirs, and let's face it, watching rehearsal is demanding. But even if only a few stragglers came to rehearsal, I think it's worth it. Open rehearsals signal a radically new audience relationship. The audience that most understands our process – a process that continues through performance – is the audience we are looking for.

What if there were no openings, but an audience presence throughout the entire theatrical process? Consider going beyond rehearsal. What about play selection, design meetings, casting?

In Howard Barker's 'First Prologue' to *The Bite of the Night*, a woman from the street is obliged to 'share a little of her life with actors'. Afterward she says, 'If that's art I think it is hard work'. She comes a second time, then concludes 'That is art, it is hard work / Because I found it hard I felt honoured'.[1]

We honour an audience by inviting them into the rigour of our process. Armed with that understanding, they will know that performance isn't something we've completed, but a long process we continue to work at, in the presence of, in dialogue with, the audience.

1 Howard Barker, *The Bite of the Night* (London: John Calder, 1988), pp. 1–2.

On the death of theatre: a call to action
Tori Haring-Smith

Tori Haring-Smith is Dean of the College of Liberal Arts at Willamette University. Previously she was Executive Director of the Thomas J. Watson Foundation; the artistic director of the English language theatre in Cairo, Egypt; Chair of Performing and Visual Arts at American University, Cairo; and an associate professor at Brown University. In New York, she assisted Joseph Chaikin with Susan Yankowitz's *Night Sky* and directed *The Country Wife* at the Jean Cocteau Rep. Her translation/adaptation of Eduardo de Filippo's *Napoli Milionaria* (Dramatic Publishing) premiered at the Cocteau, and her translations of *The Seagull* and *The Miser* premiered at Trinity Rep, where she was the dramaturge from 1991–96. She has published several books and articles on writing, teaching, feminism, and theatre including the 'Monologues for Women by Women' series (Heinemann).

Theatre has lost sight of its roots and is in danger of dying. This is an ugly fact to face for those of us who love theatre, but if we continue to ignore it, we cannot analyse the causes of our demise and counteract them. In the United States, audiences for traditional theatre venues (community theatres, regional theatres, Broadway, and college and university theatres) are growing older. Theatres work desperately to attract younger audience members that will patronize the theatre in this new century. Some theatres have added baby-sitting services, in order to make it easier for young parents to attend the theatre. Others push educational programmes, busing in large numbers of students to see a play in the middle of the day. But these students are usually so thrilled to be out of school for a few hours that they cannot attend to the show being staged before them. And, of course, many theatres try to stage new pieces that speak to a sensibility assumed to be young – plays with raw, violent themes or relying upon contemporary music and costumes. And yet, theatre audiences continue to age and, in many cases, to dwindle.¹ Broadway theatres have become tourist sites, not centres of urban culture. The theatre for *The Lion King*, one of the most innovative productions to hit Broadway in decades, is nearly obscured by the Disney store in front of it that sells production souvenirs. I asked one customer in that store how she liked the show, and she replied that she had seen the movie and saw no need to 'see it again' at a higher price on stage. If we look seriously at theatre, we must acknowledge that it is moving to the margins of our communities. The vast majority of Americans view theatre as a cultural event intended for and attended by those (unlike themselves) who seek culture.

How did this happen? In ancient Rome, theatres the size of sports stadiums were filled with spectators. In medieval Europe, theatre events were the centre of religious and secular festivals. Theatregoers flocked to London's Globe Theatre. After the London fire, theatres were among the first structures to be rebuilt. Yes, there were fewer entertainments before the rise of cinema and television, but even so, theatre was at the centre of a community, not on its margins. It is too easy, it seems to me, to blame the rise of cinema and television for the death of theatre. The problem lies not with the invention and remarkable capabilities of these screen media but in theatre's attempts to imitate them.

Theatre began as a way in which a community could tell its stories to itself. In this way, the theatre event grew out of the community and was an inherent part of it. Before the use of electric lights that separated the bright stage from the dark house by a curtain of light, the community (represented by the spectators) was part of the same world as the world of the play. In Greek theatre, the chorus was a visible microcosm of the community on stage. As late as the early twentieth century, actors regularly addressed the audience. They made asides, they had soliloquies that put their essential questions in the laps of the audience, they broke character to acknowledge accolades or hisses.

However, with the use of electric light came the rise of the fourth wall that encases the audience, like the actors, inside an impermeable box. Gradually theatre became more and more like cinema. The actors were in

1 It is difficult to document this trend in precise statistical terms, but Theatre Communications Group's annual survey of major regional and New York theatres can give us a general picture. According to this survey, attendance at sixty-eight sample theatres fell 7.8 per cent from 1990–94 ('Theatre Facts 1994', *American Theatre* (April 1995), p. 4). Total income during this period rose only 0.3 per cent, while expenses increased 0.8 per cent ('Theatre Facts 1994', *American Theatre* (April 1995), p. 3). Over the next three years, the picture was a bit brighter with attendance growing 1.7 per cent overall for eighty-one theatres responding to the survey in 1997 ('Theatre Facts 1997', *American Theatre* (November 1998), p. 10). However for 1997 and 1998, audiences grew only a total of 0.1 per cent, even though the number of performances reported rose 0.4 per cent ('Theatre Facts 1998', *American Theatre* (July/August 1999), p. 6).

the light, the audience in the dark. Two very different and separate worlds, one alive and dynamic and the other sedentary and increasingly comatose. No longer could the actors see the people for whom they played. No more asides. No more talking to the audience in times of stress. Macbeth could no longer ask the audience, 'Is this a dagger I see before me?' He had to ask himself. No more could Hamlet share his suicidal musings with the audience, because suddenly he was truly alone during his soliloquies. Characters did not present their problems and their stories to the audience any more; they lived in a separate world, under the observation of paying audience members. The audience had become voyeurs. This separation must have been felt viscerally by directors in the early twentieth century. Otherwise why would an experienced director like Sir Herbert Beerbohm Tree release real rabbits on the stage during his 1911 revival of *A Midsummer Night's Dream*? Somehow it must never have occurred to him that the rabbits would do what the human actors would not – cross the fourth wall and romp through the audience. For him the fourth wall was real; for the rabbits, alas, it was not.

The use of electricity also allowed the audience to be plunged into darkness, so that the community of viewers became a group of isolated individuals. When the audience had been lit and encouraged to notice one another, they participated directly (if not always usefully) in the stage event. Spectators noticed how others among them were responding to the play. The group shared an experience. But with the introduction of the fourth wall, each person in the darkened house was encouraged to respond to the play without noticing the response of the others in attendance; the community was transformed into a collection of isolated individuals, each ignoring the others as much as possible. From this point of view, the fourth wall is no longer restricted to proscenium stages. Even thrust stages or large arenas with darkened houses can isolate the audience members from the stage and from each other.

It is no coincidence, I think, that theatre was retreating behind the fourth wall at the same time that cinema was being commercialized. As refinements in electricity ensured the permanence of the fourth wall as a feature of theatrical presentations, the theatre began to look more and more like a cinema house. In the movies, too, actors cannot respond to the audience. But there is a difference – film actors have no choice since they are not present to hear or see the audience's response. That is a defining feature of the medium. They exist only as projections of light upon a flat wall, a fourth wall, one might say. Actors like Woody Allen may appear to address the cinema spectator at times, but of course, the projection of his image is only that – a projection unable to determine if it is facing a full room or an empty one, a raucous crowd or a silent one.

The development of the fourth wall in the theatre has produced the same effect. Audiences laugh or sigh or hiss, and actors do not explicitly acknowledge it. They proceed in their own apparently soundproof world, oblivious of the community to whom they are supposed to be talking. The audience is ignored. In this way, fourth-wall theatre violates a defining feature of theatre – the connection of the live theatre event to a living community. Like Brecht, I am arguing that the fourth wall of the theatre must be shattered in order to include the audience in the world of the play, to implicate them, as he might have said. However, I hope that the involvement of the audience will be more than intellectual, it will also be emotional and kinaesthetic.

Today, theatres continue this trend of imitating cinema. The rise of special effects in cinema has tempted theatre artists to try to duplicate their efforts. On the screen, planets explode, armies storm the highlands, close-up tears glisten on blushing cheekbones, translucent ghosts fly overhead, and blood spurts convincingly from open wounds. On the stage, chandeliers fall in *Phantom of the Opera*, helicopters land in *Miss Saigon*, and angels fall through ceilings in *Angels in America*. All of this attention to spectacle distracts theatre from its essential task of bringing a live human actor together with a live human spectator to explore issues of common concern through character and narrative.

It is understandable that theatre might want to emulate cinema and other electronic media. Films attract large audiences. Just as citizens of Elizabethan London flocked to the Globe, the Swan, and other live theatres, today's citizenry flocks to the latest movie extravaganza. And once a film is created, it requires no more production work. No one need worry about actors being sick, or a prop turning up missing, or lines being forgotten. Actors who like cinema acting enjoy not only being well paid, but also working to get their scenes perfect. Once they're satisfied, the moment is preserved for endless repetition, frozen perfectly in time. It's a sure thing and never needs re-enacting.

But the permanence and perfection of cinema are the very things that should distinguish it from theatre. Cinema is essentially an inanimate art. Theatre is an animate art. On the cinema screen, actors never age and events recur endlessly. Theatre, on the other hand, is constantly changing in response to the circumstances of human life. Two individuals seeing the same film on two different nights expect to have the same experience. Two individuals seeing the same theatre event on two nights have the same expectation. But they should not. We all know that actors have good and bad nights, that the mood and size of the audience can affect the actors' intensity and the pace of the piece. Rather than seeing theatre's inconsistency as a defect to be eradicated (thus making it more like cinema), we should embrace theatre's participation in the unpre-dictable stream of life. Some of the more successful new theatre groups have done just this. The Blue Man Group, for example, shapes every show quite explicitly to the members of the audience present at that time. Instead of ignoring their audience, hidden behind the fourth wall, the Blue Man Group addresses the audience, making them part of the show. Community and players once again share a world.

In addition to attracting large audiences, films are easily duplicated and distributed. Demi Moore can entertain thousands in Boston, Los Angeles, and Chicago, all at once. And some theatres are trying to emu-late this feature of cinema as well. As I write this, the Broadway version of *Rent* is showing in London, New York, and Chicago; all productions designed to deliver the same show. New actors must pick up the same intentions, actions, and timing as the previous actors. The cast inhabits the show; the show does not change because they have been added to the cast or because the cast has moved to a new and very different town. The assumption that different casts in different locations should give the same show threatens to ignore the actors as well as the audience. When cast members must duplicate some other actors' performances, not develop their own, they become automatons, no more alive than the projections of light on a cinema screen. A locally produced staging of Paula Vogel's *How I Learned to Drive* or Shakespeare's *Romeo and Juliet* should look very different in the rural South than in San Francisco. It should literally tell a different story because it is contextualized by a different community. Travelling shows rarely speak to local audiences in the same way – they provide a glimpse of what others are doing, but they do not grow out of and speak to the local community.[2] While films can be distributed world-wide (subtitles and dubbing allow them to be understood everywhere), theatre must remain local. That is its heritage.

Our modern society craves predictability, permanence, and univer-sality – the assurance that Big Macs will be available throughout the world and always taste the same. Perhaps theatre is dying because it just cannot be predictable enough. Yet, there are trends that indicate audiences still appreciate the unusual and the unexpected in their entertainment. People still travel to see the unknown. Live sports events continue to draw large crowds. Talk shows and reality shows on television are popular because the spectator does not know what will happen next. And children's

---

2 Perhaps this is why Theatre Communications Group surveys indicate a consistent decrease in attendance at booked-in events for the last five years 1995–99, falling 28.1 per cent from 1995–97 and 20.5 per cent for the next two years. (See 'Theatre Facts 1997', *American Theatre* (November 1998), p. 10; and 'Theatre Facts 1998', *American Theatre* (July/August 1999), p. 6.)

theatre, where young and unsophisticated members of the audience may join the action at any time, remains very popular.[3] The most successful of the experimental theatre groups in America and worldwide also speak for and to local audiences. They do not hide behind a fourth wall, but integrate their lives with the lives and concerns of the community. Cornerstone Theatre organized communities throughout the United States to reinterpret and stage classic plays in ways relevant to their own situations. Visit the small towns where they worked, and you will find that everyone remembers those performances. One of the most popular theatre troupes in Cairo, Egypt, has developed an acting style that actively includes the audience in the play. Using narratives taken from ancient Egyptian epics, the El Warsha theatre troupe connects the tale to the tellers and the audience. The actors sit on the floor in front of the first row of the audience, which is usually configured in the round or in two sections facing each other. Actors rise, seemingly from the audience, take on characters, speak to the audience, and are guided by the musicians, who are also intermingled with the audience. The community member (the actor) takes on a character, embodies it, and then returns to the community, thus sewing the theatre event into the ongoing life of the spectators. Audiences for performances like these want so much to be involved and not ignored by the theatre event that they are willing to trade a little predictability for a recognition of their shared humanity.

In order to survive, theatre must revisit its roots. It must remember that it was born so that communities could tell their stories to each other. It goes back to storytelling, in which the story changed to suit the audience and the place. It was never the same two nights in a row. Above all, theatre is a human event. It relies upon breathing, changing human beings – an actor and a spectator– coming face-to-face. It is a living, transitory art. No one likes to be ignored by other living human beings, and theatre must break down the fourth wall that threatens to ignore the audience. Similarly, it must acknowledge that changing actors and changing locales requires changing a performance in the most fundamental ways. Let's face it, theatre will never be as replicable, as permanent, or as cinematically spectacular as cinema. You just can't out-cinema cinema. And theatre must not try.

---

3 According to the Theatre Communications Group survey, attendance for children's series at sample theatres rose 21.8 per cent from 1990–94, 17.9 per cent for the next three years, and 10.5 per cent for the last two years of the millennium. (See 'Theatre Facts 1994', *American Theatre* (April 1995), p. 4; 'Theatre Facts 1997', *American Theatre* (November 1998), p. 10; and 'Theatre Facts 1998', *American Theatre* (July/August 1999), p. 6.)

Dancing with the dead man: notes on a theatre for the future of Europe

John London

John London is the author of several historical and critical studies, such as *Reception and Renewal in Modern Spanish Theatre* (Modern Humanities Research Association, 1997). He is editor of *Theatre Under the Nazis* (Manchester University Press, 2000). Among his ten performed texts are his translation of José Sanchis Sinisterra's *Ay, Carmela!* (1992) and his own play *The New Europe* (produced at the White Bear Theatre, London, in 2000).

I Changes

Amidst the champagne celebrations bubbling from the ostensible collapse of communist regimes in 1989–90, it was difficult to hear any ideologies beyond the clinking glasses of advanced capitalism. Here was a series of revolutions, largely peaceful, but so overwhelming as to signify the political reorganization of a whole continent. Nothing as important had occurred since the 1940s.

There was only one side to take and the battle seemed to be over: you could not defend corrupt, repressive regimes or their sadistic, arrogant leaders wearing outdated, ill-fitting suits to accompany their faded ideas. Now there was apparently little to fight for or against. This was not the Russian Revolution, the Spanish Civil War, the Second World War, Vietnam or even the Falklands – all of which produced their own theatrical treatments. The visible struggle came to an end so quickly and the rejoicing was so wholehearted that this period of transition – unlike previous events of similar proportions – produced no vast literature of commitment and debate.

II The end of drama

Theatre was faced by the usual problem in such situations of having to compete with a reality offering a much more powerful spectacle. Why be stuck in a theatre when (in the east) you could be out on the streets enjoying your new-found freedom or (in the west) observing the cataclysmic changes on television?

There was momentary relief to be gained by voicing in public the private thoughts of years under dictatorship. When I went to Bucharest, weeks after the bloody death throes of 'living socialism', I saw shows with overt parodies of the Ceauşescu couple and of folkloric festivals (promoted by the deceased regime). But the excitement from such satire was muted by the fact that the enemies under fire were now buried (or had changed their allegiances and were thus not so easily identifiable). Meanwhile, the productions with hidden political messages of opposition, which stayed in the repertoire from the previous decade, seemed too abstruse for the present circumstances. The Romanian National Theatre version of Goethe's *Torquato Tasso* was an example of this genre.[1]

III   English reactions

In the same year, 1990, theatres in the British capital witnessed three assessments of the political transformations, all by well-known authors on the left.

Caryl Churchill went to Bucharest with some drama students and wrote *Mad Forest*, an account of the Romanian revolution with ironic Brechtian framing techniques, a dash of fantasy and a cleverly interwoven personal plot. There was even room for an assessment of the aftermath of '22nd December 1989' and the anti-Hungarian and anti-gypsy racism brought out into the open. Rough at the edges, but generously wide in its scope, *Mad Forest* questioned the past and the present of political systems, while leaving the future troublesomely undefined. The other two contributions had little of Churchill's acumen, despite superficially more detailed approaches and grander productions.

Moscow Gold, by Tariq Ali and Howard Brenton, was given the epic scale it demanded at the Barbican Theatre. There were actors swinging in the air, a rotating stage and huge images (such as a paper Berlin Wall for Germans to break through). With a palpable nostalgia for the experiments of Piscator and Meyerhold, this was history writ large: Lenin, Mayakovsky, Andropov, Honecker, Ceauşescu, Yeltsin – all were there, with Gorbachev at the centre. But the stylistic echoes entailed a lack of political originality. Proudly declaring themselves 'socialist writers' (while conveniently omitting to define what that now means), Ali and Brenton painted a portrait of a largely innocent Gorbachev, desperately fighting for a new, but non-Western version of his country and repeatedly saying he wants his 'conscience to be clear'.[2] Gorbachev's origins in the KGB and his refusal to allow open elections did not seem to be real issues. In an optimistic alternative ending (the antidote to a finish with Gorbachev's

---

1   See John London, 'In Bucharest', *Plays International*, 5, No. 11 (June 1990), pp. 33–4.
2   Tariq Ali and Howard Brenton, *Moscow Gold* (London: Nick Hern Books, 1990), n.p. ('An Explanatory Note': 'Socialist Writers'), pp. 29–30, 45, 61 ('Conscience').

assassination), America, not Russia, was ironically viewed as having an atrocious human rights record.

David Edgar's *The Shape of the Table* took a much more pedestrian, and directly dialectical approach at the National Theatre. Although no country was named, the peaceful nature of the changes depicted and the inclusion of a returning leader made Czechoslovakia the most obvious reference. Largely consisting of verbal debate – some of it fairly plodding – much of the discussion about the future (after communism) was dominated by a somewhat antiquated anti-American rhetoric. 'I sometimes think we are the only Europeans left', says one character. 'We in the so-called Camp of Peace and Socialism. Since the West became a New York colony.'[3]

The new leaders of the unnamed country want to bring it back into Europe, but in his search for a Third Way between rigid socialism and the free market, Edgar has a dissident communist voice further criticism of the democratic region of the continent: 'Now I'm told there's the equivalent of our whole population unemployed in Western Europe, and every major city's full of people sleeping under bits of cardboard in the street'.[4] Most significantly, in what constituted a quasi-lament for the *ancien régime*, Edgar had the most Stalinist character heroically face up to the consequences of his past actions, instead of compromising with the new political structure. (This was wishful thinking, given the fate of many leaders.) It was as if Edgar were still in an East–West/communist–capitalist argument instead of dealing with the reality of the contemporary situation.

IV In Europe

On the Continent, depictions of the process of adjustment lacked British naïveté, but seemed, in their own way, trapped in the past. Beyond condemning the cheap banality of Western culture (an undertaking in any case fulfilled by numerous Western writers), it appeared that there was little that Russian dramatists, such as Galin and Kolyada, could now offer to a post-communist world.

The most important German dramatist after Brecht, Heiner Müller, always had a broad palette, incorporating major historical figures and ideological movements, even when they were wrapped up in classical or Shakespearean parallels. Given this ability, his posthumous, superb *Germania 3* (premiered in 1996) was disappointing from a political

---

3 David Edgar, *The Shape of the Table* (London: Nick Hern Books, 1990), p. 60.
4 Edgar, *The Shape of the Table*, p. 73.

perspective. A kaleidoscope of European events included Stalin, Hitler, the pre-war communist leader Ernst Thälmann and his successor Walter Ulbricht. But amidst the disconnected scenes from the Second World War and East Germany, there was a recurring metatheatricality which detracted from the political impact. One whole scene, set in the Berliner Ensemble, has three widows of Brecht in argument with each other and directors debating theatrical policy. Only the appearance of a Croatian peasant, working in Germany, brings the action into the present, but the potential for any illuminating contemporary reflection is denied by most of the content of his staccato monologue ('I work in Germany. After two years work in Germany I'm going back to Croatia ...').[5] The terms of the debate were essentially the same as they had been ten years before.

V   The new ideology

Perhaps the momentous changes will never find expression in a collection of dramas worthy of the scale of the events. In Britain, it looked as though theatre audiences were more interested in David Hare's vague attempts to condemn post-Thatcherite society.

By the late 1990s, in the new 'in-yer-face' style of dramatists such as Sarah Kane and Mark Ravenhill, political issues seemed to have disappeared amongst the overt (or covert) influence of Quentin Tarantino and the thrill of seeing anal sex or mutilation on stage (with a good dose of heroin injection). This is not an exclusively British phenomenon: such plays (especially Ravenhill's *Shopping and F***ing*) have been translated into several languages, and are particularly popular and influential in Germany. Arguments for the politics in these texts tend to be based on the assumption that the performance of something previously taboo automatically implies criticism of a whole power system. Moreover, the voyeuristic elements in this new drama, when linked to video screens or the internet, can be viewed as shots fired against the late capitalist system which has produced and cultivated such gadgets.

All this cannot detract from the fact that policy, argument and ideology – the essence of meaningful discussion – are nowhere to be seen in these plays. That is only logical, since it reflects a more general public apathy, particularly in younger generations, towards party politics. Falling voting figures (reaching their nadir in the European elections of 1999), and an increasing disregard for debates in national and local government, have been accompanied by the virtual disappearance of ideological positions on the mainstream right and left.

5   Heiner Müller, *Germania 3: Gespenster am toten Mann* (Cologne: Kiepenheuer & Witsch, 1996), pp. 40–2.

The tragic irony of this lack of creative and public interest in public politics is that, in the meantime, a major development is transforming Europe. While everybody still seems to be recovering from communism, a new ideology has occupied centre stage: the ideology of greater European integration. The increasing powers of a European government and the consequences of economic unity are gradually changing the face of the continent. The process may seem too slow, too bureacratic and too visually unimpressive to be dramatic. Yet, unlike the collapse of the Soviet empire, there is room for radicalized for-and-against argument here. Extremes seem evil: the xenophobic nation against an anonymous super-power. But extremes are always theatrical and definitions about democracy need to be made and discussed. Does enforced unity dissipate or exacerbate national tensions? Will a larger government structure mean more or less freedom?

Against a backdrop comprising the ruins of a terrifyingly violent century, a plot of huge political power shifts is being played out. Many of the characters, such as the Austrian Freedom Party's Jörg Haider, hardly need dramatizing. The actions of lorry-drivers and fishermen involve a mass appeal. Many of the issues, such as the fate of British cows, even have a good deal of intrinsic humour. Granted, it is not a simplistic battle of left versus right. But it is an ideological and practical debate of real importance for the future of politics. Those who call themselves political writers would be irresponsible if they ignored it.

Black theatre at the turn of the millennium
Kia Corthron

Kia Corthron's work as a dramatist includes *Splash Hatch on the E Going Down* (Center Stage, Yale Repertory Theatre, New York Stage and Film, Donmar Ware-house, London); *Digging Eleven* (Hartford Stage Company); *Seeking the Genesis* (Goodman Theatre, Chicago, Manhattan Theatre Club, New York); *Life by Asphyxiation* (Playwrights Horizons); *Wake Up Lou Riser* (Delaware Theatre Company); *Come Down Burning* (Long Wharf Theatre, American Place Theatre); and *Breath Boom* (Royal Court Theatre, London). She is also a member of New Dramatists.

I sit across the table from Denise Wong, artistic director of London's Black Mime Theatre Company, in the storefront side of Ninth Avenue Zen Palate. Denise, who'd seen the London production of my *Splash*

Hatch on the E Going Down, one of three plays by US authors presented in the Donmar Warehouse Theatre's American Imports series in early 1998, is visiting New York and called to get together for coffee which, for me, is juice. She is black, dark.

'Your name doesn't sound English', I remark. What a wit.

'My father is Chinese.' She begins chatting about limited black theatre in London and how she is here to see the work of New York black theatres and I nod and sip my cranberry and feel a growing embarrassment. Prickles of a panic, and a prayer that my flash-thoughts will telepathically deter Denise from her own thought path.

'And what black theatres are functioning in New York now?'

'None.' My anxiety so focused on thwarting the question that its inevitable utterance ironically spurs the instant reply. I chuckle, shame, my face warm and unfortunately light enough to colour.

'*None?*'

'Tiny little companies pop up now and again. But the closest major venue is Crossroads. Jersey.'

She is taken aback. Confusion, vague betrayal. 'Then it's worse than in London.'[1] I nod. Probably, probably. If Mecca was ever here, it left. I am the doomed messenger, not only disillusioning an outsider with romantic American visions but upsetting my own equilibrium; I am catapulted into consciousness of that overwhelming, exhausting reality which years ago had been banished to my unconscious: New York theatre in the 1990s and moving into the third Christian calendar millennium, a system wherein organizations that once nourished black work have faded into near oblivion, replaced by an integrated structure – with the season's offerings of any given Off-Broadway being all white save the single slot earmarked for whichever lucky minority is selected this year. I do not shirk my own responsibility, guilt – sudden memories of grad school ambitions: founding a new black theatre. When did my social idealism fizzle to individualist efforts that go no further than offering helpful suggestions to a theatre's outreach and publicity coordinators for bringing a black audience to my own productions?

So far the only black theatre Denise has seen, or known of, in her five days in New York (this is early October 1999) was a reading of a play with a black cast – by a white writer. Cue Kia: wrack my brain and finally I remember my own two-hour trek to the Long Wharf two weeks before – black production of *Much Ado About Nothing*. She's interested. I'm relieved. Yes, there *is* African-American theatre in New York. It's in Connecticut and written by Shakespeare.

1 Denise's reaction may have been more about initial disappointment than reality: Black Mime, for example, is on hiatus pending funding.

Fourth floor of the Mid-Manhattan Public Library, microfilm flying to
the theatre pages. Among the fifty-six Off- and Off-Off-Broadway listings
in the January 1, 1970, *Village Voice*:

> *The Harangues* by Joseph A. Walker, a Negro Ensemble Company
> production at St. Mark's Church.
>
> *Ceremonies in Dark Old Men* by Lonnie Elder at the Pocket Theatre
> (Lower East Side; space no longer exists).
>
> *Sambo* (!) by Ron Steward at the Public Theatre.
>
> *Slave Ship* by Leroi Jones at Chelsea Theatre Center in Brooklyn
> (space no longer exists).

In addition to these black pieces, a production of Maria Irene Fornes'
Promenade with music by Al Carmines.

If Denise idealized America, Kia's romance is with the past. Not just
the thriving NEC and New Lafayette Theatre and birth of the New Federal Theatre later that year; in 1970 a pulse beat across the theatrical
board: the *Voice* Broadway listings include *Hair, The Front Page* and *The
Great White Hope*.

To make the deadline for this article, the closest to the new millennium *Voice* edition I can peruse is December 7, 1999 (covering events of
1 through 7 December). I find two African-American listings:

> *In the Blood* by Suzan-Lori Parks at the Public Theatre.
>
> *The Trial of One Short-Sighted Black Woman vs. Mamie Louise and
> Safreeta Mae* by Marcia L. Leslie.

I'm going to cheat away from the consistency of my *Voice* comparison
because of an interesting discovery in the *New York Times* Sunday,
28 November 1999, Arts and Leisure section (covering events of 28
November through 4 December). These listings were overlooked in the
Voice:

> *It Ain't Nothin' But the Blues* on Broadway.
>
> *The Absolution of Willie Mae* by Joseph Walker, produced by the
> Negro Ensemble Company Off-Off-Broadway.

The obvious fascinating coincidence about the latter piece is its echo in
playwright and producer of my 1970 finding. Especially interesting given
the NEC's peripheral presence on the contemporary theatre scene – both
it and the New Federal producing only sporadically, the New Lafayette
long gone.

A few venues supporting artists of other colours appear to be somewhat fiscally healthier: Intar Hispanic American Arts Center, for example,

and Pan Asian Repertory Theatre. (I can't help but to remark upon Pan Asian's single entry in the October 1999 [season preview] issue of *American Theatre*: a revival of *The Teahouse of the August Moon* by John Patrick – a name about as Asian as those of the creators of *Miss Saigon*.)

The contributions of other artists of colour cited in the aforementioned 1999 *Voice*:

> *The Double Auntie Waltz* by Aurorae Khoo at Lower East Side Tenement Theatre, described as 'the strange encounters experienced by a woman visiting her two elderly aunts in Chinatown'.

> *Enter the Night* by Maria Irene Fornes, part of Signature Theatre's Fornes season. (Of the theatre's nine seasons, each devoted to the work of a single US playwright, seven of the writers have been white and male; the remaining two, Fornes and Adrienne Kennedy, are, interestingly, both female and non-white.)

> *Facade* and *Moondance Café*, one-acts by Jerry Rodriguez.

> *Qué Felices Son Las Barbies!* by Wanda Arriaga.

> The Satellite Project, biographical plays by women of colour at La MaMa E.T.C.

> *Entre Mujeres* at Thalia Spanish Theatre in Queens.

> *The Chunga* by Mario Vargas Llosa.

> *¿Quién Mató a Hector Levoe?* produced by Puerto Rican Traveling Theatre.

There are 178 theatre listings in the December 9, 1999, *Voice*. Ten pieces by artists of colour (twelve if we throw in the *Times*) hardly reflects a city in which 56.8 per cent of the population is nonwhite. The argument, of course, goes that 1) the subscription audience majority *is* white, and 2) subscription audiences keep US theatre alive.

Despite the fact that American theatre administrators are haunted by visions of governmental gold coins raining on European colleagues, London theatres seem to suffer fiscal crises as often as those in the US. Still, Lucy Davies, former literary manager of the Donmar Warehouse, remarks that London would never institute a subscription audience system as this would narrow the audience pool along socio-economic lines and ultimately (here I reach my own conclusions based on the American model) artistic decisions would be heavily influenced by a given script's projected demonstrability for motivating a sixty-year-old white of the upper middle classes to renew her or his subscription. Frankly, as I glance at posters for past Donmar productions – Sondheim, Sondheim, Sondheim – I realize that the American Imports series, and in particular my contribution of an all-black play, are anomalies on this stage, subscription system or no. But in examining other venues, the Royal Court, for example, my head pivoting a slow one eighty from my eighth-row viewpoint, I guess ninety per cent of this single-ticket audience to be in their twenties to forties.

Age, a crucial factor that has terrorized American theatre professionals for many years now and thus one I felt compelled to mention, is not the demographic on which I've focused this essay.

Theatre is *not* a white thing. There are several black regionals filling their seats at least as well as white counterparts. In addition, we could hardly overlook the ever sold-out 'urban circuit' extravaganzas at the Upper West Side 3,000-seat Beacon Theatre. The feelings of threat these popular shows inspire in black writers whose work style is legitimized (whether or not produced) by the Off-Broadway/regional community echoes hostilities earlier in the century between W.E.B. Dubois with his 'new theatre' of 'Outer Life' (Dubois' term), in which black society was idealized in defiance of reality and reality was rebuked in agitprop speeches; and Alain Locke's promotion of an 'Inner Life' theatre whereby folk culture was more accurately portrayed but, the overall aesthetic purpose being strictly amusement, only the *humorous* side of folk life was revealed – the result being a perpetuation of white society's blackface minstrel shows.[2] Both extremes have moderated: urban circuit pieces, though clearly geared for entertainment through one-liners and song (as in Inner Life plays), exhibit a measure of politics if only through blatant moral commentary on contemporary issues; the 'legitimate' writers, on the other hand, frequently commended for addressing 'important' issues, are concomitantly discouraged from overt politics.

In considering the stock subscription audience member in season programming, an artistic director will be influenced by a play's politics – how radical and in what way (since certain radical thinking may be 'in' one year and 'out' the next) – at least as much as the quality of its writing. This tendency is particularly significant for artists of colour who on the whole, I would argue, infuse their texts politically more often than do whites.

My friend Janet freelances in technical editing in Washington, DC. Recently she emailed me information she'd garnered from her current volume: the projected disappearance of our common race in the coming

2 From Samuel A. Hay, *African American Theatre: An Historical and Critical Perspective* (Cambridge: Cambridge University Press, 1994).

decades. Her words: 'By 2050 America will be a very light beige with fading black margins.' Trying to look on the bright side, in typical Us–Them American fashion, I suggest: 'But won't the white people disappear too?' She realizes I'm right and, checking her facts, at an 'even faster' rate.

So perhaps in the new millennium this essay (and all of my plays for that matter) will be useless, at best a curious historical artefact. We will all be equal because, despite all efforts to the contrary, we not so suddenly all *look* equal. Utopia by default.

Not likely. There will always be differences, subtle to outside eyes perhaps but, should the will to Jim Crow a particular group surface, sufficient. (Yugoslavia.)

With respect to present reality and the coming decades, the already minority New York white population will continue to shrink in percentage, and the already senior-citizen white theatre subscription audience will continue to age, and theatres will have to make some imaginative, pivotal decisions very soon if we are to have a US theatre half a century hence. Should the subscription system prove to be a merry-go-round impossible to step off of once you are on (which I personally doubt), then perhaps the slate will be wiped clean and by 2015 all of the theatres functioning today will have ceased to exist, replaced by a new Off-Off-(Off-?) community more reflective of the diversity of our culture.

Whatever it takes. And I believe it will take; the pendulum always swings back. I'm optimistic.

The crisis of label

Alice Tuan

Alice Tuan is a playwright. Her *Last of the Suns* and *Ikebana*, have been seen at Berkeley Rep, and East West Players, respectively. Her one-act play *Some Asians* was a winner of Perishable Theatre's 5th Annual Playwriting Festival. Other plays include *Coastline* and a solo piece *New Culture for a New Country*, performed as part of *Secret History of the Lower East Side*, produced by En Garde Arts in New York. She is the recipient of an NEA/TCG Residency with East West Players in Los Angeles.

Marx's words are like bats: one can see in them both birds and mice. (Vilfredo Pareto)

In his philosophical introduction of *Alienation: Marx's Conception of Man in Capitalist Society*, Bertell Ollman acknowledges Marx's peculiar use of words and finds Pareto's bat analogy 'profound' in articulating the difficulty thinkers have had in pinning down Marx's meanings.[1] I sometimes think Asian-Americans, exposed to contradictory Eastern and Western influences, experience a similar slipperiness. Whether defining self or being perceived by others, Asianness tends to be marked on the surface as either ethnic custom (to be compared with American tradition) or as political reaction to otherness through historical injustice. Much of Asian-American expression has been an explanation of the experience in our exclusionary and commodifying culture, which naively promises equality in light of market forces. I wonder if it is possible to look deeper into Asian-American works, for their sensibility rather than their cultural ambassadorship. For their Paretoan 'batness' instead of either 'birdness' or 'mouseness'.

In theatre, the great plays traffic in the mysteries of ambivalence, where two or more interpretations are equally applicable. The indecision of Hamlet, the Pinter pause, the cross-castings of Caryl Churchill. Yet in our univalent culture, where we prefer to have one winner and one loser, to allow a tie of scores feels somehow anticlimactic, less bang for the buck. Complex characters, brimming with contradictions, are reduced down to hypocrites: they leave us confused and we can't trust them. It is no wonder that Asian-American plays tend to fall flat, the characters explaining to the audience (or perhaps to themselves) why they are the way they are. It is a theatre of perennial immigration, a constant clawing to ground zero. I wonder if the artists are not imagining themselves a lusher terrain of existence or if it is the funders, producers and artistic directors that don't trust their audiences will be interested in the Asian-American artists' sensibilities.

It is no mystery that our society values profit. That which can sell, we do more of. That which we can't sell, we label, demystify, translate into marketable language, or spin core qualities towards intrigue, sensationalism, hipness, exoticism, entertainment. Is anything immune to the auction blocks these days? And if an entity is fresh and original, does it have spine enough to continue from its raw core without being commodified? Or if it is not deemed worthy of purchase, does it have spine enough to continue from its raw core nevertheless? The crisis of theatre, and here of Asian-American theatre, is actually a crisis of capitalism and decisions made solely through the bottom line.

1 See Bertell Ollman, *Alienation: Marx's Conception of Man in Capitalist Society*, 2nd Edition (Cambridge: Cambridge University Press, 1976).

This past year, I have been burrowing myself out of the hole that is identity politics in the theatre. I was self-consumptive, a snake eating its own tail, when I tried to think through my assigned label of 'Asian-American'. After fifteen years of multi-culturalism, the label became clunky, meaningless, a hollow representation of something that started out ideally to include, but never left its naïve state, for more sophisticated terrain. In her essay 'Wounded Attachments: Late Modern Oppositional Political Formations' Wendy Brown posits that identity politics is a distraction away from a true critique of capitalism.[2] This illuminative article made me realize that the label was more for funding and quota purposes than any reflection of my work as a playwright.

Still, somehow, I cannot completely discard the label because it does literally describe my make-up (and productions have happened because of it, i.e. the Lila Wallace grant to produce Asian-American works at Berkeley Rep for *Last of the Suns*). And as a writer, I am better left to write plays than to critique capitalism directly. Instead, I would like to turn the label of Asian-American inside out, see what the innards might be, give the skinside a rest, and see Asian-American more as a sensibility than a label. As a playwright, I strive to provide an American view through an Asian-American lens, and perhaps help widen the angle for artists and audience (both a, aa and non-a) involved.

Let me tell you, I admire the sisters and brothers who are unconcerned with the label, unencumbered by its association, unclaimed by it in their work. I wish I could be free of it, like I wish I could be free of market forces. But somehow, I resist the abandonment of the label because, as self-consumptive as the making-peace-with-one's-label can get, I would rather light a fire under it and reinvent its meaning than disassociate from it completely. American itself is hard to pin down, although it seems the culture is led more by economics than not, more willing to genetically alter things away from their natural being than change the dynamics of late-capitalist machinery.

Enough of the capitalism bad, compassion good diatribe. (Though, I would like to agitate for a more compassionate capitalism, one that will make choices through a more sublime thought process than 'it sells'.) Here I will describe one moment and four pieces in theatre that I found compelling in their implications of Asian-American.

The first moment has to do with language. I admit within the aa realm (I will herein use the lower-case abbreviation as a way to temper the

2 Wendy Brown, 'Wounded Attachments: Late Modern Oppositional Political Formations', in *The Identity in Question*, ed. John Rajchman (New York: Routledge, 1995), pp. 199–227. Originally published in *Political Theory*, 21, No. 3 (1983), pp. 390–410.

clunky label and also not confuse it with Alcoholics Anonymous or American Airlines), I have more insight into Chinese-American than other Asian cultures umbrellaed under the same label. As you might know, Chinese (in this case Mandarin) has four tones: a neutral tone (a dot), an ascending tone (/), a curved tone (a check mark) and a descending tone (\ ). Mandarin Chinese is complicated by the fact that words of completely different meaning might have the same exact tone (context is everything), so that the same sound with a different tone exacts a different meaning. In a play that was directed by a non-Mandarin-speaking director, a Chinese-American character learns of the concept *run* (*a check mark*), which means endurance. The Chinese-American actor who is recalling this concept unintentionally makes the American sound of *run* so that the concept relayed is not that of sustaining, but rather of fleeing. In this difficult moment, the message was more of a western flavour than its intended, very Chinese notion of long-suffering. Played to this American audience, perhaps the character felt more western in her attempt to walk away, when in fact she was making an attempt to struggle through. One word, a tone off, gave a contradicting message.

This is a very aa moment because it questions facial authenticity. What is the responsibility of our face? Because we look it, is our misfiring of information excusable and adding a shoddy 'whatever' quality to the work? This is a conundrum that I have encountered, where when someone finds out I am Chinese, they expect a sort of Cliff's Notes version of Chinese history from me. I passive-aggressively inform them that I was schooled like them, here in America, in the Los Angeles Unified School District and was not taught Chinese history. I suppose if I were the good student my label advertises for me, I, too, could be an ambassador for these curious folk. I was not at that time interested in Chinese history and further fuelled a particular brand of aa disenchantment. Perhaps this is a difference between Asian-Americans and American-Asians: a willingness to thrive in ignorance to the detriment of being.

On the topic of American-Asians, who tend to be lumped into the aa category, I find that those who were formed in an Asian-majority culture have an assurance in identity that the Asian-Americans lack. This is a distinction I make in trying to articulate aa. I think our culture does embrace the American-Asians because they have a more critical eye in their point of view and, with a more solid mindset, tend to be better writers. The American-Asians have direct experience of Asian culture (even if they have not fitted into their home country) that provides a firmer foundation than those of Asian descent formed and schooled in American.

The first piece I'd like to discuss has to do with casting. Los Angeles East West Players produced a Chungmi Kim play, *Hanako*, on the historical topic of Korean comfort women during its 1998–99 season. This issue play deals with three former comfort women who reunite in the United States for a New York rally that brought the atrocities of Japanese sexual enslavement of Korean women during the Japanese occupation to the attention of America. One of the most startling details was spoken by the toughest of the three septuagenarian women of how she could not stand the taste of milk because of the quarts of semen she was forced to endure. Two of the three actresses who played the Koreans were Japanese-American, the third was Chinese-American.

At first I wondered where the Korean actresses were, but then found myself entangled in the notion of authenticity. (Dian Kobayashi was particularly powerful in the toughest of the three roles.) Only in America, where there is not the historical, national, or emotional attachment of the brutality, could Japanese-American women be portraying the victims of their own perpetrators' race. Is this the evolution of democracy, where we can disassociate from the history of our origins and free ourselves from the past? Does this complicate the question of what aa is? Is this an American brand of working through guilt? Is this the result of a dearth of roles and merely a result of competition? Or did anyone even notice?

As a small note, *Hanako* was produced in a heavily issue-oriented season at East West Players which also saw productions of Cherylene Lee's *Carry the Tiger to the Mountain* about the Vincent Chin incident as well as Tim Dang and Joel Iwataki's musical *Beijing Spring* about the 1989 uprising in Tiananmen Square. This small note concerns the funders' vision of aa, which seemed to create a season of Theatre of Guilt and kept new audiences from being interested.

The second piece has to do with audience perception. In the 1998–99 season, New York's Joseph Papp Public Theatre produced Diana Son's *Stop Kiss* to rave reviews. Son's play tells of two straight-identified women who fall in love, one of whom suffers gay-bashing violence on the night of their first kiss. The two lead roles were deftly played by Jessica Hecht and Sandra Oh. Callie (Hecht) is a traffic reporter, detached from herself, a casualty of our ironic, Teflon age where real feelings slide off the surface. Sara (Oh) is a St. Louis woman, a newcomer to New York, who has accepted a teaching position in the Bronx. I remember sitting in the audience, particularly drinking up Sandra Oh's performance of a sprightly, quirky woman who is beaten into silence, not because of her ethnicity, but rather because of her sexuality. (Many have wondered why it was the aa character that was victimized, but do people wonder why Japan was bombed during World War II when it was Germany that was the main aggressor?) Not once did a surface marker of Asianness appear. There was something revolutionary about seeing an American who happened to have an Asian face on the American stage.

This is a new kind of aa play, unencumbered by the standards set up before it. It isn't that there isn't an aa sensibility around it: I found Hecht's Callie, the one who swerves around road kill instead of straddling it, to have the quality of being invisible to self that interfaces with an aa tendency. The refreshing air of Son's play is that it foregrounds human qualities rather than aa qualities. I saw more of Sandra Oh's invention of being rather than a chain to the discomfort of being aa. The point here is that the aa canon was opened up to feature a sensibility not steeped in the quagmire of identity. Those who feel the play lacks Asianness are reminded that one play does not define the whole identity. The more points of view in the stew, the healthier the meal.

Which leads to the question, how did aa's aesthetic get defined? Even the Public Theatre, one of the leaders of open and cutting-edge work, has been historically narrow. Joseph Papp did bring David Henry Hwang to the nation's attention and christened a whole new genre in the theatre. Starting in 1979 with Hwang's first play *FOB*, the Public Theatre exclusively produced Hwang as the Asian-American voice (his next four plays were produced between 1980 and 1983). But then for ten years there was nothing. Not a peep. Until Jessica Hagadorn and Han Ong's performance piece *Airport Music* in 1994, followed by Chay Yew's *A Language of Their Own* the next year, with a schedule of one aa play a year up to the present. Hwang's success has heavily influenced the genre, and institutions like the Public must be commended for presenting new work. The question is, can it be more than one slot a year, when there is quality aa work aplenty?

I know there is an abundance of new work. I am privy to a gamut of developing voices as a workshop facilitator at East West Players' David Henry Hwang Writers' Institute. There is raw, tough comedy in Euijoon Kim's plays, a presentation of the yolk trash in Judy SooHoo's *Texas*, brotherly rivalry in Lucy Kim's *Leon and Clark*, middle-class paranoia and fetish in Annette Lee's *Cul de Sac*, downsizing and closeting in Daniel Cariaga's *Sleepwalk*, and fierce intelligence in Henrietta Chico Nofre's *Driving Lessons*. Even East West Players, with its older subscription base and funders bias, cannot put these new works on its new stage at the Union Center for the Arts in Little Tokyo. I must say, to the credit of Artistic Director Tim Dang, Euijoon Kim's rowdy, fast-talking, profane *My Tired Broke-Ass Pontificating Slapstick Funk* was recently premiered, bringing a new young scene into the theatre. But how to keep the new audiences attending? This now is the challenge of the theatre, particularly Los Angeles theatre, whose young citizens do not have the habit of going to see live performance because of prohibitive costs, commute, the plethora of movies, or the fact that one bad play does spoil future theatregoing.

I'm thrilled to say there are young theatre groups who cannot wait for institutions to invite them in to develop work which most likely will not get produced. I am speaking of groups like Los Angeles' Here/Now, a comedy troupe of talented aa actors under thirty, and New York's 2nd Generation, led by actor/producer/writer Welly Yang. Some of the most alive and thriving theatre is in these self-produced, hands-on, bare-bones productions of new work.

I was particularly excited to see Jason Fong's *Fentor,* which I had the privilege of watching develop in the East West writers' workshops. The play tells of a family, Asianness unspecified. This is a 1950s brand of American family, never a discouraging word, even with the disappearance of the mother. The play is told from eight-year-old Fentor's point of view, he himself barely speaking eight words through the play (a stunning portrayal by Eric Tran). The subtext of the family's drama is played by the bickering furniture in Fentor's room. The beanbag chair is forever competing with the square chair for Fentor's attention. (Sit on me. No, sit on me.) When a Japanese-made table enters the picture, the chairs are threatened, not knowing what it is. Fentor is visited by his angelic mother: we've found out she's died in the hospital but no one has reached the psychically retreated Fentor about this. She leaves him a package and exits. Fentor screams for her return, his fury shown through the destruction of the talking furniture. The package turns out to be a step stool, silent and wooden, for Fentor to elevate himself on, because the paper aeroplane letters he'd been sending his lost mother 'didn't quite reach'.

An elegant production directed by John Miyasaki and produced by Here/Now (of which Jason Fong is an actor), this production subtly portrayed aa characters with narrative stealthily depicting Fentor's alienation from the world. I had heard that the actors themselves could not pinpoint what was aa about this play, because they themselves are used to playing the surface markers. The strength of *Fentor* is in its showing of sublimated feelings beneath a cartoonish, pop surface. The dynamism of the object's drama versus the staidness of the people rang true not just from an aa sensibility but from that of capitalism's residues, where objects are imbued with more attention than the common human. This to me read as a young playwright with a new aa sensibility, that of the next generation coming up, even further saturated by television and computers than my own, attempting to reach and express emotion. I sometimes feel new plays are criticized because the theatrical language is hard to pin down, the knowledge of what is trying to be conveyed in its own terms dismissed. This is an example of actors, artists, writers, funders, producers, artistic directors, and audience needing to reinvent terms and labels for new work to make sense.

Finally, we have *Medea Macbeth Cinderella,* a co-production of two Los Angeles mainstay ensembles, Cornerstone Theatre and the Actor's Gang. The ambition of this piece required the mammoth moxie that is lacking in so much of theatre today. (Even Broadway spectacles are all huge stagings of light pieces.) That Bill Rauch and Tracy Young led their respective ensembles to present all three plays at once is a miracle. This play could only happen in Los Angeles, a naturally post-modern city with no apparent centre, disparate juxtaposition and pop culture as bright as the sunshine. Medea is played by an Asian woman (Paige Leung), Macbeth (Shishir Kurup) by an Afro-East Indian man, and Cinderella (Rodgers and Hammerstein's) by a lovely redhead (Evie Peck). Yes I am guilty of labelling here, but the beauty of this piece is you never even had time to notice, there was so much going on all at once. If one must keep track, then one has lost the reason for why this piece exists.

A volume can be written about this piece, there are layers of implication, but I will describe the moments that struck me, mostly concerning the interface of the three disparate worlds. It starts with a pageant of all three play worlds, the audience introduced to the characters in a pinball-like fashion. An immediate feeling was that one was always drawn to the musical; in a mass of confusion one goes to the simplest most beloved story with the sweetest of melodies. The set provides the contradictions: designer Rachel Hauck placed what seemed a stairway to heaven smack in the middle with an elevated tilting ramp behind it, hugging the back wall, then curving around and onto the ground. The kings and queens of all the plays were all placed in the throne area up high, and at points of the play switch crowns and take each other's seats. (Ah the dilution of monarchy.)

After the play worlds are established, the first interfacing is 'The Prince Is Having a Ball' number from *Cinderella.* How surreal to have Medea and Lady Macbeth (the ever sublime Christopher Liam Moore) to remain in dilemma character, yet go through the motions. (Are our private dramas held in as we entertain with a pleasing dance?) In Macbeth's daggers speech, he hallucinates by seeing Cinderella's paring knife as she sings in her corner, then turning away sees the knife that Medea prepares in killing her children. (Might the objects in one's mind be benign in one context and horrific in another, so that we must see clearly the references and meaning, and not react to all in the same manner?) The drunken porter in Macbeth no longer sees boundaries between the play worlds, he actually sees Cinderella's stepsisters and Medea's chorus on stage with him. (Is drunkenness seeing into other worlds that we make boundaries for when conscious and sober?)

I was witness to an extravaganza that punched away boundaries and impossibilities. It challenged the audience to look beyond a mere story to implications and juxtapositions and disorientations that are so a part of our heterogeneous culture. This to me was an articulation of American, and dared one to go beyond a univalent mindset and endure, engage, enjoy multivalance for three hours. The crowning moment, though, was the response of a group of Marshall High School students I was doing playwriting workshops with through the Audrey Skirball Kenis Play-wrights-in-the Schools Project. 'It's kind of like watching TV, listening to the radio and doing your homework at the same time.'

Bingo. All talk of dramaturgy-this and thruline-that fell away. The young audiences are out there. They get the complex narratives. They've been channel-surfing all their lives. The borders are perforating. The bloods are mixing. The authenticity is no longer at the surface. New products of the same old thing appear on shelves and screens faster and faster. The young are consuming as fast as they can. But will we allow the truly new to emerge, to have its time to process, to be thought about and nurtured before it comes to full natural being?

I agonized over the semantics of a term. But language is an organism that needs to be infused and updated, to be enfleshened with new mean-ing. If the greatest crisis calls for the greatest reform, the greatest reform is in language, how we choose to think about old terms, how to find the language to reinvent. Leon Trotsky describes artistic creation as 'the com-plicated turning inside out of old forms'. He says that 'the artist is the nat-ural ally to the revolution, and we believe, that the supreme task of art in our epoch is to take part actively and consciously in the preparation of the revolution. But', he continues, 'the artist cannot serve the struggle for free-dom unless he feels in his very bones its meaning and drama and freely seeks to give his own inner world incarnation in his art'.[3] In this sense, inner worlds must be allowed to be revealed and emerged.

And so, the snake, now mouth free and tail a rattlin' has spun into a bat, turning inside out, hanging upside down, bouncing its radar, and blind to the literal. As for you, artist, for you, producer, for you, funder, and for you, dear audience, in looking at the bat, can you see the mouse in it, can you see the bird in it? Better yet, can you see both at once?

---

3   See Paul N. Siegel, ed., *Art and Revolution: Writings on Literature, Politics and Culture* (New York: Pathfinder Press, 1970).

Notes on opera at the end of the century

Ricardo Szwarcer. Trans. Caridad Svich and Judy Herbert

Ricardo Szwarcer is a freelance London-based opera producer and artistic consultant. He has been General Manager of the Teatro Colón de Buenos Aires (1986–99), Artistic Director of Lille Opera House (1991–99), and Production Director for the International Theatre Festival of La Biennale di Venezia (1994–95). He was previously Administrator of the Teatro San Martín (1975–82), and of the Teatro Colón (1982–86) in Buenos Aires. At the request of the Municipality of Santiago de Chile, he has completed a study of Santiago de Chile's Opera House related to cultural policy.

Recently a huge book of predictions for the twenty-first century fell into my hands. It was written by one of those prophets of doom who were much in vogue at the end of the 1960s. After flicking through this book, I realized that there is nothing more tedious or grotesque than a volume full of miscalculations.

With this precaution in mind, I approach the subject of the future of opera. I hope that what follows will be understood as a series of reflections on opera today. I think it is necessary to consider firstly the general context in which these reflections are made, so that later on I may discuss the broader theme of the mission of lyric theatre and its principal characteristics. I will end with a bit of lyric fiction of my own, musing on the latest developments in the genre and its possibilities for the future.

General axiom

I think that for various reasons theatres dedicated to producing opera have lost their sense of direction, given that they are involved in trying to solve such problems as political survival, profitability, union wages, image, and perceived success. The artistic process itself does not enter into the discussion. In fact, if I may exaggerate a little, we could say that no one is at all interested in the work itself.

An example. In my last year at the Opera Theatre in Lille, I was asked to devise a new programme for the general operation of the theatre. The instructions I received from the political body who oversaw the decisions consisted solely of a series of parameters that were regulated by the demands of the overall budget. I had to take into account raising the number of performances necessary to meet the budget; the appropriate range of ticket prices in which to do so; the obligation of co-producing certain shows, configuring an alliance with other theatres; developing educational programmes for children, the unemployed, and senior citizens; offering a 'performance' opportunity for amateurs; developing an audience; providing work for young professionals; reducing the average costs per show; estimating the profit from renting performance spaces when they were not in use, etc.

However, when I asked what the artistic mission should be, I was told: 'That's your problem. Within those parameters, do what you wish. But make sure that it goes down well with the press.' This could be interpreted to mean that I was given a free hand. But such was not the case. Instead, there was a general uninterestedness which I perceived as a lack of belief in the art's worth in and of itself, or even an avoidance of discussing what its value could be. And, in addition to this apathetic response, there was much ignorance of and boredom with the subject.

I was able later to confirm that this general state of affairs is endemic regardless of the country. I believe that in this context, it's honestly impossible to guarantee the realization of an artistic project – which for me is the only essential thing – because after all without the art itself the rest would have no reason to exist: neither the economic needs of a theatre's daily operations, nor the social visibility and standing of an organization. Any artist – musician, painter, writer, etc. – needs basic conditions to create their art. Today, theatres dedicated to producing opera do not have in their day-to-day infrastructure, nor can they ever guarantee, even the most minimal working conditions for an artist.

What is worse is that they have forgotten what these conditions are. And without meaning to, by obeying the old maxim that the show must go on and the curtain must rise, the management slips towards hypocrisy.

It is time to reprioritize – to place the making of art at the centre of the discussion.

Culture and the market place

The end of the twentieth century offers us a plethora of changes and social mutations which occur at a great speed, driven by the rhythm of the globalization of the economy. The freeing up of the market place seems to be the sole governing philosophy, and it is questioned only when unforeseen economic imbalances begin to make themselves felt in different parts of the world.

Faced with the urgency of positioning themselves competitively in these markets, of raising their productivity and diminishing relative costs, different countries see no option but to drastically cut public expenditure. In this context, any investment in culture is questioned from the outset. Moreover, this is because, traditionally, the political establishment associates culture with luxurious expense, whose contribution to society – even at a moderate level – has yet to be substantiated.

That is why besides the traditional budgetary restrictions, political bodies now require that institutions also provide aims and/or cultural objectives which reinforce or make visible their social roles: those aims which contribute to the elimination of social barriers; which take into account pedagogic services necessary for the development of audiences for today and for the future; which are interested in professional staff development and are based on principles of simple, efficient management, orientated towards commercial viability via marketing policies and the evaluation of results.

These changes are occurring simultaneously with a crisis which is affecting creativity in different realms, in some of which the difficulty of reaching audiences is constantly in evidence.

Culture and the market place have antithetical objectives. The market place tends towards standardization; the cultural realm towards the personal and unique. The goods in a market place are consumed; cultural goods are not. They are appropriated, and they do not disappear through appropriation.

Thus, the methods of both realms must necessarily be different. Failure to recognize this runs the risk of gravely confounding things.

It is not shocking, therefore, that in this state of affairs there is a great confusion in regard to the use of the word 'culture', and its possible social value. Even in the media, the word has come to be associated with notions of 'importance', 'prestige', 'difficulty', or 'elitism'. And here I would like to share a definition I once read, which seemed to me enlightening: 'Culture is the way we regard things.' A cultural difference is, therefore, a difference in perspective. And this is a definition which does not take into account any of the notions cited earlier, or just the work of art itself. This definition is about the relationship between the work and its audience, which is neither more nor less the very mission of a lyric theatre.

Opera today

To create the conditions wherein this 'conversation' between the work (the lyric opera's repertoire) and its audience takes place – this is the mission of an opera house. There is no other.

Exit the manipulation of stars; the carnival of the rich and famous; the important speeches vacuous of content; the nostalgia for a past, which all of us know was never 'better'. If anything, it was different. And irrecoverable. Exit, then, also the falseness of those who wish to preserve 'authentic values'. As a philosopher once said: we never visit the same river twice. The river is different. And so are we.

The conditions which must be created in theatres are almost non-existent today, save for the exceptions to the rule.

Said another way: you can count on the fingers of one hand the theatres that take it upon themselves to move forward with a truly artistic mission, characterized principally by the search for new forms in regard to the musical and scenic presentation of the operatic repertoire, and by a willingness to constantly renovate it. This necessarily implies the taking of risks, at least from the public's point of view.

Another paradoxical example is that of the Santiago de Chile Opera House. At the request of the Chilean Parliament, I undertook an analysis of the overall performance of theatre in the region. The outcome was undeniably clear. If we were to compare the proportion of their own revenues (box office, sales, sponsorship, etc.), it exceeds the results of the best European theatres. The Municipal Theatre of Santiago functions so well that it finances in part the salaries of its permanent staff from the collection of its box office alone. This is why it cannot take any kind of artistic risk, because one failure would mean its staff would lose their jobs. This example serves to show us that the politics of an 'efficient effort', in respect to marketing and sales, typical of any enterprise which manufactures a product, does not resolve the problem. On the contrary, sometimes the problem is aggravated, because the marketing policies in culture generate confusion in the audience about the real value of the work, thus reducing the market and asphyxiating creativity.

The problem does not get resolved either through a voluntary political design, like the French one, which went on investing resources in the cultural system, without having generated a proportional return in terms of creativity. The problem is much more subtle. Talent and sensitivity are good advisers. Moreover, it is important to place the artistic mission as a central priority. A priority which all parties must share – government officials, the critics, the public, the unions – in order to help design an artistic policy which would be pedagogic, and steeped in cultural traditions, without losing sight of international trends.

The mission

The artistic director of a theatre dedicated to presenting opera must ask himself:

- How to contribute to the development and evolution of this particular art form. The question requires answers to at least three issues:

- What is the visual aesthetic by which one presents repertoire from the baroque period?
- What does one do with the reinterpretation of the classical and romantic repertoire, taking into account the exhaustive theatrical explorations already undertaken during the second half of the twentieth century?
- How does one contribute to the creation of new operas?

The artistic policy and the programming of opera in the future must concern itself primarily with and provide answers to, these questions, always paving the way to new paths.

The future

There is a joke that goes like this: in lyric opera, over time, the protagonists have changed. At first the most important artist was considered to be the librettist, then the composer, much later it was the singer (or the diva), and later still the conductor, who was robbed of his glory by the stage director, who then gives it up to the theatre's artistic director, who was then replaced in turn, in order of importance, by the Minister of Culture …

Who then will be the next great protagonist? The sponsor? The financial director? Or the marketing director?

Given what I have stated, I think that three types of opera house exist, according to their different aims:

- Those that have an artistic mission, characterized by a programming policy which evolves over time, and whose artistic decisions are achieved through a spirit of adventure, innovation and risk. They seek, thus, to finely tune the production instrument – that is the theatre – creating an internal culture, a 'way of making art', where both artistic and technical bodies are integrated. In this category mention must be made of the Salzburg Festival, the Théâtre de la Monnaie in Brussels, Le Grand Théâtre of Geneva, and Amsterdam's De Nederlandse Opera.
- Those who dedicate themselves, especially in major cities, to presenting the lyric repertoire in a rather traditional way, those that have a big tourist audience and whose main concern is the smooth functioning of the complex production machine that operates without any flexibility.
- Those devoted strictly to entertainment, who approach their task with a superficial artistic focus, and whose priorities are purely social or commercial.

I think that in the future the lack of funding will continue. Despite efficient management or the additional funding that could come from private benefactors or commercial sponsorship, the truth is that the political
establishment wishes to withdraw from giving to the arts, convinced that
art is an activity for a small minority, which should be funded by that
same minority.

In this context, it is more than likely that many mid-size theatres and
smaller theatres will lose the ability to produce work, and will thus
become rental houses for touring productions. This phenomenon has
already started to happen in Europe and in Latin America – visible in theatres in São Paulo, Rio de Janeiro, and Caracas, and to some extent in
Argentina's Teatro Colón.

As a result, co-productions among theatres will increase as will the
proliferation of privately funded works, which will become available to
theatres through a distribution circuit. It would not be strange in the
least, then, that the multinational entertainment corporations (Disney,
Spielberg, etc.) will resort to this method of presenting and distributing
their spectacles, as they already are doing with their musical comedy
productions.

These major investors will not stop exploring the spectacular side of
their endeavours, among which they will seek the advancement of new
audiovisual technologies, and anything involved in the realm of 'special
effects', as they have already done in film.

I doubt that technological innovations will guide new artistic forms
in the future. I think that, as always, the exploration of the purely human
is what will lead us toward a new concept of theatre. Of this we can
already see signs. What is new today centres on a non-linear narrative
line and naturalism in acting – but with a gestural and musical rigour
which is extreme – and above all, a return to poetic expression in all its
manifestations.

It is a fragile and, as yet uncertain, way forward. It is uncompromis-
ing. Will it be able to survive in the jungle of the market place?

It is possible that the only path left to this expression is the way of the
catacombs.

What's to be done? Theatre off the map

The question of culture
Peter Sellars

Peter Sellars is a theatre director and a professor of World Arts and Cultures at UCLA. His most recent work as a director includes *The Persians* (1993), *The Merchant of Venice* (1994), *Peony Pavilion* (1998) and *The Screens* (1999). In opera he is perhaps best known for his collaborations with composer John Adams (these include *Nixon in China* (1987) and *The Death of Klinghoffer* (1991)) and for his work with Handel (*Theodora* (1996) and *Giulio Cesare* (1985)), Mozart (*Così fan tutte*, *Le Nozze di Figaro* and *Don Giovanni* (1984–90)) and Stravinsky (*The Rake's Progress* (1996)). This piece is adapted by Maria M. Delgado from a lecture given at the Fourth Elia Conference, 'Reflections on the Human Face', held in Lisbon, 13–16 November 1996. The conference's three major themes were Multiculturalism in the Arts and Society, New Technologies in Arts Education, and Current Developments in Arts Education.

Anything in life that occurs, occurs through dialogue and not through monologue, which is indeed our very point when we use words like multiculturalism. If anything that you are doing is not multi then it's not anything. Multi is the definition of being a human being and surviving on the planet, and not only surviving but doing better than that. Let's be more ambitious than survival. We can, I think, get beyond the cats and dogs phase of 'What are we going to eat next?' If we're asking ourselves a larger question, then we're into the question of culture. Even if we're thinking about our next meal, probably we're into the question of culture. Culture is by definition multiplicitous because all of us as human beings are, by definition, multiplicitous and multifarious. When we talk about motivation, when we talk about intentionality, none of us really know our own motivations or our intentions; much less the motivations and intentions that we are imputing to others, because in fact we don't know ourselves at all. So to announce that I'm here to represent this or that culture is outrageous because all of us represent lots of cultures all the time.

We're in a very complicated situation with European culture because from the nineteenth century on, a lot of European culture developed along nationalistic lines, to defend a certain political identity. An identity politics meant that then Hitler could say, 'This is what Wagner is', and reduce Wagner to that. And Wagner could play along. Great film music for a genocide.

So we have to ask ourselves what our products are doing. What are we writing the film music for? What is the movie? We have to understand when we hear a Bach suite that a saraband, the most beautiful poignant movement in a Bach suite, is, of course, traditional North African trance music. It shows up in the Baroque, a period where in Europe all of these cross-cultural currents were in evidence. But few people talk about what it means to live with an Arab presence in Europe and what we were always brought up with in our schools as the Dark Ages. You have Rome, then the Dark Ages and then suddenly the medieval period, revival of learning, and the Renaissance. The Dark Ages are obviously when Europe was Islamic. So could we open a window and turn on a light; it's not all that dark as it turns out. Whose darkness are we talking about?

I think it's very very important to understand that great classical French culture is, of course, this incredible intersection with the Crusades. The decoration on a Gothic cathedral or in classical French manuscripts would be unimaginable without the contact with Arab culture. The very roots of what we call European culture are non-European.

Examine the labels on your clothing. The coffee that we drink takes us to Guatemala, it takes us to Brazil. My Nike shoes were made in China by Chinese prisoners, so the fingers of Chinese prisoners are touching my feet right now. Any time we tell ourselves that we're separate from the rest of the world and 'this is Europe', well, excuse me! This is the 14 per cent of the world's population that is consuming 80 per cent of the world's resources. So could we get a little more honest, instead of saying 'Oh, people in Africa and India should have fewer babies', while we consume their bauxite, their rubber, their wood, their silver, their gold. Could we deal with multiculturalism not as a fad but as a reality. The fact is that your life is inseparable from the lives of people elsewhere on the planet; economically and politically you are responsible. It becomes your karma.

We are now living in the generation of what Martin Luther King called 'four hundred years of unpaid wages'.[1] Those wages are now coming due in this period. And the question is: what will the currency be that they're paid in? There's a lot of pain, aggression and violence behind our comfortable standard of living, and we're shielded from that because we're in a materialistic culture where we're never asked where anything came from or the cause of anything. All we want to know is the product.

In America we specialize in the culture of special effects. I think of the case of Oedipus Rex, for example, who at the moment of self-knowledge tore his own eyes out. In the Greek theatre you're not allowed to show that moment of violence. So Oedipus Rex has to go off-stage and when he comes back on his eyes are gone. Now if Steven Spielberg or Martin Scorsese were making this film, of Oedipus gouging his eyes out, there would be thirty special effects experts called in to give you a close up of the exploding eyeball: what particular green liquid spurts out in one direction, which little red glob goes another way, what this little layer of skin under the cornea looks like, all in maximum close-up. This is because we're a culture that's all about the effects. All we want to know is about the effects. What we don't want to know about is the causes. In Greek theatre you weren't permitted to show the moment of tearing the eyes out because that's not the point. The point is not that someone tears their eyes out, the point is why would someone tear their eyes out. This is the big question that our society doesn't want to ask. We want to say, 'Yes, we hate crime', but nobody wants to say, 'Wait a minute, what created crime? Why did somebody do something?' If we're talking about Clytemnestra and Electra, the statistics of daughters who kill their mothers, sociological study won't help. You have laws and you can pass new laws and you can punish people accordingly and it won't help. In fact your laws are helpless in front of the most profound and basic human phenomena. The Greeks invented theatre in the West as a way of supporting a democracy, as a way of saying, if we are going to have people vote, what are they going to vote on the basis of? What does an Electra need to know in order to vote? What do we have to have in order to have a democracy? First of all we have to have the presence of many voices, we have to have the feeling that we're hearing multiple voices and dialogue. But dialogue from the people you least want to meet, dialogue from the source you

1 For further details see *A Testament of Hope: The Essential Speeches and Writings of Martin Luther King, Jr*, ed. James M. Washington (New York: HarperCollins, 1986).

least wanted to talk to. Talk to the prisoners in the last war that you took and mistreated. Aeschylus and Euripides create plays about the people you least wanted to talk to. And when they speak to you they don't just give the statistics or the facts, they speak in poetry. They speak in the broadest, deepest way to activate a moral and ethical sense.

There's been a lot in this current American and British phase of trying to prove that the arts are useful, saying, 'Well, the arts improve your critical skills, your thinking and your maths scores.' So we can justify teaching the arts because the kids do better in maths which, I would add, is true. But that's a small part of the picture because what happens is the kids do better in life not just maths: they're equipped to live. Otherwise, out of these schools, we're producing massive numbers of people who are simply not equipped for life. They're technocrats and they have created the nightmare social and political policies that we now have of giant structures in this society and a giant prioritization of funding that does not serve the society. In fact that has been a disaster. In the world's largest democracies we're now in the midst of a situation where the governments themselves have run out of ideas, have run out of steam, are in a state of paralysis. No leader has more than one or two per cent so nobody can make a bold move. We're in the triumph of the bureaucracy and the government is, if not the enemy, the irrelevant mistake.

Our art institutions are in fact producing the same thing: a whole bunch of things that didn't need to be done. Mostly what we're teaching our students to do is perform for their grandparents. Who needed to know any of those things? Are those things helping? Who are those things helping? What are they learning when they are learning those techniques? Techniques that basically our generation failed with. Instead of starting our teaching with our presumed success to impress our students, I think it would be far more effective to start with our failure, the failure of our generation to communicate effectively in a society. The fact that the arts are totally marginalized in our societies is a demonstration of the failure of our generation. We've failed to get through, we've failed to connect our self-absorption, our smug self-satisfaction, and created a complete crisis in which the art that we practise is likely to be wiped off the face of the earth. If the Royal Opera House at Covent Garden has difficulty getting through a season because they don't have the funding, that's pretty serious. Right now the big companies that you imagine will be here forever, won't.

I'm coming from the United States of America and, as always, I'm proud to report that we're in the forefront of so many important moves. Just as we pass our laws to attack immigrants, I'm pleased to see that within a year or two Europe is able to follow suit. Just as we tear apart our health-care system, just as we tear apart the very social fabric that creates a society, I'm happy to see that Europe is doing its best to keep up. So I come to you as an American very pleased and honoured to talk here in Europe simply because I'm coming from where these things have been enacted. This is not some dystopic nightmare future, this is the present. In Los Angeles I have seen hospitals, parks and libraries shut down while the building of new prisons has been prioritized. We're spending five billion dollars in the next four years in the state of California to build new prisons. We're spending thirty-five billion dollars a year to keep the existing prisons going. Our 'three strikes and you're out' law means the third time you're arrested you're put in prison for life, for things like stealing cookies. We're willing to spend thirty-five thousand dollars a year keeping a twenty-year-old black man in prison for the rest of his life. We're not willing to spend three thousand dollars a year on his education. The same law, which is now being applied all over the country, removed the education system and even body-building equipment from prisons. So you are in prison for life but you cannot get an education there. You can exercise neither your mind nor your body. This is the social priority. We don't have enough money to keep a hospital or a school open, but we do have enough money to construct five billion dollars worth of new prisons. It's a society where the prison is the priority over the school. Now a prison is a great image for a society because, as we know, in art everything is not just a reality, it's also a metaphor. And it's that metaphor which I wanted to talk about, just for a moment.

I do feel very, very happy to be alive at a moment where almost for the first time in the century, in the West, art is actually necessary. The social collapse is so extreme, the political collapse is so extreme that actually people do need ways to communicate. People do not know how to articulate what they are now feeling in this society. The absence of articulation is what creates violence. If you can't express something, or if your voice is unheard, you of course resort to violence. The ability to move against violence is the ability to create forms of expression where nobody has to be killed in order to say something.

Now I come from a city, Los Angeles, where we had an uprising in 1992; I know what it is for people to set fire to their own city: a gesture that Antonin Artaud would call 'signalling through the flames'.[2] It's comparable to the Buddhist monks protesting the Vietnam War, who immolated themselves as an urgent signal that something needs to be done. Most of our cities are in flames anyway; you just can't see them, but Elijah could. You have to look with the eyes of a great prophet and suddenly you

2 See Antonin Artaud, *The Theater and Its Double*, trans. Mary Caroline Richards (New York: Grove Press, 1958), p. 13.

see a ring of flame around you. Can you sense those flames? Art, of course, is the ability to articulate that which is invisible, because that which is invisible is more present than that which is visible. Those flames are more present than anything else, but how many people can see them, can touch them, can articulate their presence? That question of visionary prophetic engagement is what artists are here for. They're here to see the fire on the mountain, to see the ring of flames, to understand the flames that we're feeling.

I would stress that one of the things that I find so important and one of the reasons I make all of these operas about contemporary events is because of the presence of CNN, our current media. We have not lived through our own lifetime. We do not know the events that have taken place during our lifetime because they're presented to us, if and when they're presented to us, in this supposedly objective, impersonal way. 'Three thousand people died in India in a plane crash' – the man or woman reading the news shuffles the papers and then they're onto the next item. What has been erased is the emotional power of the events of our own lives, because television and the media announce they present it objectively. The minute anyone tells you they're objective, watch out; that's a dangerous person. No human being is objective; that's built into the system. There is not one objective human being on the face of the earth. Another reason why I think the arts need to play a larger role in public life, is to emphasize that there is no such thing as objectivity. Once and for all let's get that clear. In fact this pretend objectivity has only served to obscure the political realities that surround us – people's real choices in life, where they could make a difference, where there are structural things that could be altered. It's also engendered this sense that it's not worth voting. The 1996 election in America had the smallest turnout since 1926, because most people realized that it's not worth voting. There's nothing to vote for; there's nothing to participate in.

That's the reason why I'm advocating the arts as pure activism, pure participation. If Picasso's working on a painting and there needs to be some red in the upper left-hand corner, he doesn't write a letter to the editor of the newspaper, he doesn't call his mother and complain, he doesn't sit in the corner of the bar and get drunk with his friends; you take some red paint, you squeeze it out, you pick up a brush, you put it in the red paint and you go and put red paint where there is some red paint missing.

Our task in the arts is to find something that needs to be done and do it. It is pure activism. It is giving people permission to take back their own society, their own lifelines, their own lifetimes, not as spectators but as actively engaged participants. This is one of the big crises that so much arts education of the last two generations has been about, as Ananda Coomaraswamy would say, appreciation being more important than experience.[3] In fact the art training that has been about appreciation has almost killed the arts. Most art-making activity that gets grant money has almost killed the arts. What's so fabulous about the arts is they survive anyway in some underground form where Brezhnev couldn't touch them. The forces of a giant meritocracy and bureaucracy, like so much of education, the art world and government, simply say, 'I am going to keep my job no matter what', so policy is put forward that does not perpetuate the art, it perpetuates the institution. Right now we're saving our institutions and killing the art forms. Like our governments, we'll be left with just big institutions that aren't serving a purpose.

Hence my wish to get active, this grass roots energy that says that a single human being is immense not small. The media world tells you that you're just one small insignificant person, and anything you thought is your problem, you're a pathological exception. Art is about a pathological exception like Vincent Van Gogh expressing himself and then a whole bunch of other pathological people saying, 'Oh my God, that's the most beautiful thing I ever saw', and then beginning to notice that each one of us is a pathological exception. If the twentieth century has taught us nothing else, it is that mass culture is a contradiction in terms. Not one of us is a mass. Nobody is a mass. Everybody is unique. You are the only person who can possibly bring what you're bringing into the world. You are not replaceable. There is nobody who duplicates you in any way. And that is powerful. That is the empowerment that first comes out of our art programmes, where a single human being feels their immensity, and where we understand that one thing created by somebody in isolation or with a small group of friends turns out, four centuries later, to be kind of important. What's so beautiful is that art goes against the terror of numbers that this century has introduced, where everything must be quantifiable and the biggest numbers are the most important. We know McDonalds has served more hamburgers than anyone else ever, but if you are confusing that with cooking, we do have a problem. The numbers aren't what's important. Think of two people: one is whoever is on the cover of *Newsweek* this week, and the other is a Tibetan monk in a cave in the Himalayas praying for world peace. Who is doing more in the world?

Art is about elevating the power of prayer. It's understanding that prayer does change things, does change lives and is the most powerful thing we know. It's a lot more powerful than the people who have armies, and the people who have giant marketing plans. At the end of your life,

3 For further details see Ananda K. Coomaraswamy, *Christian and Oriental Philosophy of Art* (New York: Dover, 1956).

on the Day of Judgement, will you be able to say, 'I sold eight billion tubes of toothpaste', or will you be able to say, 'For a few minutes I brought a little more justice into the world?'

The subject of justice is what I want to get at, because, frankly, right now in America most people have to vote to decide 'Do we want art?' and the answer is 'No, we don't need it, thankyou, take it away'. So with Congress shutting down the National Endowment for the Arts (NEA), how will artists survive without federal money? The message now being given to artists in America is: 'If you are an artist, get a day job'. This is not such a bad idea.

When Bernice Johnson Reagon was asked a few months ago what she thought about the crisis in the NEA and the crisis in the arts, Bernice calmly said, 'What crisis?' She remarked that it's going to be a sad period because we are going to lose a lot of institutions that we loved, but at the same time maybe artists will begin to identify with people who've been under attack for a long time, people for whom being under attack is not a recent development. They might begin to notice what the other side of the street looks like, and they might actually have to include subject matter in their work.

We've been in a terrible period where Herbert Read announced that art begins where function ends.[4] So anything that had no function was elevated as art and anything that you could use, like a pot, was called a craft, particularly because it was made by women and wasn't signed by anyone. If they didn't have a giant ego problem, it can't be art! I'm reminded of this great story of Coomaraswamy who was the first great curator of Asian art in the Americas; one of those great Gandhi figures, educated partially in Oxford, partially in India, who could teach one world about the other. He presented an exhibit of a Chinese painting in Boston in the 1930s, and he wrote this beautiful thing at the beginning of the catalogue where he said that to the Oriental the Western conception of art is a little strange. It's as if a traveller hiking in the mountains comes to a place where the path forks in two directions and there's a sign that points with an arrow that says what's this way, and another arrow that says what's that way. The traveller looking at the sign immediately asks, 'When was it made and who painted it?' He then proceeds to cut it down and take it home and put it over the mantelpiece in his home and says, 'I have some art here', ignoring the fact that it's no longer functional.[5]

---

4 This is discussed at length by Read in the following texts: Herbert Read, *Art and Society* (London: Faber & Faber, 1967); Herbert Read, *Art and Industry: The Principles of Industrial Design* (London: Faber & Faber, 1953).
5 This is also discussed in the fourth chapter of Coomaraswamy's *Christian and Oriental Philosophy of Art,* pp. 89–101.

What I think is so exciting right now is that, as art is under attack all over the world, we are going to have to demonstrate that we are functional; we're going to have to demonstrate that we add something to people's lives; we're going to have to demonstrate that we're not a luxury, decorative item but that we're essential and that we're dealing with deep issues of survival. Art is not the dessert part of your menu, it's the protein. It's not what comes after; it's what comes first. Art is the capacity to create a vocabulary where communication can take place across different people. Every single human being is different: nobody who you meet can you know anything about, so how will you communicate with them? What language will you use? Until that communication, those lines are open, until there is first a cultural life, there can be no economic, political or social life. In America we made the world safe for business, and now it's a really bad business climate. You can't do business in a place where the society is collapsing.

I was having dinner with Bernice Johnson Reagon on the first night of the LA uprising, the first night as the city was going up in flames. All these people were calling her all over the place. Because she's a great leader within the Black and many other communities in America, her phone was ringing off the hook and people said, 'What will we do? There's no Martin Luther King anymore, there's no Malcolm X.' Bernice's answer was: 'If you are waiting for a leader then you are not hearing the sound of your own voice.' What does it take to empower people to hear the sound of their voice? What needs to be changed in this world doesn't require an advanced degree. You don't have to be a rocket scientist to tell when something's wrong. You have an inner voice that tells you. Don't be afraid of acting on that inner voice. You're so afraid that the rest of the world is going to strangle it that you strangle it first. The task of being an artist and of being a human being is the ability to hear your inner voice and act upon it. It's about acting on your conscience. When we're talking about why art is essential in a society, it's because it represents a conscience, an ethos, a moral presence that everybody needs. If you're living without it, then you're not living. We're talking about offering people not just food so they eat for another day; we're talking about food that nourishes a lifetime.

I teach at the department of the University of California at Los Angeles entitled World Arts and Cultures. I'm very proud to teach in this department; it's a department which understands that the culture of Papua New Guinea is as important as the culture of southern France, and it's treated accordingly. So the department is interdisciplinary and intercultural. It's understanding that all the education of artists has to be interdisciplinary and intercultural: that poets have to know music, musicians have to know dance, filmmakers have to know literature, that whatever you're doing you have to know something else, and as a human being you have to know people who are not like you, which means everyone. It's about trying to live in a mode on this planet where there are no more enemies lists.

The amazing image of our period is Nelson Mandela. It is Mr Havel. Both took the people who tried to kill them for thirty-eight years and are now making a government with them. Now that they have the chance to get their revenge, they don't. Now that they have a chance to kill their enemies, they won't. It's Mozart's *La Clemenza di Tito*, his last gift to the world; the opera that everyone thought was undramatic and undoable. Here the wise ruler is such a nice guy that people kill him at the end of the first act and set fire to the city. In the second act he survives the assassination attempt and says, 'Find the people who tried to kill me and who set fire to the capital.' They're found, they're brought in front of him, and the opera ends when he says, 'I forgive you. Now let's make a society together, because no one can be safe until we can do that.'

Art is ultimately about talking to your enemies. It's about human interaction. Like a relationship that you have with anyone, like any work of art, if communication's only going in one direction we have a crisis. Communication is reciprocal, it has to go in two directions in equal amounts. Art has to be about communicating across lines of communication that are closed. Those enemies are sometimes far away, sometimes they're close. The other way I think of the need to say painful things in a society is: 'Who's going to tell Dad what Dad doesn't want to hear? Who in the family is going to tell Dad and how do you do that?' How do you communicate something unpleasant and difficult, where everybody is going to have to change in order to absorb this?

The LA Festival which I've been associated with, worked very closely with, was only possible because of, the World Arts and Cultures programme at UCLA, where the students became the front line of the LA Festival. The World Arts and Cultures programme at the university has students engaged in off-campus projects every year as their primary activity, so that they have to learn survival skills in the real world and work with, and learn something from, different communities across the city of Los Angeles. Most artists want to tell the world everything, but what would it be like to listen and to set that up as an element of arts education. In UCLA we're trying that. This idea is a very different paradigm from the university I grew up in. I went to Harvard and trained under the last of the great old professors who knew everything, the experts. Now in our society the one thing you have to admit is every field is expanding so rapidly that nobody in any field can possibly know everything of what is going on in their own field. So in fact now we have to enter every conversation not with what we know but with what we don't know. That's what we start with. We have to start from what we don't understand. So education becomes not just giving students expertise, but giving students the ability to cope with what is unknown, and to learn gracefully in an atmosphere where you can't know anything, where no master narrative is acceptable any longer, where everything has a question mark, where everything has to be re-examined, and where the first step is to acknowledge your ignorance.

I think of the art that is made in this period as not accomplishing the discussion or the negotiation that needs to take place in our society right now. We need to look to the beginning of the Vietnam peace talks in Paris in the 1970s, where they spent the first two years arguing over the shape of the table that would permit all parties to sit down and everyone to feel they were being heard. In our generation now, and in the generation of our students, the question is: what is the shape of the table that you can bring all the elements of our society together at? So that everyone will feel they're being heard, they're being valued, they're being understood because of their positionality. That's the architectural project. So I don't expect art to solve the question yet, I just expect art to get to the place where people could articulate what it is they're looking for.

The last LA Festival was curated by 350 people. I may have been the artistic director, but what you see in the LA Festival is not what I think is important. One of the first steps that all of us have to learn is literally, if you're in the position of power, learn how to give it away. The first step involves stepping aside. Look at the person in the room who is not saying anything and create conditions in which they could say something. As in community organizing, the first step is to go with the person who is causing the most trouble, who wants to hijack the meeting. Fine, let them talk, don't silence them. Go with the greatest anger. Let yourself as the person of power in the room be attacked and don't take it personally. Listen. Listen to what is being said and ask yourself: 'What can I do?'

I first met the Salvadorean artists living in Los Angeles in a wonderful way. In the 1990 LA Festival we invited a group of Latin American poets to come to Los Angeles because in Latin America poets are great national figures – much more important than any politician. A committee that read a lot of poetry invited their favourite poets, and from El Salvador they invited David Escobar Galindo and we happily announced that he was one of the ten poets from Latin America we were inviting to Los Angeles. Los Angeles has the largest population of Salvadoreans outside of El Salvador, because all the people escaping the death squads came here. Of course most of them are 'illegal', and they came here running for their lives. David Escobar Galindo turned out to be the right-hand man of Mr Cristiani, the leader responsible for the death squads. So the Salvadoreans in Los Angeles were not amused by our choice. I came to work one morning to find my office occupied by fifty angry artists. My desk was taken over and the entire place was occupied by angry artists. That's how I met the Salvadorean artists in Los Angeles. You have to be willing to make a big mistake because it leads somewhere. You'll meet people you needed to meet. Allow that to happen. As it turns out we invited Alfredo Urias who was in exile in Canada to join the programme chosen by the Salvadorean exile community in Los Angeles. And then Mr Galindo didn't show up, but it was a discussion. The *Los Angeles Times*, which would never have printed an article about Salvadorean poetry in a million years, suddenly had three articles about Salvadorean poets. So it worked out very well. Controversy is your friend. Allow it, encourage it, live with it; it's keeping you alive. The minute there isn't any controversy something smells bad. Allow people's rage to be present, it's genuine and you will learn something from it. And it is an incredible incentive to making art. How rage is processed into art instead of into violence is a really important issue in our societies right now.

One of the artists I met did a big project with the festival. The LA Festival Memory Projects involved teaming up artists with different communities in Los Angeles to help to do something that needed to be done in the community. I always remember my first visit to the Soviet Union in the bad old Brezhnev years, when I, for the afternoon in Moscow, dodged my official KGB colonel host, and with a poet went around parts of Moscow. This poet was an 'unofficial' person. We would stand in front of an apartment building and he would say, 'See the third window to the left on the fifth floor, that's where this painter lived. Over there the sixth window to the right is where that composer lived.' All these people were 'non-people', because they didn't meet the current media criterion, but in the community people remembered. Art exists to keep a memory, a song, a painting; it keeps a memory alive that the rest of the world wanted to extinguish. It's a focal point for communal identity.

One of our Memory Projects was made by the Salvadorean artist Dagoberto Reyes, a sculptor who had less than a day's notice to leave El Salvador because three of his closest friends were killed by the death squads, and it was clear he was next. He left with his family in one afternoon. If you're a sculptor you can't bring too much sculpture with you as you're trying to get across the Mexican border at night. For thirteen years he worked in Los Angeles, not as an artist because he couldn't prove to anyone that he was a sculptor; he was in factory jobs. And in those factories he was not allowed to work a machine; he had to do just janitorial work. In the LA Festival we commissioned his first work of art in his new country. It was a bas-relief called 'Why We Emigrate'. He did it at El Rescate, the Salvadorean refugee centre in the Pico Union area of Los Angeles. This is the most densely populated area of the United States: highest crime rate, most intense drug infestation. Three nights a week Salvadoreans living in exile in Los Angeles, would come to El Rescate and bring photographs, drawings, memorabilia, bits of music, cassette tapes of what reminded them of their real home, what they had lost, family members who were missing, and records of their new life. These evenings grew across six months, to these extraordinary community meetings of exchange. People were weeping and weeping, sharing things they'd held in and held in for years, because they thought it was just their problem. But the minute you're sharing, it isn't your problem anymore, and so much of the weight of it can be carried differently.

Out of this he made a bas-relief sculpture that had two halves. One half showed El Salvador: the death squads, the people hanging from the trees, the open graves, the prisons, the women and children running around crying. Every inch of the ground was filled with footprints. Then the centre of the sculpture was the fence of the Mexican border: a woman climbing over the fence who had just been shot by the border guards, which became a crucifix image with a pregnant woman. The footprints were there because for centuries their ancestors have been making this migration from south to north, and from north back to south. And they were following in the footprints that were already there. The American side of the bas-relief showed the cars, showed rooms of children, with twenty kids watching television because their parents are frightened to let the children out, in case the immigration police pick them up. They're frightened to let their children go to school, so the children stay at home all day watching television. It showed people polishing the machines in the factory that they're not allowed to operate. It showed people picking lettuce in the fields. In the American half of the bas-relief you don't see anybody's face, you only see the backs of their heads, because in America they become faceless; they lose their identity; no one knows they're here. They can't even tell themselves they're really here.

That statue is now put in the main park in the Pico Union area. We installed it with the LA City Council. It is the first marker of the Salvadorean community in Los Angeles and in the United States. It says 'Why We Emigrate'. Buried underneath it in the park is a time capsule filled with everything that was brought to the community meetings for six months at El Rescate. So that one hundred years from now their descendants can dig up the photographs, the songs and everything else underneath this statue, and learn why there are Salvadoreans in North America.

The 1993 festival we announced on the first day of the Gulf War and two months before the LA uprising. The LA Festival of 1993 focused on Arab, Jewish and Black art. We set the 1993 festival at the intersection where the first fires were lit in the uprising: a place most people in Los Angeles would never dream of driving to, because they're so frightened. They would never drive through it, much less park. For five weeks we put four hundred shows at that intersection, so the people from Beverly Hills for the first time in their lives visited the part of the city that set itself on fire. They found that the people living there actually want the same thing for their kids that you want for your kids, that it's not such a frightening place, that people like you live there, that it's not a Hollywood crime movie.

When we started setting this up it took a year of work with people living in that community, so we didn't come in opportunistically, because believe me those communities have seen that: big institutions get their grant proposal and people come in to be black for the month, and then leave, pocketing the grant money and leaving the community worse off. It took a year of working with local businesses, police, and residence associations, gaining people's trust.

When we first went into that intersection we noticed that if we're going to have a big arts festival here, it's dark at night. People will be very frightened of coming here, so we need street lights. It turned out that there were street lights there, but the bulbs had not been changed for ten years. We said, 'Oh, all this garbage is going to be off-putting.' It turned out there were no regular city garbage collections. It turned out the fountain in the park had never been turned on, the trees had never been trimmed, the plants had never been tended. We went to the Los Angeles City Council and said, 'We're doing an arts festival here. *Time* magazine and the *New York Times* are going to come. We need the trash picked up and the lights turned on.' And we got for that community basic city services that they had not seen in ten years. That's what the arts can do. The arts create a point of focus, create a point of attention, create a point of commentary, create a point of discussion for that which goes undiscussed. The arts can show that these citizens are not asking for special rights, they're asking for what they should have had all along.

One of the important projects that we did in that festival, in our Memory Projects, was a theatre project with homeless gay and lesbian teenagers living on the street, working as prostitutes on Santa Monica Boulevard. Another 'underrepresented' group in the city was kids living on the street. We made a year-long theatre project with them. The first six months was writing, because the first step is get your story straight. You tell yourself and your friends, 'I was kicked out of my home because of my sexuality and my parents.' This is true and tragic in one way, and in another way maybe that's not the whole story, maybe there's more to it than that. Maybe there are things you did with your parents; there are other things your parents did with you. What really happened? Go back, look at it. A blank piece of paper means you have to actually get your story to be more interesting and more real than the story you tell all your friends. Because we all have the story we tell everyone, but what really happened is a lot more interesting and a lot more human.

As you know if you've worked with homeless people, homeless people primarily are very alone and very isolated. They don't talk to other people. When they do talk to other people it's a monologue, not a dialogue. What does it take to get homeless people to talk with other people and not to them? What does it take for society to talk with homeless people and not about them. Because we are all willing to talk about everything, we're never willing to talk with someone.

For six months those kids wrote, and wrote critically to understand. The discipline that writing brings is understanding. It's a deepening of your perception of your own life. The second six months was making a show. The kids made a musical comedy that was hysterically funny, and made you cry the entire time. It had no self-pity at all. It was really smart. And the rule for making that show was that no one was allowed to enact their own material. You had to take someone else's life and become that person. It turns out, of course, that you knew more about another person than they knew about themselves. It turns out another person knew more about you than you knew about yourself. It turns out that things you thought you were the only person this ever happened to, happened to someone else. It turns out they have another set of insights about it. And gradually, while making this show for these kids in homeless shelters, what started to happen was the creation of exactly what they didn't have in their lives, a family. When you went every day to rehearsal, there was someone there for you, who cared about you and, meanwhile, you had to be there for someone else to care about them. You were responsible for them. And so it created this network of interdependency, mutual responsibility, communication, honesty, and pleasure.

The show itself was tremendous, and we toured it all over Los Angeles, and throughout all the high schools in Los Angeles so that kids could talk to other kids about their sexuality, because that wasn't happening and we needed a forum that was authentic. Meanwhile what that programme did was what no social programme, like welfare, can do for the homeless. It addressed the issue of why people were on the streets to begin with. It addressed what was missing in people's lives. It addressed their ability to articulate their own situation and understand it and then change it. Nobody in that project is living on the street today.

In the arts we can offer the society what the society needs and can't get through political channels, what people need and they can't get through economic channels. These questions of identity are what enable people to move forward in their lives and define points of contact with others. Without that every one of us is powerless.

So what I'm talking about now is a question of civil rights instead of public relations. What does it take not to say the smooth political thing that smoothes over everything. What does it take to go into the heart of the problem. What does it take to be there present with the crisis, to live through the crisis and create a way of sharing that courageous experience with other people that permits them to engage their own set of crises.

I will end with two little things. When I talk about justice I talk about this need for justice that people feel. When there's no justice around you, you can feel it. There's this beautiful, great Vietnamese epic from the 1820s, *The Tale of Kiêu*.[6] The heroine, a young woman named Kiêu, is being addressed by a young man who wants to have sexual relations, and he's really hot and anxious for quick action, like everybody in this world: 'Let's have something fast now.' Her reply to him is about the difference between a one-night stand and a lifetime commitment. In the arts we're talking about a lifetime commitment. In the arts we're not talking about instant results. We're not talking about anything that's going to appear in the next twenty-five minutes. We're talking about spending your lifetime working. He finds her little pin that she dropped on the ground and that's his excuse to go see her and say, 'I found your pin.' Mozart uses that one. And what she says to this hot young man is: 'Thankyou for returning what I lost. A pin is not worth much, but beyond price is a man's sense of what is right and wrong.' Where does that sense come from that has no price? What activates that sense?

We're sitting on top of the one thing that the world needs and we're wasting it day after day after day. We have not begun to release the power, beauty, grandeur, hope, courage and danger that is present in the making of art. We are sitting on it. It will only be released when things get so bad that people have no choice but to take it out and use it, because there's nothing else left to work with. After people have exhausted every other option, they'll notice that the solution was always here. I think of it like those windows that you see which have an axe in them, and it says 'In case of emergency, break glass'. I would suggest we're at the time where it's

6 Nguyên Du, *The Tale of Kiêu: A Bilingual Edition of Truyên Kiêu*, trans. and annotated by Huynh Sanh Thông, with a historical essay by Alexander B. Woodside (New Haven and London: Yale University Press, 1983).

appropriate to break the glass. Reach in, let a little blood flow off of your knuckles, because it's not a bad thing to mix a little blood in your paints. It's not a bad thing to let the art be part of your bloodstream and let your bloodstream be part of your art.

This question of art making practice with blood comes to me because I've just spent the last week in Utah, in Bryce Canyon, in Zion National Park: incredible places. Then you realize that most art is made by people trapped in cities, and most people are looking at man's creation and not God's creation every day. They don't get that there's something much bigger going on with every sunrise and every sunset. It's not about an accumulation of objects. In fact the objects are no big deal; they'll always be here, and if they're not, what a relief! Get them out of the way!

Most societies on the face of the earth have not accumulated objects. In Africa a work of art is a comb and it's carved for you by somebody who loves you. So every time you comb your hair you have the presence of an ancestor in the handle of your comb. You're reminded that your ancestors are with you, trying to whisper things to you every day. You are reminded just by touching a comb that you are loved by someone and that you have to love them back. You're reminded of the invisible presence in your life every time you comb your hair. You're reminded, while you're combing your hair, that the only things that matter in your life are invisible, that everything you touch in your life reminds you of something that's really important. That sense that you get in traditional African society that everything you touch reminds you of something important, that's what we can now do as artists released from the need for self-importance, understanding that we're here in a service capacity, and it's important to learn how to serve.

If the world doesn't like what you are doing and gives you trouble, that's usually a good sign. I will mention one last story of my friend Boetheus. Fifth-century Boetheus was the chief of staff for one of the last Roman Emperors in multicultural Rome, where the Roman Emperor was in fact a Goth, Theodoric. Boetheus was, by all accounts, a good person. Then there was a palace coup and a new bunch took over, and Boetheus was thrown into a dungeon, and people said, 'Well, okay, we've silenced him for ever.' For five years he lived in this cell and people came in and tortured him once a week. He wrote during that time on toilet paper something called *The Consolation of Philosophy*, in which philosophy as a woman came into his cell every day and sang songs about the nature of justice. These songs he transcribed. Finally after about five years the people that put him in the dungeon decided that he'd been around long enough, and they killed him. They took huge clubs and beat him into jelly on the ground. Five centuries later, in the Middle Ages, that book, *The*

Consolation of Philosophy, became the most copied manuscript of the age. The centres of learning that were trying to oppose the feudal containment and proto-fascist control of knowledge, used the image of Boetheus to keep themselves alive. Fifteen centuries later Boetheus' *The Consolation of Philosophy* is the only book written in the fifth century that is available in paperback.[7] I'm talking about the power of art being so much bigger than the powers of this world. The courage of those of us who run large institutions is going to be to ally with the powers of art, not just the powers of the world.

7 Boethius, *The Consolation of Philosophy*, trans. V.E. Watts (Harmondsworth: Penguin, 1969).

The crisis of theatre? The theatre of crisis!

Dragan Klaic

Dragan Klaic is Professor of Theater Studies at the University of Amsterdam. Until 1991 he was Professor at the University of Arts in Belgrade and then until 2001 Director of Theater Instituut Nederland in Amsterdam. Educated in Belgrade and Yale, Klaic has been working as a theatre critic, dramaturge, festival and production adviser, editor, researcher, lecturer and trainer. He was the founding Co-Editor of *Euromaske*, the *European Theater Quarterly* and serves as a Contributing Editor of *Theater* magazine (USA). Among his several books are *Terrorism and Modern Drama* (co-edited with J. Orr, Edinburgh University Press, 1990, paperback 1992), *The Plot of The Future: Utopia and Dystopia in Modern Drama* (Michigan University Press, 1991), *Shifting Gears / Changer de vitesse* (co-edited with R. Engelander, TIN Amsterdam 1998) and *Exercises in Exile* (forthcoming). An earlier version of this article appeared in English under the title 'The Theater of War' in the Zagreb magazine *Frakcija*, No. 14 (Summer 1999), pp. 26–31.

Rather than to dwell on the perennial issue of the crisis of theatre, I would prefer to turn the tables, as it were, on the prophets of theatre's doom and explore what theatre can do in the situation of acute crisis. The proverbial crisis of theatre usually means that theatre has become conventional, repetitive and uninspiring, caught in obsolete institutional moulds, styles, genres and conventions, what Brook decades ago called a 'deadly theatre'.[1] Perceptions of theatre as superfluous and marginal, irrelevant to the social reality and to the prevailing interests and obsessions of the public are sometimes well founded. In periods of affluence, prosperity and relative social stability, for instance, theatre usually really does not

1 Peter Brook, *The Empty Space* (Harmondsworth: Penguin, 1968), pp. 11–46.

have that much to offer – except to add to the overwhelming self-satisfaction and serve as another outlet for the peddling of the prevailing ideology, be it the American Dream or the New Economy. The more theatre churns out its stuff in unison with the other factories of collective consciousness, such as film or television, the more irrelevant it becomes. The diagnosis of crisis is either a minority opinion of dissident artists, demanding critics and discriminating viewers or, more commonly, a facile prejudice of those who hardly ever go to the theatre.

In the situation of the acute crisis of a society, where there is a major turmoil, natural disaster, economic collapse, epidemics, civil unrest and war – can theatre claim a special role, can it do something very valuable for the society? Usually, under such dire circumstances, theatre offers an escape from the problematic and troublesome reality or ceases to function altogether, deprived of some elementary material and logistic preconditions. In some situations of social tension, trouble and conflict, theatre could emerge as a combative force, with a strong and clear advocacy line, but runs the risk of preaching to a small group of the converted.[2] This engaged, political theatre, focused on pressing issues and driven by an allegiance with the interests of a particular social group, has in principle its validity, ideally both aesthetically and politically, but often displays a pathetic discrepancy between the sharpness of its stances and its artistry; it fails to escape 'the galloping treat of a message'.[3] It can move, mobilize some social groups, clarify some issues, chart out various courses of action but the impact is short-lasting and the coalescence of people united in ideas and enthusiasm tends to evaporate quickly. Even if the Belgian (1830), Hungarian (1848) and Cuban (1896) struggles for independence did explode in theatre (or rather, theatre was used to jump-start them), theatre did not become the headquarters of these revolutions. Soon after the explosive moment of glory, theatre only followed the events and mirrored them in a triumphalist manner. The Velvet Revolution of Prague in 1989, although directed from a theatre for a while, very soon could not be contained by it, so the stage again found itself at the rear end of the events with not much more of a role than to quickly produce once-banned plays by Havel and his fellow writers, turned politicians.[4]

There is in theatre an inherent difficulty to shape an immediate, adequate response to a social crisis. That is at least what I learned during

2 See Baz Kershaw, *The Politics of Performance, Radical Theater as Cultural Intervention* (London and New York: Routledge, 1992) and Kees P. Epskamp, *Theater in Search of Social Change* (The Hague: CESO, 1989).

3 Howard Barker, *Arguments for a Theater* (London: John Calder, 1989), p. 57.

4 See Jane Machalicka, 'Czech Theater from 1989 to 1996: Discovering Terra Incognita', in *Eastern European Theater after the Iron Curtain*, ed. Kalina Stefaniova (Amsterdam: Harwood Academic Publishers), pp. 43–57.

the 1970s and 1980s, while still living in the former Yugoslavia, and being involved in theatre that was following, interpreting and to some extent even anticipating the contradictions of the Yugoslav maverick socialism, its failures and accumulated conflicts. In my experience then, theatre was pretty good in invoking some collective traumas of the recent past, piercing some societal taboos on issues, personalities and events, and even sketching in a rather oblique manner the perspectives of disintegration and catastrophe that ensued. But it was not very articulate in formulating a response to the protracted economic and political crisis. It certainly did try to do so but within some imposed limitations, often confused by fast changes of circumstances, intimidated by the reality's contradictions, uncertain whose side to take and where to lay the blame.[5] Then, at the very end of the 1980s, as the crisis intensified, when blocked political institutions could no longer contain the political forces set on a collision course and when parallel nationalist frenzies entered a phase of full escalation, sustained by the media and used both by the communist and anti-communist political elites, when tensions rose and finally armed conflict became a daily occurrence, theatre slid into a vulgar chauvinist cabaret or sought refugee in an artistry that was as much as possible detached from any social reality. The crisis of the society and of theatre coalesced in a prevailing moral complicity of many politicians and artists.

I am sure plays will be written and productions staged to understand and explain why the former Yugoslavia disintegrated and why it happened in such a violent manner. These are projects for the future. Throughout the 1990s, while the Balkan conflict remained hot, as if were, there were several attempts by theatre people in the countries of the former Yugoslavia and elsewhere to react to the occurring violent events and the mass suffering they caused. In the most recent phase, during the NATO attacks on Serbia and Montenegro in March–June 1999, I was again confronted in my Amsterdam exile with an urgent question posed by colleagues and students: what can theatre do in the time of war? This bizarre war, waged by a mighty military-political alliance without the sanction of the international legal order (UN), and not in self-defence but in the name of human rights protection, posed many political and moral dilemmas and tested the sense of civic and professional responsibility of theatre people.[6] Let us do something as theatre professionals about the most recent outburst of war in the Balkans, suggested an English friend

5   See Dragan Klaic, 'Czy teatr przeczul wojne', *Dialogue* (Warsaw), No. 5 (May 1999), pp. 112–24.
6   See Boris Buden, ed., *Bastard, Global Edition* (a selection of press and internet reactions to the NATO campaign in English) (Zagreb: Arkzin, 1999).

of mine. Let us put together an international theatre team and develop a production exploring the ongoing conflict, investigating the victims and the perpetrators, measuring the moral goals, the political objectives and applied means, and seeking the venues to peace and justice.[7] I experienced déjà vu.

Responding to the siege of Sarajevo

Haris Pasovic, a theatre director from Sarajevo, came to my Amsterdam house in May 1992, a few weeks after the war engulfed Bosnia and Herzegovina. Seeking a chance to work in peace and with concentration, he had left Sarajevo a few months earlier, together with his students from the Theater Academy, and found shelter in the Subotica Theater, on the Serb-Hungarian border where the previous summer he had directed two productions. Then, joining his students with the ensemble of the Subotica theatre, he made a forceful, scatological *Ubu Roi* in March 1992. When soon afterwards Sarajevo came under siege, he felt increasingly uncomfortable in Serbia, whose government was deeply implicated in the assault on his city. So he decided to go somewhere else. Ljubisa Ristic, the director of the Subotica Theater, with whom he had worked in harmony until then, understood his problem and helped him get out by sending him to me.

Haris and I knew each other but not too well. He is a decade younger but started directing early, earning a name while still a student. I saw several of his productions in Belgrade and Novi Sad. His *Waiting for Godot* premiered in Belgrade on the eve of Slovenia's disassociation from Yugoslavia in June 1991, which marked the beginning of the war. After the premiere, a large company of colleagues was sitting in the theatre café knowing that our own castigating Godot would certainly come. Tomorrow. Without any postponement or mercy. And that all hell would be let loose.

Two months later, while the war moved from Slovenia to Croatia, Haris adapted Danilo Kis' story 'Simon the Magus' from his book *The Encyclopaedia of the Dead*. The production was staged in the sand dunes, a few miles outside Subotica, close to the border with Hungary, in darkness, which was suddenly dispelled with torches and noise. It was a biblical miracle in the middle of nowhere, with fire and water. A few minutes after the performance ended, a huge storm descended suddenly from a clear summer sky, and a biblical flood engulfed us as we rushed to cars and buses to return to the city. Another warning from heaven of the forthcoming catastrophes which would befall us in the years to come.

---

7 Michael Kustow, *Theater@risk* (London: Methuen, 2000), pp. 67–9.

Now, in May 1992, Haris was in my house, glued to the television set, watching CNN for hours, staying up late, waking up at noon as if from a nightmare, and then having to face another nightmare of the reality. Watching him for weeks going almost crazy from anger and anxiety, cut off from his mother and sister in Sarajevo, I said at some point that we should try to do something but within our profession, theatre. Political initiatives and humanitarian assistance would be taken care of by others, we should concentrate on our own *métier*. For a few evenings Haris and I sat at the computer, constructing an outline for a production on Sarajevo, with the city as a hero and martyr. We discussed the history of the place, its mentality and lifestyle, its multicultural character, its humour and music, its literature and its slang. Sarajevo embodied the values and attitudes that the war in Yugoslavia had been systematically destroying, and now this city had become its symbolic and factual target.

At the peak of the summer I sent our proposal to several colleagues around Europe knowing that most of them would not be in their offices at that time of year to receive my fax. Once the proposal was made and sent, Haris lost his patience and decided to go to Ljubljana or Zagreb in an attempt to get back to Sarajevo. I could not hold him. A few weeks later there had been several responses to our proposal. Haris returned at my urging telling me how in one moment he succeeded in Zagreb to board the plane carrying the Bosnian President Izetbegovic to Sarajevo, only to be removed at the last moment by security. In the meantime, our project was advancing slowly. Goran Stefanovski, a successful Macedonian playwright, living between Skopje and the UK, joined us as the author. In October, at the meeting of IETM, a large European theatre network, in Ljubljana, the interested parties got together. Chris Torch, a Stockholm colleague, took it upon himself to put the production together. A Hamburg summer festival was interested and London's International Festival of Theater (LIFT) as well and most importantly Antwerp that was the next spring to become the European City of Culture for 1993. Stockholm became a production base, Haris and Goran moved there into an apartment near the Town Hall and made it an unofficial Sarajevo embassy. They were pulling together books and music, working intensely, while Chris Torch was seeking money and partners and completing the team, and an international cast was quickly put together.

Sometime in November I was asked by my friends at the Antwerp City of Culture organization to talk to their board chairman, a bigwig from the harbour, and to the mayor. My Flemish was still less than rudimentary at the time, as I had just finished an intensive beginner's course, but I decided I'd pitch the production idea on the power of conviction, not rhetoric, and they'd have to accept it as the opening event of Antwerp

'93 on their political instinct, not on the arguments. The artists involved were unknown to them, the mechanics of an international co-production they could not grasp, the production was still in development, but politically and morally it made sense to inaugurate their city as the European City of Culture with a homage to the city that was on everyone's mind as a place of death, destruction and suffering. It worked.

I stayed in the background, following the process from a distance, but talking regularly with all the people involved. Haris went for Christmas to Ljubljana to stay with friends and before New Year he suddenly disappeared leaving a message on the answering machine that he had to return to Sarajevo, that his place was there and not in Stockholm nor Antwerp. Months later he told me how he tried to board some of the UN flights from Zagreb, then travelled on buses through Croatia and Herzegovina, continued on foot through dangerous terrain and on the evening of 31 December reached the UN-controlled Sarajevo airport. He succeeded in avoiding patrols and searchlights, and, crawling across the tarmac, sneaked into the city to surprise his mother and sister in their house just before midnight.

The pretzel dramaturgy

It is a miraculous story but we did not know it at the time. With Haris' sudden departure the project was in a deep crisis, the production partners in turmoil. After some hasty consultations, Slobodan Unkovski, a Macedonian theatre director who had often worked with Goran Stefanovski and did the premieres of most of his plays, was invited to take over. Courageously he accepted, aware of all the risks involved in a work with both the concept and the cast chosen by another director. Some time was lost, the work was speeded up and in March, *Sarajevo, Tales from a City* opened the European City of Culture programme in Antwerp, in a newly restored Bourla theatre. Before the opening, there was a moving ceremony on the square outside, with video interviews of Sarajevans projected onto a wall, and flowers and candles brought by many. Haris was not among the people interviewed, but I was thinking of him the whole evening.

The production received a lot of publicity. For me and many others it was a moving gesture, a cry of outrage, mixed with some humour, some nostalgia, engulfing the audience in pain. The company went on to perform it through the spring and the summer in several European cities, performances usually followed with discussions, sometimes harsh and confrontational. In July 1993, at LIFT, I took part in one of these talks, at the Riverside Studios, and I was pleased to see how the performance

focused and clarified the moral and political issues involved. It went
further than just squeezing empathy from the audience; it reinforced the
sense of responsibility and metaphorized the urban texture, and the
lifestyle and values being destroyed in Sarajevo. It did not attempt to
compete with the gruesome television images that had by then become
commonplace, but individualized the peril, reinforced and transmitted
the anguish. Goran Stefanovski, whom I have known for years as someone who does not like speaking in public, surprised me with a new eloquence and a sharpness of formulations; in the discussion he was precise
and astute, challenging and direct. I remember he was talking about the
dramaturgy of a pretzel: about theatre not being able to reach to the very
core of the pain and horror of the war but constructing its action around
it, developing a discourse around the catastrophe. Of course, the production could not stop the war nor lift the siege of the city, but it brought to
the European theatre public an idea of what Sarajevo was like before the
outbreak of the war and helped the audience understand why the city
became the main target of the assault.

With the passing of time, I was becoming more aware of the production's shortcomings, caused not only by the switch of directors but by the
shortage of the time needed for an international cast to come together
and build cohesion and coherence of style, and to find its vigour in dealing with the complex issues and to push its emotional response further
towards a specific theatre aesthetic. I learned that time is a crucial factor
of success for an international co-production because the participants
need extra time to work through their cultural differences and their
distinct theatre traditions and habits, to coalesce their stage conventions
and fuse their work routines. Also, I learned that theatre needs time to
distance itself from the event in the reality it wants to address. Making a
theatre production on the destruction of Sarajevo while the assault was
still going on turned out to be an endeavour taxing both the human and
the artistic strengths of those involved. After the war, with some breathing space recovered, some time-distance built in, theatre would have
more of a chance to dramatize the wartime experience than trying to
dress an open wound.

Distancing methods

Goran Stefanovski understood that himself for he had recently made a new
version of Sarajevo for a British company, Theater Melange. Dusan
Jovanovic, a Slovenian playwright and theatre director, also understood the
need for a distancing device. In 1993 he wrote a version of *Antigone*,
responding to the ongoing war in Yugoslavia but seeking the necessary

distance in the Greek myth and its old dramatic renditions.[8] He cast the conflict of Eteocles and Polynices as one which had been dragging on for a very long time, so long in fact that everyone had forgotten the original cause of the feud. The hatred was transformed into a blind, almost visceral passion with no evident cause and purpose. In Jovanovic's Thebes the violence had become so pervasive that it had imposed its own construction of the reality, which was in turn internalized by all those affected. It had become transgenerational and only some intervention from outside the system could break the spell. That should be the role of the deities but in Jovanovic's play they remain in the background as a source of evil, refusing to assume the role of either arbiter or rescuer. Systematic, protracted violence appears as the great leveller, abolishing differences among the people and their positions, nurturing their opportunism and cowardice rather than heroic capacities, so that even Antigone's space for resistance becomes extremely narrowed, almost non-existent.

In another play, written during the war, *The Puzzle of Courage*, Jovanovic turned to the inherent limitations of theatre in dealing with the turbulent reality, mocking the inability of the stage to catch up with the fast-evolving crisis in real life.[9] He shows a theatre company prompted by the war in Bosnia to stage Brecht's *Mother Courage*. The actors are eager to find inspiration in the plight of the Bosnian refugees. Their exploration of the dynamics of war and the refugees' suffering and humiliation brings them, however, no guidance or inspiration because they can not absorb and rework the refugee experience fast enough. Moreover, the refugees are not standing still either, their own experience and conditions shift and evolve. While the actors are in rehearsals, the refugee woman whom the principal actress sees as her inspiration and model turns into a real-life Mother Courage, becoming an entrepreneur and war profiteer amidst misery and loss, compassion and bungled humanitarian relief, and develops her own small business by exploiting other refugees. In every phase of the production process the actors are confronted with a reality that resists their preconceived notions and their Brechtian models because it is more complex than the stage rendition and develops much faster than the production in progress could follow. Jovanovic's play about a theatre production that cannot catch the elusive and shifting truths of the reality is a satire on the inherent shortcomings of theatre that seeks an instantaneous response to the ongoing war and sketches out the demise of good intentions and moralistic engagement. Those who are prompted by some new crisis somewhere in the world to articulate an immediate

8   Dusan Jovanovic, *Antigona*, German trans. Klais Detlef Olof (Ljubljana: SNG, 1993).
9   Dusan Jovanovic, *The Puzzle of Courage*, trans. Lesley Wade Soule, in *Contemporary Slovenian Drama*, ed. Blaz Lukan (Ljubljana: Litterae Slovenicae, 1997), pp. 153–91.

theatrical response to it would do well to read carefully Jovanovic's sceptical play. In his earlier works Jovanovic demonstrated what theatre is
good at, in dissecting the traumas of the past such as World War Two
(*Liberation of Skopje*, 1978) and the Tito–Stalin conflict (*Karamazovs*,
1981) and in anticipating society's collapse in terror and violence (*The
Military Secret*, 1983, and *The Soothsayer*, 1987).

There were other plays about the war in the former Yugoslavia but
I have not read or seen all of them. Goran Stefanovski later wrote an
adaptation of Euripides' *Bacchae*, trying to understand the suspension of
civility and the bursting out of violence that grabs collectives and blinds
them while making them mad. Again with Chris Torch and thanks to
his insistence and his ability as a producer, the play was done as a co-
production with Macedonian and Macedonian-Albanian actors. It took a
Swedish (actually an American) producer to bridge the gap of silence and
mistrust that has been marking Skopje for years, splitting its theatre and
artistic circles into self-enclosed ethnic and linguistic communities.
Today, the production echoes as an omen of the dangers that have only
escalated after the NATO Kosovo operation. In another play, *Casabalkan*,
Stefanovski dealt with the war's aftermath, reuniting the war victims, the
perpetrators and bystanders, the profiteers, and the incidental participants on a ship turned into a floating casino. Seeing this play in Stockholm in 1998 I could follow it in Swedish since I'd previously read it but
the dry, timid actors of the Municipal Theater could not render the passion and the fury of the play nor its grotesque, eerie tone. Yet the essential
distance from the recent horror was there, and with the action firmly
placed in the problematic aftermath of the recent war, without real vic-
tors except war profiteers, the theatre could handle with concentration
and competence a cluster of individual misfortune and betrayal without
having to toss it like a hot potato.

The Zagreb playwright Slobodan Snajder wrote in 1994 a play *Snake
Skin* (*Zmijin svlak*), about the mass rapes occurring then in Bosnia.
Roberto Ciulli staged it originally in his Theater an der Ruhr in Germany,
radically devaluing its biblical metaphor by placing it in the theatrical
surrounding of a circus. Nothing could be more at odds with the theme
and the circumstances of the play, but paradoxically, this saved it from an
excess of pathos and added a grotesque tone to the central issues of mar-
tyrdom and redemption. Within this framework, the excessive and the
extreme become tamed and manageable; violence and the continuation
of life balance each other in the sand of the circus arena where the
ordinary, the banal and the exceptional fuse as a matter of routine.

Ciulli, an Italian *Gastarbeiter* in Germany, had through the 1980s
many ties with the Yugoslav theatre, working and touring there regularly

with his German company and we had become close friends. His voluntary exile to the icy German theatre landscape preceded for many years the exile of many Yugoslav theatre people, whom he received, helped and supported together with his dramaturge Helmuth Schaefer and the entire company. When I left Belgrade in 1991, I went to Vienna and then to Ciulli before settling in Amsterdam. In 1993 he organized a small meeting of his post-Yugoslav friends and we met for a few days of intensive talks, in neutral territory, as it were.[10] In all those years I only met Snajder, a very old friend, in Muelheim. Ciulli's understanding of the virtues and contradictions of the pre-war Yugoslav cultural space, that has become through the years uniquely his own, made him extremely sensitive to the fatal consequences of its shattering. Behind the rough texture of his production of Snajder's play there was his own understanding of pain, his own sense of loss.

Mirad

Reflecting on strategies that enable theatre to encounter an ongoing or recent war in an effective way, I still wonder how such a powerful response came from a Dutch author and director of children's theatre, Ad de Bont. In 1993, during the worst phase of the war in Bosnia, he wrote and staged a play, *Mirad, a Youngster from Bosnia*, in his company for children, Wederzijds.[11] The play caught on quickly; several Dutch companies produced it simultaneously in order to bring to as many children as possible an idea of the brutalities of a war and of a child caught up in them. The play was translated into more than twenty languages and later had more than sixty professional productions in Europe, North America and Australia, and there were Dutch, Hungarian and British television adaptations. By a strange coincidence, I saw an early preview for theatre colleagues with Haris Pasovic, who, for the first time since his disappearance from Ljubljana, returned from Sarajevo to Amsterdam in November 1993 at the invitation of Mayor Ed van Thijn. One afternoon we went together to the former school, where Wederzijds is based. I whispered the translation into his ear and we were both very moved.

De Bont found a theatrical modus that could deal with the complexity of the events, with the violence permeating them and with the cultural specificity involved, in such a manner that they became comprehensible even to an eight-year-old. He deployed minimalist dramatic and theatrical means, limiting the action to two actors and giving it a retrospective

---

10   See Dragan Klaic, 'Reconnecting in Ruhr', *Theater*, 2 (1993), pp. 112–15.
11   Ad de Bont, *Mirad, A Boy from Bosnia*, trans. Marian Buijs (Harlow: Longman, 1996).

point of view, so it could run as a reconstruction made out of two complementary narratives, and interwoven with third, that of Mirad's. In fact, Mirad, a Bosnian youngster, does not appear in person in the first part at all, his plight is retold and re-enacted by the two actors who impersonate his aunt and uncle recounting their own traumatic experiences. They lend their voices to Mirad's tale that only comes through in the form of his diary entries and letters. Reduction, distance and an indirect style of discourse serve the purpose to cool, as it were, the hot material of a family dispersed and killed, martyred and exiled. The uncle and aunt are reunited and brought as refugees to the Netherlands and *Mirad* ends there as well. The local and familiar frame in which the characters appear brings the story from the distant locale back home and serves as a means of familiarization.

At the same time, de Bont conveys to his audience who the refugees are: those traumatized, suffering folk who have to restart and reshape their lives and find emotional energy for this whilst still in the process of mourning or in a post-traumatic stupor. The uncle and the aunt represent this transition with accompanying hesitation, insecurity and self-doubt. At the end of the first part the author refuses a calming and harmonious ending – that of a fourteen-year-old boy finding a replacement for lost parents in his uncle and aunt within the comforting Dutch circumstances. Instead, he makes Mirad, who witnessed the death of his father and sister, return to Bosnia to take revenge and find out what happened to his mother.

In part II, written and staged some months later, the same means and the same reductionist techniques are used. The direction of the action is reversed: from the Netherlands to Bosnia. Mirad and his mother are the two characters assigned to the two actors, who, just as in the first part, lend their voices to other supporting characters involved. Here, the mother's and son's narratives complement each other and, running parallel, complete the sequence of events. Mirad's craving for vengeance brings him back home but even the act of vengeance, once committed, cannot by itself fill the emotional void. His mother, raped, abducted, pregnant, expecting to be confronted at birth with a monster from within, discovers with tenderness a baby which helps her relaunch a new life. Only after these false starts and betrayed expectations can personal redefinition of the experience occur. Mother and son are reunited so that they mutually reinforce their capacity to think beyond the past and envisage a life after the war.

The entire play oscillates between the past with its traumas, its myths and negative experiences, and the future that must be disengaged from the past as much as from the butchery of the present. Violence and hatred are dealt with as burdens that must be discarded if a meaningful future is to be conceived at all. While frequently even the most talented artists indulge in obsessive celebrations of violence, displaying astonishing moral turpitude, de Bont confronts violent deeds not as some quintessential, irrational but seductive evil, and not as a bizarre force that suddenly bursts out from the feeble foil of civilization to overwhelm reality with is inherent spectacularity. Violent deeds are introduced as moments which annihilate the border line between childhood and adulthood. From the perspective of de Bont's intended public, children in the primary schools, the play shows what it means to grow up suddenly through the experience of horror and suffering, pointing out the protected nature of the childhood role and at the same time its vulnerability in the proximity of a war or any other calamity. The play deals with essential childhood fears: loss of parents, home, friends. It makes the war understandable not as a distant catastrophe but as a wild sequence of events that can be triggered off amongst the most civilized circumstances.

Mirad plastically shows the reshaping of personality through the tumultuous breakdown of normal social life (neighbours become henchman, boys killers, loved ones victims) and maps out the path from destructive emotions to understanding and reflection. And it clarifies the identity of a refugee beyond the stereotypes of an intruding, threatening other or a hopeless zombie, the stereotypes promulgated by reactionary politics and media. While television clips and front-page photos in the papers bring terrifying or disgusting images of violence as some fatality one can avoid by not looking at, be it Bihac or Sarajevo, Grozny or Monrovia, de Bont's play confirms the theatre's ability to induce reflection and broaden experience, and offers an emotional and cognitive linkage with misfortune, bringing us to the threshold of the tragic experience we are capable of sharing as our own.

Beyond theatre

Haris came to Amsterdam that time in November 1993 to tell the mayor and his distinguished guests, which included G. Konrad and Salman Rushdie, what culture and the arts mean in a besieged city.[12] He was a theatre professional experienced in working under war conditions. After sneaking back into the city as a lonely returnee on New Year's Eve 1993, while so many of his fellow Sarajevans were attempting to escape, he quickly found his role within the difficult circumstances. His instinct was

---

12 Ed van Thijn, *Stemingen in Sarajevo. Dagboek van een waarnemer* (Amsterdam: Van Gennep, 1997), pp. 9–10.

right. Instead of rehearsing with an international cast and performing to the audiences across Europe in a production about the war in Sarajevo, he had an urge to create theatre in Sarajevo, with his colleagues and students, for Sarajevans, as a form of spiritual resistance and moral encouragement. In a furious tempo, he organized concerts, film screenings and performances, and hosted foreign artists who dared to come to the city to perform. He was working with Susan Sontag when she came to rehearse *Waiting for Godot*, under the light of candles, with actors tiring quickly from malnutrition and cold.[13] Afterwards, Haris established a film festival, created his own company, and made new productions. In the cellars of half-ruined buildings, during daytime, without any heat, often with candles or battery lamps, performances were made and given and always attended beyond capacity by exhausted, hungry and despairing and yet admiring and passionate audiences.

In this and subsequent visits to Amsterdam, during the war and afterwards, I learned from Haris how the situation of siege and constant threat to life fosters self-composure rather than panic and disorientation; how one achieves the utmost concentration and an increased speed of doing things under duress and with practically no resources.[14] I learned also that under these extreme circumstances a performance matters less artistically and more as a form of communion. It is a short intensive, reinvigorating gesture for the benefit of the community, which is in turn rebuilt, recomposed and strengthened by the sense of solidarity and common values, becoming united in suffering but also in the desire to resist. In a besieged city, theatre was one of the very few functioning institutions of civil society, based on the courage, imagination and determination of just a few people, who by getting together made theatre produce an extra energy and share it with their fellow citizens. After the war, someone counted that more than one hundred productions were created in Bosnia and Herzegovina between April 1992 and the Dayton agreement at the end of 1995. Some were amateur, some professional productions, some mixed both and they were made in several cities, some of which in the pre-war time had never had much of theatre life. People wrote plays and did plays, and even staged the musical *Hair*.

Haris, for instance, reached out to his pre-war passion, classic Japanese theatre, and staged some No drama. One day someone brought

13   See Erika Monk, 'Reports from the 21st Century: A Sarajevo Interview', 'Notes from a Trip to Sarajevo', 'Only the Possible: An Interview with Susan Sontag', *Theater*, 3, 1993, pp. 9–36, and Susan Sontag, '*Waiting for Godot* in Sarajevo', *Performing Arts Journal*, 16, No. 2 (1994), pp. 87–106.
14   Miroslav Prstojevic, *Sarajevo, Survival Guide*, eds. M. Razovic and A. Wagner (Sarajevo: Fama, 1993).

him a novel by Paul Auster, which a foreign correspondent had left behind saying that this was a novel about what had been happening in Sarajevo. Reading *In the Country of Last Things*, Haris realized that Auster had anticipated the breakdown of Sarajevo, the pulverization of normality, and decided to make a stage adaptation. In the summer of 1994 he left the city temporarily with his company at the invitation of Peter Brook and his International Centre of Theatrical Research, to perform these two productions in Paris and elsewhere in Europe. Everywhere they were received with respect and appreciation, and with a special warmth by theatre professionals. Yet I felt that these productions with their strong ritualistic component could never have nearly such a strong meaning and impact on audiences living in peace as they had on the people in Sarajevo under the siege. They were taken out of the context in which they were created, that had prompted them and made them essential there: abroad they were slightly different, a bit special, almost a bit of an exotic feature in the rich and diversified theatre programming of any large European city.

In the following few years Haris was in Sarajevo and also in Amsterdam, he made some productions but increasingly turned to publications, events, documentary films, and the theatre festival he ran in Sarajevo which he left to some younger colleagues.[15] For someone who was so passionately immersed in theatre and who was known even before the war for his fanatical work rhythms and long intensive rehearsals, it was a strange change of heart. Slowly, through many conversations, I understood that having reached some far-out end, some pinnacle of theatre making under the most extreme conditions, Haris could not imagine returning to theatre directing as merely a profession, a job, a regular artistic pursuit, going from one play to another, stacking premieres, tours and prizes one on top of another. After the exceptional period when theatre mattered so much to him and his collaborators and especially to his Sarajevo public, theatre as business as usual lost all attraction, all appeal to him, especially in the midst of nationalist politics and NGO-aided wild capitalism, dominating the post-Dayton Bosnia and Herzegovina, with its unfinished war and underachieved peace.

Back to Karl Kraus

A few years later, with the most recent outburst of war in the Balkans, with Kosovo in flames and NATO bombing Serbia and Montenegro, the question of what theatre can do against such misfortunes was posed again. I felt more reserved and more sceptical than in 1992. During the

15 See Thijn, *Stemingen in Sarajevo*, pp. 11–13, 166–9, 220–1.

NATO campaign, there were no means to make theatre in Kosovo as it was possible to do in Sarajevo during the siege. There were colleagues from Western Europe who wanted immediately to go to make theatre in the refugee camps in Macedonia and Albania, with the aim to help people overcome their traumatic experiences and regain a sense of the future. It was logistically difficult to do so and I was sceptical of such an effort so quickly, so soon. Once the Albanian refugees returned to Kosovo, rebuilding some sort of theatre life became again a meaningful project but I hear very little of a few old theatre colleagues of mine who I know are trying to do exactly that in Priština nowadays.

If you do not happen to live in the Balkans, what do you do as a theatre professional in your own surroundings? Perhaps pull out an old play and stage it as a provocation? So many of the ancient Greek tragedies would do. *The Trojan Women* by Euripides, for instance, imprinted on my memory as Andrei Serban's 1973 production that conveyed a tragic experience of defeat, loss and forced exile I have been re-experiencing in the last few weeks, watching the flood of Albanian refugees from Kosovo. On a recent visit to New York I saw that it is being brought back to La Mama where it originated. Joshua Sobol's *Ghetto* comes to my mind too, but I discarded the idea fearing trivializing analogies with the Holocaust, refusing to slide into the rhetorical figures which politicians nowadays propel, talking about genocide, Hitler, Munich and Chamberlain when they refer to the current Balkan mess. Too many images of past conflicts and wars crowd the contemporary imagination when facing the most recent Balkan quagmire. Or should it be Salacrou's *La Terre est ronde*, where wild youngsters rampage through Renaissance Florence, burning paintings, mirrors, jewels, and cards as objects of vanity, their fanaticism inspired by the fire-and-brimstone preaching of Savonarola? Salacrou comes close to the contemporary manifestations of a fundamentalist faith, invoking the Taliban terror in Kabul more than the paramilitary's plunder and terror in Kosovo. Then better Musset's *Lorenzaccio* squaring the tyrannicide with faceless mediocrity, something which reflects NATO's desire to eliminate Milosevic without taking too many risks. Even *The Massacre in Paris*, the forgotten play of Christopher Marlowe, comes to my mind. Written as a relatively fresh response to the systematic slaughter of the Huguenots on St. Bartholomew night, with the Duke of Guise as a typical Elizabethan villain, this cardboard tragedy – some poetic passages notwithstanding – appears as an early precursor of the genre popularized by *Saturday Night Massacre* and similar titillating horror films.

Plunging into my library, I could probably come up with more plays, each of them inadequate for some reason, either too distant or too narrow for the war situation. Those inside the conflict zone, in Belgrade for instance, could have reached for Euripides, or better Aristophanes, the despairing and mocking commentator on the prolonged folly of the Peloponnesian War that went on for twenty-five years, bringing utter ruin to Athens. Shakespeare's catastrophic imagination is broad enough to cover any misfortune. Just a few weeks before the NATO bombing started, a Belgrade theatre staged an adaptation of Agota Kristof's *Le Grand cahier*, a cool, meticulous record of kids mercilessly training themselves to match the cruelty of the engulfing war. If it works in Belgrade it could probably work in Priština, Podgorica, Skopje and Tirana as well. But here? What theatre adventure, what gesture makes sense? That is what my British friend asks.

I try to stimulate his imagination and at the same time plead for some distance through time in order to benefit from theatre's proven ability to function as an instrument in the re-enforcement and reconsideration of cultural memory.[16] To those too impatient to wait so long; to those theatre students I spoke with in Utrecht during the NATO campaign, who wanted to do something at once; to the colleagues who thought I must have a ready-made answer because I am in theatre and I happen to come from the Balkans, I tended to say: don't try to restage the war, it is too complex and too gruesome and, thank god, it is at a safe distance even if television makes it explode in our living rooms every evening. Deal rather with the media coverage of the war that is so ubiquitous. Dramatize and run through a gamut of genres and styles the avalanche of war reports, the endless parade of television punditry, the solemn statements of the politicians and the daily briefings of the military spokesmen, the voyeuristic exploitation of human misery and humiliation, the jerking of emotions, the barrage of lies and half-truths, the twisting of facts, and the upstaging of some issues and events and the blackout of some others.

That is what Karl Kraus did during World War One and afterwards in his megaplay *Die letzten Tagen der Menschheit*. Start, for instance, with this cosmic drama of hundreds of scenes, take it one by one every day or week and you'll have plenty of material to keep you busy for the months to come. Probe the fresh media footage, newspaper articles and commentaries by bouncing them off against Kraus' grotesque exploitation of bellicose propaganda and jingoism. Theatre in all probability cannot stop war nor correct injustice but can show how power and might lose the firm moral ground, how fantasies of omnipotence cause blindness, how supposed winners turn into losers once their triumphant phrase begins to sound shallow. Euripides and Shakespeare as seasoned theatre professionals knew in their best moments how to use these powers of theatre,

16 Kustow, *Theater@risk*, p. 69.

but today's theatre maker seeking to articulate promptly a theatre response to the war had better seek to start his apprenticeship with a more contemporary master such as Karl Kraus. Well before radio, television and the internet, he understood that modern warfare was being waged on the home front, with the media as the primary weapon.

The crisis of theatre might well be its constant condition, determined by its own fatigue and opportunism, the economic constraints of show biz, the fragility of the inspiring artistic talent tending to slide into routine, and orchestrated by the overwhelming indifference to theatre of most potential viewers. But the theatre of crisis, the theatricalization of a crisis, is no fancy and no myth but a viable option, given some distance, necessary for the collective and individual memory of the traumatizing experience to settle only to be unsettled again by the strikes of the stage acts. And the theatre of crisis, be it war, hunger, epidemics or civil unrest, can make sense if the artists focus not on the unfolding tragedy itself but on the ways it is being presented, reported, perceived and metaphorized by other dominant discourses. 'Theater is not a disseminator of truth but a provider of versions.'[17] It is up to theatre professionals to use the weakness of their medium, its marginal position in society, as a point of strength, taking a maverick stance: to slow down the incessant parade of blitz images, to magnify them one by one, reveal their falsehood, deepen their shadows, rearrange their assigned context and add unexpected voices and commentaries.

17   Barker, *Arguments for a Theater*, p. 44.

Scavenging for home (or, how I learned to take refuge in live theatre while worrying about the bomb)

Lisa D'Amour

Lisa D'Amour is a playwright and performer, originally from New Orleans, Louisiana. Currently, she resides in Minneapolis, Minnesota, where she received a Jerome Fellowship, and a McKnight Advancement Grant. Her plays and performances have been produced at Salvage Vanguard Theater (Austin, TX), Annex Theater (Seattle, WA), and Raindog Playwrights Project (Portland, OR). In 1998, she participated in Eugenio Barba's International School of Theater Anthropology Conference in Lisbon, Portugal, and travelled to Belgrade, Yugoslavia, to observe and train with Dah Teatar. She is a core member of the Playwrights' Center of Minneapolis, and a member of New Dramatists. This article was originally printed in the *Austin Chronicle* in January 2000 during the run of Lisa D'Amour's solo performance installation, *Slabber*. It was then adapted for this volume.

I was sitting alone at a table at the Bryant-Lake Bowl in Minneapolis when I saw it. I was waiting for my breakfast dates, Sharon Bridgforth, visiting from Austin for a reading of *The Bull Jean Stories*, and Megan Monaghan, former Austinite and Lab Director at the Playwrights' Center. I was feeling downright hopeful about the world, sitting at my favourite table at my favourite diner/bowling alley with a hot cup of coffee and the sun on my face, pondering Sharon's transcendent reading the night before. As I daydreamed, I happened to glance over at the daily paper sitting on the next table. The half-page photo showed an historic building on fire. And the headline read 'BELGRADE BOMBED'.

Thank god Megan and Sharon were old friends, sisters-in-art, for when they arrived a few moments later, I was a mess. I had spent a month in Belgrade the previous autumn, studying with Dah Teatar, the powerhouse collaborative theatre company that wowed audiences in Austin during the 1996 RAT conference. There had been threats of air strikes during my visit, but the company members were convinced it was just government posturing. And when the bombs started dropping on Yugoslavia four months after my visit, none of us thought the bombing would reach Belgrade. It would be like bombing Washington, DC.

Suddenly, bombs were being dropped blocks from the homes of my dear friends/mentors. Their lives and their art were in grave danger. Their planned international US-funded tour (through the Artlink programme) was cancelled. The company scattered to four countries: China, Great Britain, the United States, Yugoslavia. At home in the US, I wrote letters and attended protest rallies. I expressed my views on the bombing whenever I could, but for the most part, my life went on eerily unchanged. And in Yugoslavia, in the midst of nightly bombing, the members of Dah who remained in Belgrade began creating a new theatre piece.

How did the NATO bombing affect my career as an artist? Did it make me give up playwriting to become a full-time activist? No. Did I immediately change the thrust of my performance art from conceptual to overtly political? No. As a relatively itinerant, relatively poor, relatively experimental playwright, the NATO bombing forced me to examine the intention behind my art, and my reasons for being an artist. My friends in Yugoslavia were making art, sincerely and defiantly, in the face of death. Their art was their means of survival. Why was I making art? Was my commitment to my craft so unrefutable?

Some important things Dah taught me, ostensibly about performance

1] There are many ways of resting besides just stopping and proclaiming 'I'm tired'. The body must be in constant motion, in a constant state of readiness. If you let yourself sink into your exhaustion, you are defeating yourself – it takes more energy to get yourself started again than it does to keep your body going ...

I make my life writing plays and creating site-specific performance. Like many of my colleagues, I have roamed from city to city, making my home in small theatre companies and organizations committed to new, often experimental work. Currently, I live in Minneapolis, MN, where I develop most of my work through the Playwrights' Center and renegade theatre companies like the Red Eye Collaboration. Minneapolis, however, only constitutes about one-quarter of my home base: I spend almost as much time living under the 'roofs' of Austin Scriptworks, Frontera@Hyde Park Theater, and my collaborator Katie Pearl (all in Austin), New Dramatists (in New York City) and my partner-in-new-deep-south-performance, Kathy Randels (in New Orleans, my town of origin).

More often than not, I feel as though I am scavenging my career from the resources and creative support offered by these generous colleagues and organizations. All of the above-named organizations operate on a different currency than most of the United States, 'buying' their place in the world with talent, energy and persistent effort. I truly believe in this currency. However, when one is saying 'fuck you' to the dominant method of getting what one wants/needs, it is easy to get exhausted. It is easy to sit around one's house and grow bitter, proclaiming oneself a martyr-for-the-cause, making loud noises about the ills of mass media and the death of live theatre in general. And while it is easy to sink into such an artistic rut, it takes quadruple the energy to pull oneself out.

In order to avoid the rut, an artist must find a way to sustain a constant state of creative energy. For me, this means identifying the principles of live performance that I hold most dear – the principles that make what I do essential for the well-being of the world. At the risk of making a brash generalization, I'll proclaim that all the principles which I hold dear can be boiled down the notion of immediacy: of the writer/director/performer's intentions, of the relationship between performer and audience, of the relationship between an audience of strangers gathered together to witness the theatrical event, of their surrounding theatrical space.

Everyone knows that we come to the theatre to experience the unique immediacy of live performance, right? No one comes to a theatre expecting to see a TV show. While this is true, my artistic exhaustion sets in when I feel trapped in a mainstream performance culture that takes the immediacy of the theatre for granted. *The seats are there, the stage is there, and we will do plays right there in front of them. Of course it's an immediate experience. We're producing live performance. Plays with a track record, of course. Dependable plays that 'work'.* Suddenly, the immediacy is squashed by strategies to make the theatre foolproof and easy to predict.

I make art because of the artists who exploit the immediacy of live performance. Three moments in the theatre I will never forget: being duct-taped into the theatre in Frontera@Hyde Park's *Weldon Rising*, watching Japanese No master Akira Matsui make his No mask change shape, texture and emotion by simply moving his head one-eighth of an inch, watching The Wooster Group's Kate Valk deliver Gertrude Stein's dialogue while simultaneously and exactly mimicking the movements of an actress in a 1950s soft-porn video shown on a nearby monitor, with every movement amplified by extremely sensitive body mikes turned up LOUD. In each of these performances, the intention behind the action was so complex, three-dimensional and *fierce*, that I was absolutely engrossed in it. I'll never forget these moments, but I also don't remember watching them. In each case, I was pulled so completely into the moment that the act of watching fell away, giving way to pure experience.

> 2] Always keep your body moving in two directions at once. The oppositions in your body create a tension that makes a performer fascinating to observe – the audience may not know why they are looking, but they will not be able to look away.

In my continuous quest to define exactly why my art is essential to myself and others, I find I feel most satisfied when I have worked to the absolute limits of my ability to bring that kind of pure experience to an audience. Working to the limits of my ability means intense, quiet concentration on my part, and a great deal of intense collaboration.

My closest collaborator over the last four years has been the director Katie Pearl. In our site-specific performance installations, Katie and I attempt to create complete, theatrical worlds composed of bodies, story/ text, visual images and sound/music. In each of our collaborations, Katie and I make a pact with each other to create a performance which respects our audience while challenging it, and which asks audiences to reimagine the physical and emotional boundaries between themselves and the performer. We strive to create an experience that is at once intimate and communal by inviting audiences into a story-world that can only be completed by their presence, commitment and imagination.

In our latest collaboration, *Slabber*, audiences meet a character known as 'Our Lady', a mysterious pilgrim on a quest for information and the source of her own past. In our shared search for immediacy, Katie and I conceived of *Slabber* as a series of studies: each incarnation of the piece is its own unique study of character and space, revealing different facets of 'Our Lady' according to the circumstances under which she tells her story. Our first two studies yielded incredibly different results: the Minneapolis *Slabber* became a high-tech indoor/outdoor performance/ installation/fair; the Austin, Texas, *Slabber* turned into a study which could fit into several suitcases, to be unpacked before an audience at five different, secret locations over the course of five nights.

I am obsessed with the perpetual challenge of these studies, even though it means, essentially, that I must rewrite the piece each time we do a new production: a process I know is impractical, time-consuming, and, well, a little bit insane. I know I cannot place the same demands on all of my plays, and I wouldn't want to. However, I am obsessed with the challenge because it is in direct opposition to everything that contributes to my mainstream artistic exhaustion: the studies are neither dependable nor predictable, they require Katie and I to rigorously examine our intentions each time we mount a new study, and the studies are not in any way designed to make money. If I tried to figure a number of hours worked to dollars made ratio on this project, I'd sink, no, nosedive, into that bitter artistic rut faster than you can say *Death of a Salesman*.

Working on these studies, and working with Katie, helps keep me alive and filled with energy. Our work requires me to be perpetually, undeniably alert, because everything about our process and aesthetic is filled with contradictions. Success never means money. Story never means spoken narrative arc. Collaboration never means absolute agreement. Our process and performances require that we not only be open to the demands of our present circumstances, but also have faith that our present, with all its contradictions, holds everything we need to create a performance that is immediate, theatrical and, once the audience arrives, whole.

> 3] Always make your body as precise as possible. In striving for precision, the body becomes alive, filled with energy.

Perhaps the thing that irked me the most about the NATO bombing was that it was so damn easy to ignore. I remember one day at the Playwrights'

Center, when Belgrade was hit for the second time, I walked into the common area and said to a group of people hanging out in front of the copy machine: 'All my friends just got bombed again'. I think one person looked up and said, 'Really?' as two other people banged on the automatic feeder, trying to get the copier to work again. Later that night, as I thought about the incident, I realized that what made me the most angry was not their indifference, but that I walked away from them without saying a word, as though I expected nothing less from them.

It is easy to monkey around in this country, especially for an over-educated upper-middle-class white girl like me. It is easy to say things like 'I am a playwright', 'I am experimenting with the form', 'I am challenging my audience', and never follow through with the full intention of those statements. As I follow in the footsteps of my mentors – steadfast itinerant playwrights of the big, cheap theatre, Eastern European experimental artists salvaging art from the rubble, Japanese No masters summoning beauty out of rigour – I try to the best of my ability to do precisely as I say.

In a recent article in the *Austin Chronicle*, Erik Ehn noted that 'the culture that once received plays has evaporated and has been replaced with commerce'. I agree, and would add that this commerce creates and thrives on distance. As we make our lives in this country, there is more and more distance between what we buy and who makes it, what we watch and who creates it, what we live in and who built it. This distance brings with it fuzzy intentions, botched communication and the ability to ignore anything that isn't causing you immediate pain.

My current quest for precision in my own life is connected to my longing for a culture rooted in awareness and immediacy. Live theatre is one of the last venues in this country which demands such immediate consistency: saying and doing exist in the same moment, face to face with your witnesses. If I am going to participate in creating the kind of culture I want to live in, a culture that will appreciate my craft, I must act out my values as precisely as possible, with the blind faith that others will follow in the way that I have followed those who have inspired me.

4] 'Dah' means breath in Serbian. For the artists of the group, Dah means to breathe in, to gather strength, to preserve, to be spiritual, to keep the spirit of life-warmth, movement and creation.

Dah Teatar came to the United States in February and March 2000 for their second US tour. They toured *Documents of Times*, the piece created during the bombing by the members of the company who remained in Yugoslavia. Dah calls the performance 'a record of lived through reality bites, carved on the performers' bodies, vanishing when they leave … the record that remains in the souls of the audience who witness the piece'. The members of Dah could not stop creating, even when their country, indeed their lives, were in danger of disappearing at any moment. And as soon as it became an option for them to travel again, their US company member, Kathy Randels, began organizing a six-city US tour (which included a stop at the Iowa RAT conference, thanks to Erik Ehn) *by herself*, in her office/bedroom in New Orleans, LA. When I look at the international collective intention of Dah how can I possibly allow myself to sink into the rut, or whine about the difficulty of my chosen path? How can I do anything but stay fiercely true to my intentions and create, forging relationships and homes as I work, *hard*?

The NATO bombing of Yugoslavia brought war home to me – which is a silly thing for me to say, really, because I was so very far from danger. But for the first time in my life, cities I had visited were disappearing, and people I knew were in grave danger, and I was forced to examine the way I lived my life, and the ways I stood up for the things that meant the most to me. The bombing and Dah's perseverance throughout it forced me to reckon with the complexities of my chosen path, and in this examination, gather strength, determination and a deep respect for the people and organizations that I hold dear. My wish for us all: that through tireless, precise work, we will gather the collective strength needed to build a home for ourselves: a home that crosses international boundaries, a home which welcomes contradictions, a home which allows us to create and share the work we love in awareness and peace.

Stealing kisses
Paul Heritage

Paul Heritage is Professor of Drama and Performance at Queen Mary, University of London, a founder of the Theatre in Prisons and Probation Centre at Manchester, and formerly a director with Gay Sweatshop. Since 1992 he has been working in Brazil, directing Shakespeare and developing theatre projects in Brazilian prisons. He is director of People's Palace Projects, which is working on theatre projects in Brazil, Burkina Faso, Sri Lanka and the East End of London. His publications include work on contemporary Brazilian and British theatre, sexuality and performance, AIDS, etc. He has edited two collections of articles for The British Council in Brazil: *Mudança de Cena: teatro e desenvolvimento social* and *Mudança de Cena/Changing the Scene II: theatre building citizenship*.

To witness an event is to be present at it in some fundamentally ethical way, to feel the weight of things and one's own place in them, even if that place is simply, for the moment, as an onlooker. (Tim Etchells, *Certain Fragments*, London: Routledge, 1999, p. 17.)

I have been a privileged onlooker to certain events in Brazilian prisons since 1993. This chapter attempts to bear witness to just one performance that took place in a Brazilian penal institution, to feel the weight of things and to think about my own place in relation to what I have seen. Tim Etchells provides me with a point of departure to think about the relationships between performance and the act of witness, but a certain fragment that has survived from a performance in 1993 could just as well serve to begin this chapter. Carved on a wooden plaque are the names of the men who took part in the first performance I staged in a Brazilian prison, and underneath they have chosen to inscribe the following:

A arte não reproduz o que vemos, ela nos faz ver.
(Art does not reproduce what we see, it makes us see ourselves.)

In very different ways, both Etchells and those prisoners provide words that resist ideas of representation and reproduction that are bound up in the mediatized world in which we live. In most instances we have lost the human capacity to experience our lives directly and must be content, it seems, with living them through the various technological media that the twentieth century has bequeathed us. I imagine that those of us who still make or make ourselves present at performance do so because we still insist on seeing it as a resistance to that phenomenon. Rather than merely seeing theatre as a failing competitor in the global economy of cultural exchange which is inevitably doomed to lose out to the rival forces of cinema, video and television, we see performance as offering something different from other representations of the world. Tim Etchells from the British performance group Forced Entertainment has characterized the call that comes from the most radical in performance as: 'be here, be here, be here …'[1]

In the liveness of the theatrical event we are not looking merely for the spectators of the mediatized world, we are trying to create witnesses. A witness is an active participant, as Brecht discovered, and has responsibilities that go beyond the moment at which that event takes place. With every step that television and cinema take to find technological ways to bring crime and violence closer to us, we are ever more distanced from an active and therefore an ethical relationship with the original event. We have spent a decade watching wars in the Malvinas, the Gulf, Serbia,

1 Etchells, *Certain Fragments* (London and New York: Routledge, 1999), p. 18.

Rwanda, and East Timor, becoming with every edit, every close-up, every computer simulation more the spectators and less the witnesses of our age. The work I want to present today is, in contrast, an evocation to the spectator to become a witness of something that can only be played by those people that are in that room and that particular time. And because of this, the call that performance makes is to *feel the weight of things and one's own place in them.*

The American theatre director Peter Sellars has spoken about why it is important for him to work with a multicultural cast. He explains how living in a multicultural society affects the ways in which we live our lives, and therefore the classics that he works on. Shakespeare, Mozart, Aeschylus, and Brecht, he maintains, can only be seen today in relation to that multiculturalism: its pleasures and pains. He invokes an idea of creation that is collective, in which the text can only be weighed and balanced in relation to our contemporary society when the cast itself feels that weight, can bring their own experiences of that world into the creative process.

> I make theatre because I want to work through material that I feel is in the society, and I need a group of really powerful people in the room to work though it with, because I have a very dim view of my own capacity or expertise. Theater is not a solo activity. It's actually the understanding that we will never be able to understand any of these issues until we search for a collective understanding. Individual expertise or point of view is no longer adequate in this world, if it ever was. Knowledge has to be an understanding, has to be conceived much more as Plato would, as an ongoing dialogue. So the question is, where is the dialogue and how can that dialogue be as rich as possible?[2]

I would like to start with this question – *where is the dialogue?* – but move on from the process of creating theatre in the ways that Sellars here imagines, to look at the creation of meaning produced from making theatre in situations away from the spaces in which theatre is normally sanctioned. My starting point will be same as Sellars': the working through of material that is in society. My basis is also that the strength of theatre relies on the strength of the group of people in that room together, but I want to extend beyond the performers to think about the witnesses and to think about how performance can matter. And perhaps to ask the biggest and most romantic of questions: where and how does performance make a difference?

2 Peter Sellars, 'In Conversation with Michael Billington at the Royal Exchange Theater, Manchester, 18 November 1994', in *In Contact with the Gods? Directors Talk Theater*, eds. Maria M. Delgado and Paul Heritage (Manchester: Manchester University Press, 1996), p. 226.

I am therefore not interested so much in the process of creation that concentrates on the speech and how it is delivered or the context that is created by the director to give that speech meaning. I shall be looking here to find the two-way process by which that speech performs its meaning at the moment of utterance. Clearly, when I talk of the act of witness, performers/writers/directors themselves are already making their work with the hope and intention of being those witnesses of our age that will have resonance and impact. We can all think, I am sure, of the plays or productions that mark themselves out or have been identified as the witnesses of their times. But here I am thinking more of the work that activates the witnessing by the audience: the work that creates in the moment of performance a responsibility for those who watch. My interest lies not in the way in which performance constitutes or describes itself as an act of witness, but rather in the way in which the audience and the actor perform this act. In other words, I want to think of performance as doing – performing – an activity that is in itself that moment of witness.

The performance that I am going to discuss is a staged reading of *Romeo and Juliet* by juvenile prisoners which I directed in the Instituto Padre Severino on the Ilha do Governador in Rio de Janeiro, in September 1999. Much of my own theatre work in Brazil since 1993 has been making theatre with prisoners and in some way I will be discussing seven years of this work. But I want to root it in one moment. This performance was both a continuation of other experiences and distinctively different. I have worked in various prisons in Brasília, São Paulo and Rio de Janeiro, and have usually tried to move beyond the running of drama workshops to look at ways in which theatre could become a part of the structure of the prison. A prison is a world where survival is tested at its limits. Performance is normally thought of as that which does not survive, thus in seeking to ensure a continuity of theatre in the prisons where I have worked, I seem to have been engaged in a bizarre act of negation: denying something essential in both the institution and the activity. But the survival of performance in prisons has for me become a form of resistance and negation of the system itself. If, in Britain, too often theatre work in prison has been concentrated on directing individual behavioural change, in Brazil I have instead become fascinated with exploring the ways in which theatre can offer the hope of institutional shifts. I will never be able to offer you an example of the way in which theatre has reduced crime or changed offending behaviour, but I can encourage you to go to a maximum security prison in Brasília called Papuda and visit the studio theatre that has been created within the walls. That is what I have learnt to call change.

But the work that I did with the young men in the institution known as Padre Severino was very different. Although it was part of a programme that I was seeking to establish at the time, there was no direct plan to implement regular drama work in the prison. Nor were there any obvious or immediate ways in which this particular group would be able to continue what they had done on the project. All of which I regret. But perhaps in some way its continuation is present now in the act of talking to you about it. Perhaps this moment of testimony is indeed part of its impact, of the ways in which it continues to work. I can speculate only on what impact it may or may not continue to have for the young men in the project, but here is just one of the traces left by that performance as I consider its ability to activate the witnessing of what our culture both desires and profoundly fears.

I need first to tell the story of the performance. I am mindful in doing this, that anyone else who was there would tell a different story. I wish I could bring those other stories with me. Even as I quote things that were said or show you pictures of what happened, they will not be the story that any of those participants or that audience would chose to tell. But we need a context. A point of focus. And the way I tell the story will bring out, I hope, the things that I want to say about performance: its creation, its ways of meaning and what it does.

I had visited the three juvenile prisons situated on the Ilha do Governador on various occasions during my time spent in Rio over the last few years. I will continue to refer to these institutions as prisons rather than schools, although under Brazilian law, because the age for criminal responsibility is eighteen, these young people are not actually imprisoned. But the word *school* will never be appropriate for the methodologies, philosophies or activities of these places. It has too many illusions. But I am conscious that when I talk of prisons and Brazil, there are other images being evoked that might not belong to my particular story. This is not going to be a horror story, but I cannot stop your own images and narratives playing out alongside mine. It will undeniably be a romantic tale because it is grounded in dreams, resisting the empiricism that is offered elsewhere as salvation. But this story takes as its starting point a responsibility to the events that we witness.

The production of *Romeo and Juliet* was an act in response to what I had witnessed at other moments. Tim Etchells quotes Michael Herr as saying that when he went to cover the Vietnam War, his act of looking was both crude and serious:

> Serious because I acted on it and went, crude because I didn't know, it took the war to teach it, that you are as responsible for everything that you saw as you were for everything that you do. The problem was that you didn't always

know what you were seeing until later, maybe years later, it just stayed stored there in your eyes … .[3]

If there was one moment – and there never can be – that took me back to the Instituto Padre Severino last September, it was when on a previous occasion I had been shown the new computers that had been installed for use by a very limited number of the inmates. A proud teacher showed me the work that one of the young men had done. It was technically far in advance of anything that I could produce on my computer: a full colour design of a three-storey building not unlike the one in which they were held, with a boy being suspended by his feet from one of the upper windows. The only text was a line beneath the computer-generated drawing which read: 'Will no one release me from this hell?' … *It just stayed stored there in your eyes …*

Of course the idea of staging a reading of *Romeo and Juliet* with a group of fifteen fifteen-year-olds from a juvenile prison in Rio is a kind of lunacy. I was aided and abetted in this insanity by Maria Nakano who had asked me to produce a series of events to mark the second anniversary of the death of her husband, the radical sociologist and social activist Herbert de Souza (commonly known as Betinho). During the long years of her marriage to Betinho, and in the time subsequent to his death, Maria has not faltered in seeking to make work happen that, in the inverted logic of Brazilian social reality, would be considered madness. Betinho's popular campaigns against poverty and hunger were a form of resistance to the acceptance of existing social conditions as being either necessary or natural. Therefore, on the actual anniversary of Betinho's death, we staged a football match between a team of artists led by the legendary Brazilian musician Chico Buarque and the young men and women from the juvenile prisons. Chico and the other artists were deservedly slaughtered. So when I returned to begin the process of rehearsing *Romeo and Juliet* a couple of weeks later, I could honestly tell the group of boys that had come to work with me that this was a form of revenge. I told them I would be returning with more actors – some of them from the football team – but this time we were going to play a game which we thought was better suited to our talents: Shakespeare.

The idea was simple. We would stage a reading of *Romeo and Juliet* made up of the inmates at the juvenile prisons on the island. A group of boys would work with me to look at the themes and ideas of the play and work with the text. At the end of this process they would all get to play a role in the final reading and I would bring a group of actors, most of them from the all-powerful TV Globo network, to play the other roles. As the

3 Etchells, *Certain Fragments*, p. 20.

work progressed, it quickly became apparent that most of the boys wanted to play Romeo, so we ended up with one actor for each scene in which Romeo appears. Meanwhile I rehearsed with the other actors elsewhere, and also invited a band of young drummers called Afro-lata from Vigário Geral, one of the hillside communities in Rio de Janeiro that are commonly known as *favelas*. The two parts of this strangely divided process only met for a brief time in the morning before the afternoon performance for over two hundred other inmates plus what seemed to be almost as many guests, journalists and photographers.

The mix was potent. Each of the components in this performance has their own cultural value which operates in contradictory ways within Brazilian society: TV Globo stars, Shakespeare, juvenile offenders. Globo stars are not meant to mix with juvenile offenders nor do juvenile offenders mix with Shakespeare. And the cultural economic imperatives of Brazil mean that Globo stars rarely mix with Shakespeare. Juvenile offenders are not normally associated with reading, so the idea of them staging a reading seemed an even greater disturbance of the realities with which society becomes comfortable, even while they are horrific. Of course, the young men had problems with the language, but so – and I am sure they will not mind me saying this – did some of the professional actors. That's the point. We are all distanced in some way from this language. It is beyond us. If it were not beyond us then it would not serve its purpose, which is to extend the ways in which we think and speak. Who needs this more than those members of our society that, for whatever reason, have had the expectations of how they think and speak set so low that there is no hope of them ever growing beyond these boundaries?

As artists, we are not only border-crossers ourselves, but are capable of helping other people cross borders. On rare occasions it can be a mutual process. On that particular Monday afternoon in the Instituto Padre Severino there were some powerful borders being approached. Some of them were never reached but only glimpsed. Some of them were crossed in ways that we did not expect. Some of them were crossed in ways that we did not want. Some were crossed by the young men of the institution, others had to be crossed by the actors who came from outside. I hope that others were crossed by those who bore witness.

The performance itself took place in a cavernous hall which did nothing to help the words cross the boundary between the stage and audience. Distant from the concrete stage, were rows of chairs on which sat dignitaries, guards, teachers, and journalists. In front of them on the floor sat the young men and women from the three penal institutions. On stage were the actors, seated on individual chairs: a Romeo between each actor who had come to join with them to tell the story of the star-crossed lovers. Each Romeo wore a white T-shirt bearing the character's name, and new shorts hurriedly supplied by the Institute at the last minute to ensure respectability. Afro-lata stood behind, their young faces showing little reaction to the place to which they had been brought to play. Perhaps they were too young to see the irony of where they were to perform. It is through cultural activity that they may avoid being perceived as part of the trajectory that takes too many young people from the poor communities to the prisons of Brazil. Yet it is because of that art that they were inside the juvenile prison that afternoon.

While many actors had promised their services for the performance, TV Globo's unpredictable recording schedules meant that there were sudden absences on the day. Thus it was that Leticia Sabatella, one of the major stars of the telenovellas, came to play Juliet to all of these young Romeos. It had never been intended as such when the project was planned, but it allowed for a fixed identification around Juliet while the multiple nature of her lover was acted out by the finest line-up of Romeos that I have been fortunate enough to work with. Frantic last-minute rehearsals gave Leticia the opportunity for at least one run-through of each scene with a different Romeo. She had little idea of what to expect and their abilities varied from the almost illiterate to the fluent and passionate. Each in his way presented different challenges for her and the other actors who had to work with them. And, of course, the challenges for the Romeos and their colleagues in the audience were likewise considerable. This, then, was the happening that causes me now to reflect on the performative act of witness that theatre can invoke. I cannot provide a narrative account of the performance, but would like to take some random thoughts and consequences that arose from the work of those twelve Romeos and their Juliet.

Thomas Kyd, contemporary of Shakespeare, wrote in *The Spanish Tragedy* that where words fail, violence prevails. In working on *Romeo and Juliet*, these young men were encountering a vocabulary and a form of expressing ideas and emotions that they had never been exposed to previously. It is a commonplace to see *Romeo and Juliet* as being thematically linked to the divisions and violence of other communities. Certainly we did the sort of improvisational work that found/forced those sort of connections. However, I was not interested in parallels or approximations. I wanted to see what happened in the act of speaking this language: a language that was already alien from the original in that it was in translation. I started from the premise that they would have no trouble understanding what these characters were doing or feeling or thinking. The only block might be in the way in which they expressed themselves. But that is a block we all have. How many of us have the words to express what we do, feel or think? Thus I did not want them to rephrase the text in their own words. That would merely serve to keep them in their place and we were entering this work with a desire for change. The group were already literate enough to read the text, although all of them had some problems when they first encountered it, as all of us would, whether in English or Portuguese. Even with considerable assistance, some of them could only read each word individually and showed little ability to make connections between the words. Others quickly found a fluency that would be admirable in any group of adolescents from Britain or Brazil. Much of the work with the text was like a form of physical exercise with their tongues, mouths, faces, and eventually their bodies. The first connections were thus made with the forms of the words: their shapes, their sounds, their resonances. Then came the ways in which these words were structured together and how they filled space and arrived at other bodies. None of these words are neutral or inactive as they discovered. They began to do things with language. Not to describe their world, but to be active with and within this language. They were therefore performing.

As I watched these young men engage in this process I was constantly forced to reconsider what defines the difference between good and bad acting. We recognize the great performance when it is effectively performative: when it does something. The bad actor is the one that only manages the constative act of reproduction, describing an emotion that has passed, a world that has gone. The actor that excites us is the one that makes their utterance exist only at that historic moment in which it is made by that person. In very different ways, these actors took me as close to that moment as I have ever been in the presence of a Shakespeare text. Thus my work with these young men was to try to enable them to use the language to do things.

One of the most effective challenges that the presentation gave to the audience, was the vision of these boys reading the play out loud. At least two of them read their lines with no apparent understanding on the day of the performance, as word laboriously followed word. At that moment I wondered how far I had betrayed the participants in exposing them to the ridicule of their peers and the other spectators. But as I was egotistically absorbed in my own failures, I realized that the audience was watching something completely different. They were watching them read. Even an actor with the finest diction would have had problems with the acoustics in the room, and I had failed to observe that it was not the text that the audience was really following. Indeed, when there were only Globo actors on stage the audience was at its most restless. But the moment that one of their own colleagues appeared and began his struggle with the text, there was complete attention: the sort of attention that this play is rarely given at Stratford-upon-Avon. Perhaps just one of the ways in which this performance achieved its power was in the very substitutability of the boys. While I and the other actors involved in the project experienced each of them as individuals who had managed something unique, the audience was able to see them as extensions of what they too might be capable of doing.

At the same time that the text began to expand the ways in which the participants were able to express certain feelings, their work also began to reveal the text itself in different ways. For example, in Act Three, Scene Three, Romeo is waiting, after he has killed Tybalt, for news of what the Prince will decree. Friar Lawrence returns and tells him that he is to be banished, a punishment that shows some leniency from the Prince. But Romeo's reaction is fierce and he is unreconcilable to his fate, as banishment means that he must be separated from Juliet. We began by working on the speech in a group exercise that revealed the violence of Romeo's thoughts in the battering of the verse. After a while we began to look at the meanings of the words. *Banished* was not a word that the group knew, so I talked about people who had been exiled from Brazil in the past. They were quick to add names, and although there were some historical inaccuracies, they were able to identify a variety of Brazilian exiles from pop stars to presidents. Gradually they talked about themselves as being banished and their feelings of separation and desperation. In that moment, the text was revealed for me as much as it was for them.

Such revelations were on every page, almost every line. In a wider sense I learnt something that I had never quite grasped about one of the essential differences between Romeo and Juliet. The way they are linked in the title, the prologue and the narrative tends to make them seem equally balanced in the play. Having twelve juvenile offenders play Romeo against a young and valued star from the telenovelas, ripped asunder this easy equation. Juliet is a much-prized member of her family and her cultural value is enormous, as we see when her father settles her on Paris. Romeo meanwhile may come from a good family, but the way in which others react to him, the company he keeps, and his actions in the early scenes show him to be one of the local delinquents. He is already outside of family and social control. It took this particular version of the play for me to begin to see the ways in which the play operates.

Of course the difference between these Romeos and their Juliet was exploited by the media in the widespread coverage that the presentation received in the newspapers on the following day, and in the subsequent pictures that appeared in the tabloid magazines (Illustration 1). The front page of *O Globo*, with its lead story on a prison rebellion in São Paulo, emphasized the social and political contexts within which this theatre work was being done. A typically dehumanized and animalistic picture of prisoners through bars is set above the photograph of one of the young men from Padre Severino kissing an actress with a copy of Shakespeare's text in his hand. This unexpected image tells an unimaginable story of an impossible encounter that would be beyond the reach of most Brazilians. Just to show these boys reading is in itself a cultural transformation, but it is in the pictures of the kisses that the transgressive sensation is most forcefully evoked.

As Leticia had approached her first kiss at that Monday afternoon performance, I realized that in all the boundaries that we had crossed to come to this moment, there was one border that we all knew was the subject of intense institutional, cultural and personal surveillance. The moment seemed all that more dramatic as the photographers rose, more alert than I had imagined to the verse that prepares for the first kiss, and they were as acutely poised as their sports colleagues awaiting Romário's front-line manoeuvres at Maracana. With the first kiss there was such a battery of clicks and flashes, accompanied by catcalls and cheers from the audience, that I failed to notice what had happened on stage. What I did notice was that Leticia Sabatella adroitly sidestepped the next kissing by skipping some lines (Shakespeare's text as ever directs the stage action). As she returned to her seat at the back of the stage with the other per-formers, she showed no untoward response, but while she waited for her next scene, she was carefully looking through the text. Calculating which Romeos were next in line to kiss her (they were conveniently seated in order of their entrances), she quietly got up and went to talk to each of her Romeos while other scenes were taking place. It was only later that I discovered what was happening.

At the first kiss she had been firmly tongued by her Romeo. As she said to me afterwards, her reaction was simultaneously one of being assaulted but at the same time of wanting to regain control. She did that by jumping the lines, but she wanted to anticipate what might be to come in future scenes. What she said to the Romeos that followed was this: 'You can kiss me for as long as you like, on the lips if you want, but you cannot put your tongue in my mouth. Because it is not theatre. No one will be able to see.' While I was horrified by what I had exposed her to, I was full of admiration at her response. She showed herself as brave, resilient, cre-ative and compassionate as at any moment since I had first invited her to take part in the performance. But she had also reasserted her control to the extent that even in the final scene, when, drugged on the tomb and seemingly in no position to affect how Romeo might kiss her, she still achieved what she wanted. The final Romeo kissed her on the lips in such a way that he seemed unlikely ever to stop. But he crossed no further boundary. As Leticia had explained to him, it would not be theatre. And the borders that were being crossed that day were already sufficient. I sensed then that I could never really be aware of all the complex cultural, political, social and personal negotiations that are going on when that young Brazilian uses Shakespeare's lines to kiss Leticia Sabetella.

The performances that perhaps we all most admire are the ones that involve some kind of risk for those involved. That does not necessarily

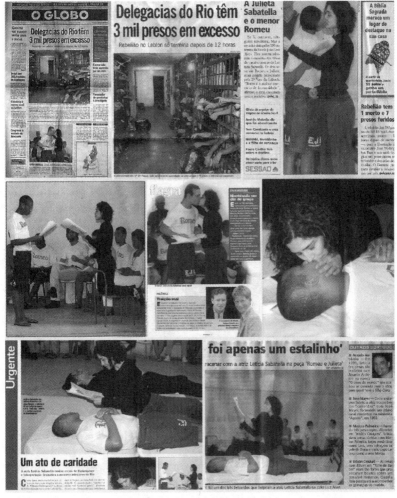

1 Brazilian newspaper coverage of a staged reading of *Romeo and Juliet* by juvenile prisoners in the Instituto Padre Severino on the Ilha do Governador in Rio de Janeiro, in September 1999

mean physical danger, but it must mean a personal investment. If that investment was tested to its limits for Leticia Sabatella, it was similarly dangerous for those young men. As the performance approached I could see how they were putting themselves on the line. To be serious about this work would in itself expose them to potential ridicule. One of the most effective moments for them all was when one of the Romeos began to speak the text without the book. He had, unbeknown to any of us, learnt his lines. He had committed himself to the work. And the audience of peers stopped the play to applaud. It would have been far easier for any of them on stage to have disrupted and disturbed what was happening. To show their 'investment' was the greatest risk. By letting the performance reveal their pleasure as well as their fear, they showed the sort of risk that we always seek, yet so rarely find whenever we go to the theatre. It is in that investment that we see the real consequences of performance that lie beyond the meaning of the play itself. Is that the moment when we are drawn in to become witnesses? When the line between the performer and the task becomes so strong that we cannot resist being pushed or dragged out of our desire to be merely spectators and become the witnesses that will ensure this event has a life beyond that moment?

For that is what a witness does. As Etchells reminds us, the witness ensures that the original moment has a life that goes on. Without the witness to the crime or the accident, it might never be known beyond that moment of action. But in theatre something else is happening because the witnessing is a continuation of the creativity. In contrast to the witness to the crime who is required to suppress all fabrication in an effort to recall most accurately what has happened, the witness to the live performance is not required simply to remember but to carry on the imaginative act. Witnessing is, thus, not simply a means of remembering or documenting, for the performance itself does that in the only effective way possible. Rather, the act of witness is the means by which perform-ance makes a difference. The means by which it matters. My romantic hope is that each of us who participated in that event and each of us who saw it – each of us who read those newspapers and saw those photographs – will carry something forward that makes a difference.

I am sure we all have our own questions that we ask of performance. What does it do for us? What can it do to others? Peter Sellars asked what the dialogue is that performance creates between the stage and society. I hope that the performance I have described shows a way in which we can extend that question and that dialogue. I want to finish with a series of questions that Tim Etchells recorded about the performances that matter to him. They have some resonance for me when I think about that Monday afternoon in the Instituto Padre Severino. Perhaps they will serve to alert us all to what is important in the work that we do:

> When this performance finishes will it matter? Where will it matter? Will the performers carry this with them tomorrow? In their sleep? In their psyche? Does this action, this performance, contain these people (and me) in some strange and perhaps unspeakable way?
>
> I ask of each performance: will I carry this event with me tomorrow? Will it haunt me? Will it change me, will it change things?
>
> If not it was a waste of time.[4]

Perhaps in this moment of those boys performing their Romeos we can see something of the promise that performance makes to us all. A promise that it will not be a waste of time. A promise that it will be carried somewhere: in somebody's sleep, in somebody's psyche. But as I have written elsewhere about theatre in the favelas of Rio, while I want to celebrate all that live performance promises, I also want to notice as it fails. It is in those stolen kisses, as Leticia Sabatella rightly said, that theatre fails: 'You can kiss me for as long as you like, on the lips if you want, but you cannot put your tongue in my mouth. Because it is not theatre. No one will be able to see.' In bringing together a group of juvenile prisoners with a supporting cast of professional actors to perform a rehearsed reading of *Romeo and Juliet*, perhaps we can have a glimpse of an act that calls on us to bear witness. In revealing the stolen kisses I do so not to break the romance of the image of what happened that day, but rather to state again[5] that it is in the 'failures' as much as in the successes that performance truly reveals its promise.

4 Etchells, *Certain Fragments*, p. 49.
5 See Paul Heritage, 'The Promise of Performance: True Love/Real Love', in *Theatre Matters: Performance and Culture on the World Stage*, eds. Richard Boon and Jane Plastow (Cambridge: Cambridge University Press: 1998), pp. 154–76.

A theatre of monsters: live performance in the age of digital media

Matthew Causey

Matthew Causey is Lecturer in Drama at Trinity College Dublin. He is a theatre and new media artist whose writings have been published in *Theater Journal*, *Theater Forum*, *Theater Research International*, *Essays in Theater*, and the *Journal of Dramatic Theory and Criticism*.

2 Trinity College's School of Drama's production of *The Apparatus*, directed by Matthew Causey

The technologies of representation created in the advent of digital elec-tronics and Internet communications have revolutionized the ways in which many people in industrialized countries process information, pic-ture the world and construct identity. Scientists are generating new maps of the interior and exterior of the human body through computerized visualization techniques. The Human Genome Project is charting the DNA structure of the human, while medical corporations patent each strand of that network, creating ownership of the biological system. Researchers now mate human cells with circuitry in a 'bionic chip' and can control the activity of the cell. These revolutions in science and medicine point toward a new construction of the biological as an inter-face with the technological. The 'new human' or 'post-organic' subject combined with the hegemony of the televisual images and virtual envi-ronments creates new manners of conceiving the world and building subjectivity. It is self-evident that as the basic tools of representation and subjectivity are changing so should our manners of creating, teach-ing and researching theatre. Brecht argued that 'the old forms of communication are not unaffected by the development of new ones nor do they survive alongside them'.[1] His argument is that as modes of

3 The Performance
   Technology Research
   Lab's production of *Faust*,
   directed by Matthew
   Causey

4 The Performance
   Technology Research
   Lab's production of
   The Bacchae, directed by
   Matthew Causey

communication change so must the means of devising performance. The theatre, if it wishes to be responsive to contemporary mediatized culture, needs to engage the technologies that have helped to occasion that culture.

The great drama of contemporary western subjectivity might be configured as the transitional process of the human from a solely organic to a technologically integrated entity (bionic, cyborg, etc.). The questions that need pursuing concern the construction of subjectivity, culture, and ideology within the regime of the virtual in the space of technology. Live performance that incorporates digital and interactive media is uniquely situated to represent the conflicts and convergences of the human and technology. What is needed is the creation of hybrid forms of performance, forms of a monstrous theatre that bridge, extend, and explore the gaps between the live and the mediated. Such a theatre would violate the norms of live theatrical performance of the 'here and now' with dislocation and fluidity of narrative, character and theme, both 'here and now' and 'not here and now'. This theatre of monsters is possible through the incorporation of the technologies of digital media in such forms as video, hypertext, interactivity, and virtual presence within live performance. The theatre of monsters is a theatre that is not theatre, but also that is not, not theatre.

The question is often posed as to whether the theatre is in crisis. I do not think that it is. The presentation of 'otherness' on the stage continues its seductive process. The technologies of representation of the theatre, from the mask to the downstage curtain, hold their power to tease and torment with metaphors of consciousness and metonymies of desire. What I have tried to argue above is that it is the human itself that is in crisis as it attempts to understand its position in the space of technology. It is then necessary to call upon the theatre as a discipline to discern the world of the virtual and the boundaries of the televisual, in which so much of western culture has found itself isolated. The dramatic struggle between the material body within a virtual and televisual space can create a dialectic that reveals the underlying issues and ideology of the changing positions of the subject in mediatized culture. The theatre is once again the test site, the replica, or laboratory, in which we can reconfigure our world and consciousness, witness its operations and play with its possibilities.

Artaud writes that 'the theatre like the plague is a crisis which is resolved by death or cure'.[2] If the theatre is in crisis at this point, it has

---

1 Bertolt Brecht, 'The German Drama', in *Brecht on Theater*, ed. John Willett (New York: Hill and Wang, 1964), p. 47.

always been in crisis, as its goal is to instil an urgent turning point in the participants. The urgent turning point of the human immersed in the televisual fields of virtuality is here. We need the theatre to represent that change so we might map the new terrain and approach the construction of a working model. A theatre of technological monsters might make this possible.

2 Antonin Artaud, *The Theater and Its Double*, trans. Mary Caroline Richards (New York: Grove Press, 1958), p. 31.

The moment of realized actuality[1]
Andy Lavender

Andy Lavender is a Senior Lecturer at the Central School of Speech and Drama, and Course Leader of the school's M.A. in Advanced Theatre Practice. Recent writing includes a chapter on experimental theatre in *Theatre in a Cool Climate* (Amber Lane Press, 1999) and *Hamlet in Pieces*, a study of contemporary theatre *auteurs'* (Peter Brook, Robert Lepage and Robert Wilson) approaches to *Hamlet* (Nick Hern Books, 2001). Recent productions as director include *The Singularity* (London International Mime Festival: a one-man show featuring fire effects, video and remote-controlled machinery) and *Blavatsky* (Young Vic Studio, London: a part-devised show combining video, Victorian illusionism and the routines of a magician).

[W]ithin our mediatized culture, whatever distinction we have supposed there to be between live and mediatized events is collapsing because live events are becoming more and more identical with mediatized ones ... What we are seeing in many cases is not so much the incursion of media-derived 'technics' and techniques into the context of live performance but, rather, live performance's absorption of a media-derived epistemology. (Philip Auslander, *Liveness: Performance in a Mediatized Culture*, London and New York: Routledge, 1999, pp. 32–3.)

1 My title is a quotation from an interview given by Peter Sellars. Peter Sellars (in conversation with Veronica Kamp-Hasler and Katrin Klingan), 'Spirituality and Theater', unpublished transcript of interview at the Vienna Festival, 20 May 1998. An edited version of the interview was published as 'The Right to Hope', *Theaterschrift*, No. 13 (September 1998), pp. 79–97. My thanks to Maria M. Delgado for bringing this to my attention.

Instance 1

[OR], presented by dumb type
Barbican Theatre, London, 26 September 1998[2]

A white cyclorama wraps round the back of the stage in three sections, to make a large central screen with an adjoining screen at either side. A woman wearing a white shift dress stands upstage centre, smack against the cyc. A vertical line of light moves round the screen from stage right to stage left; then a widescreen image, spread across the width of the cyc, appears. It shows the view from a car driving along a two-lane freeway in flat country-side, with some trees dotted in the landscape. The point of view, you might say, is that of the car, since there's no sign of windscreen wipers or the car's bonnet as there would be if you were the driver. This is pure drive imagery. There is hardly any other traffic.

With a flash of light the image changes to a hillier roadscape. There is snow on the land. The woman onstage remains stationary. An electronic beep provides an accompaniment. A band of prism-like distortion alters the image (a fault line down its centre) in a vertical strip the width of the woman onstage. A machine-like hum and the speeding landscape signal an increase in veloc-ity. There is a brief segment of computerized jumble on the soundtrack and the image gradually fades to white across the entire stage.

The staging emphasizes the physical dimensions of the woman. Her body looks small against the huge image – but oddly enough this human form is the only thing which does not move, which remains stable. The white dress 'takes' the projection so that the woman blends in with the image. The woman herself is a screen, and she is 'blank' throughout. But she remains other, different, a human in a technologized domain. This isn't simply the world of video projection and computer machinery; it is also the world of video games (the image looks something like a racing simu-lation) and the world of the car (a wider mythology, here). The imagery, then, evokes the teenager's bedroom and amusement arcades, but also seems to be escaping these things, driving out into the hills. It conjures up speed and flight, but also emptiness. It is directional – the car is going somewhere – and aimless.

The distortion of the image renders it strange and playful but also subjects it to the corporeal presence of the woman. It is disturbed in order to fit, spatially, with one dimension of the figure onstage. Woman and image are implicated. The scene might be in the memory of the woman. Or not. Perhaps she is being travelled to. Perhaps she imagines the whole thing. Perhaps she is 'irrelevant', an ironical folly in a show by

---

2 Dates are those on which I saw the respective productions.

postmodern people. But her very presence means that meanings percolate shadily without being asserted or denied. Without her, the scene would be more bland, less interesting. She is the grain of sand in the oyster shell.

Instance 2

[OR], presented by dumb type

One by one, four performers place deckchairs on the stage which show up brightly against the white cyc. They lounge in the deckchairs. A projection begins, again taking the full width of the cyc, showing images of city life filmed by a moving camera. The images are indistinct, swiftly-edited glimpses of the streets, traffic and buildings of a typical late-industrial city. The low front-projection source means that the deckchairs are silhouetted on the screen.

Evident contrasts are in play. The performers have a rhythm different from that of the images. They arrange seats and recline in them. They renounce the bustle of city life. But they are simultaneously bound up with it – their very placing on the stage implicates them in the urban buzz. Their repose might be that of city dwellers on holiday, or beach worshippers who shun the pace of the metropolis. Perhaps it indicates a state of mind, a calmness in the face of the city's relentless drive. The shadows of the deckchairs make the city seem oddly organic. On the one hand, bustle. On the other, rest.

Instance 3

10 Backwards, presented by Blast Theory
Institute of Contemporary Arts (ICA), London,
11 May 1999

The audience sits in traverse formation along two sides of a square playing area. At either end of this stage is a screen, one larger than the other. A performer sits at a table centre-stage. A photo of her younger self is shown on the smaller screen. A camera, operated by a man, views the table from high over her shoulder. The woman, meanwhile, cuts up a television listings page. This action is shown live on the larger screen. A voice-over says, 'She's making her perfect evening.' The image of the photo on the smaller screen is divided, then quartered, to include another photo image, a woman who might be the performer's/character's mother.

The image on the larger screen changes to show shots of an urban cityscape – a road, street lamps, a river. There is a Docklandish feel. It is night and the colours are predominantly greys and yellows. Onstage, the performer and the man talk. In the story, he is her stepbrother, staying over. The smaller screen now shows stop-frames of the performer in spasm and/or laughing. She mirrors these postures, facing the screen, sliding from one posed tableau to another.

The staging shows many times and places at once. We see the woman's younger self in relation to her present self and an older woman. She is indoors, whilst we see what could be the environment outside. She is a character, engaging in dialogue with another character. But she is also a performer, quoting, by her fixed postures, a body in *raptus*, moments of sudden biomechanical activity just as suddenly stopped. The snapshots echo the stop-frames – time is captured, but the performer reproduces this capture – captures it all over again – live. As with the sorting of TV programmes, things are scrutinized and fixed. In a time-shift culture, where we can create our ideal TV schedule by videoing the shows we want to watch, here is a staging which shifts a series of time-moments and spaces into a single present and place.

Instance 4

10 Backwards, presented by Blast Theory

The performer stands centrally in front of the larger screen. She has placed the camera tripod centre-stage on a revolve. She talks to the camera. The screen shows an urban backdrop of flats alongside a small park. The performer's image also appears onscreen (a chroma-key effect). The picture of the performer is paused. As the revolve continues to move, so the camera films the performer from an increasingly different angle and perspective. There is a jump-cut to a new, slightly altered image of the woman. Because of the configuration of the camera angle and subject, her body now appears to one side of the screen, looking slightly away.

The performer is implicated into the outdoors environment but simultaneously kept separate. Her image isn't in direct, proportional relation with the picture of the outdoors – there's no attempt to pretend that she is 'actually' standing in the street. Simply, there is a performer and there is a street, both appearing on the same screen, both in the same staging, but both in different proportions and spatial realms.

The stilled image of the performer instantly creates a divorce between the woman and her picture. She is live. Her image is clearly conveyed now by this particular camera – except that it is also already out of date, superseded. The woman herself becomes *more* live, therefore, in relation to her paused self on screen. By jump-cutting the screen shows the woman from a different perspective, even though the shot is continuous and the woman hasn't moved. (The vision mixer operator pauses a subsequent image of the woman, and cuts from the first still to the second.) The arrangement emphasizes the woman's static position by drawing attention to the camera's discreet movement. What is being staged here? Presence, stillness, alteration, continuity, discontinuity – all at once.

A familiar view has it that screened images in the theatre always take precedence over anything else that's onstage. They grab the eye, they are more compelling to watch, they diminish the presence of the live per-formers and the theatrical action. This is true of a fairly straightforward use onstage of film and video, which you might watch in the same manner as you watch a TV or cinema screen – that is, the screen itself con-tains everything you need in order to understand the import of its images. But in more developed (or perhaps, simply, 'established') mixed media performance that isn't the case. Here, the screened images work only by virtue of their relationship with actual live bodies, staged action and the larger theatrical space. So whilst theatre events are increasingly mediatized, elements of other media in live performance are themselves being theatricalized.

My focus here is specifically the meeting between stage and screen (so I shall use the term 'mixed media performance', rather too loosely, simply to refer to this particular combination of media). Can we still talk at all of two different media – theatre and video – coming together like partners on a dance floor in order to have their spin as separate bodies? I'm not sure. Increasingly they intermingle like liquids which colour each other. And as spectators (remembering that spectators need to be trained) we're growing more accustomed to seeing them combine. We're increasingly able to watch mixed media performance *differently* from the way in which we watch theatre, television, cinema or video (although we watch it saturated with understandings learned from all four).

I've chosen the instances above, from productions by leading multi-media companies in Japan (dumb type) and Britain (Blast Theory), for two reasons. Firstly, they show how the merging of screen and stage can achieve effects of liveness. Secondly, they demonstrate a crucial feature of mixed media performance: an intrinsic plurality-effect in representation. To put it simply, different things are happening in different ways at once. Nobody writing about these issues can ignore Philip Auslander's critically alert book, *Liveness*. Auslander, likewise, refers to Walter Benjamin's cele-brated essay of 1936, 'The Work of Art in the Age of Mechanical Repro-duction'. By way of pulling some threads together (too briefly!), I want to suggest some of the things that happen at the point of mergence between media, and consider (after Benjamin) how this might relate to our historical moment – which in turn shapes our own modes of perception as consumers/spectators.

Auslander suggests that, whilst mediatization owes much to an 'ontology of liveness' derived from the early phase of television, '[t]he ubiquity of reproductions of performances of all kinds has led to the depreciation of live presence'.[3] I am not sure of the extent to which liveness has been downgraded in cultural activity. A continuing feature of television news is its ability to go live to the scene of a significant event or a site close to centres of power – the ubiquitous broadcast from the lawn of the White House or the street outside 10 Downing Street. The growth of twenty-four-hour news broadcasting suggests a fetishization of immediacy (information – have it now!). Even instant replays in sports stadia (on one hand the displacement of the live in favour of the recorded) are designed to enhance the in-the-moment pleasure of the spectator. The fidelity and improved focus of the replay extends the moment of truth. It is a question of quality. The similarity between twenty-four-hour news programmes, the sports replay and the point of mergence in mixed-media performance is that they all guarantee you access to nowness, to the moment of actuality.

An experience of liveness is partly a question of being in fuller possession of this moment, having and holding it more completely. Liveness, and its sibling nowness, underwrite contemporary consumer culture. They are the temporal equivalent of goods and possessions. There are two ways in which we can pursue time as a commodity. The first is to attain seemingly more of it – to live longer, have lengthier periods of leisure, enjoy more 'quality' time. The second is to experience more fully the present moment – 'live in the now', as people, from Buddhists to hedonists, say. In a routinely capitalist culture we might expect to trade time – to exchange our goods, our labour or our monies for chunks of time-to-ourselves (whether on holiday or in retirement). But late capitalism has introduced diversification into commodity control and ownership. We both own more of the world, as shoppers and shareholders, and less of it, as individuals in increasingly denationalized and corporatized economies. Something similar has happened to our experience of time. We have more of it. And there is, to put it anecdotally, never enough of it. Which means that the experience of nowness has become a defining feature of our relationship to time.

For theatre, this counts in two ways. Firstly, of course, we speak of the presence of the performer. This can be thought of as a state of *being-here*

---

3 Auslander, *Liveness*, p. 36.

– distinguished, in much recent criticism, from conventional character-based theatre, where the actor is not here entirely as herself (whoever that might be) but represents someone else. In performances where characters aren't necessarily fixed or do not figure at all, we are in the face of the performer's presence rather than her 'pretence'. A phenomenological understanding of performance follows hot on this particular trail, emphasizing presence's etymological echo of nowness, the singularity of experience in the present tense. And this brings us to the second way in which presence matters – which is, of course, for the spectator. A series of effects in mixed media performance guarantees that the spectator's own sense of present-ness is expanded.

Theatre has always traded in nowness, and at various points in its history has developed new ways in which to heighten the spectator's awareness of the present moment. Think of the utterances of the chorus in Greek tragedy, the witty asides of Renaissance drama, the impressive scenic transformations of nineteenth-century spectacular theatre and the reality effects of early naturalism. Mixed media performance – in its 'established' (but not its 'early') stage – is no different. Its mediated effects, working in relation to the theatrical, help to emphasize the liveness and the nowness of the event. The spectator is made hyperaware of the presence of the performers' bodies, the configurations of stage space, the actual moment of (re)presentation. What, in traditional terms, was one's excitement at beholding the spectacle and marvelling at its achievement – an old pleasure – is achieved all over again through new means.

I am not trying to say, nostalgically, that theatre is the master-medium because it is always live. But it does seem evident that any performance in the theatrical frame is immediately subject to the theatre's non-recordedness (that is, you watch it in the present moment). Any material drawn from film, video or computer graphics (some – but not all – of which might be prerecorded) is *staged* as part of the live event. And this staging, which is tailored to the perceptual capacities of modern people, is shaped in another way by late capitalist culture.

It is difficult to say, so close to the event, whether *[OR]* or *10 Backwards* have a passive relationship to the mediatized culture which spawned them, or make space for more critical perspectives. What does seem clear, however, is that they are inherently volatile. In mixed media performance there is a state of always being simultaneously elsewhere, of being doubled, of being better (more clearly and largely represented), of immediately presenting another angle. Mixed media performance presents spatial continuity (the stage remains the same) and discontinuity (screen space is fundamentally different from stage space). This is a *multiple* the-atre, where perspectives, ontological states, and meanings themselves are not only plural but simultaneously so.

How characteristic of late capitalism. Advanced reproducibility has made for serial possession (we can all own that new marque of Nike train-ers, the complete set of Pokemon cards) and even serial being (we can all be like – well, name your favourite celebrity). More tellingly, we can eat Thai food with French wine followed by an Italian dessert and Colom-bian coffee. Damian Hirst's restaurant, Pharmacy, in London's Notting Hill, wears its name well as an eatery which looks more like an upmarket retro chemist's workshop. If you walk a little further along the high street you pass an estate agent which looks somewhat like an American diner. Ours is a culture of buildings, objects, spaces and events which advertise themselves whilst pointing elsewhere, trailing shadows whose shapes are other than their own. As consumers within this culture we are post-choice, possessing not just a single option but the whole range of options, both having and eating our cake.

It is hardly surprising, then, that the intersection between theatre and new technologies, between the live and the mediatized, between stage and screen, celebrates multiplicity at the very point of media merging. Faced with a plurality of representational modes and meaning-effects, the spec-tator experiences a frisson of pleasure – *now* – at the wonderful syn-chronicity of their realization. This is one effect of the mediatization of the theatre. It goes hand in hand with the theatricalization of non-theatre sources. And the ground of such pleasure is the evanescent live event, as palpably fabricated as it is beautifully real.

IV

Looking forward, looking back: theatre and the spiritual, messages to a new world

---

When an angel goes through the stage

Jon Fosse

Jon Fosse (b. 1959) is a Norwegian poet, writer and playwright. He has published some thirty books. His plays *And We'll Never Be Parted*, *The Child*, *Someone Is Going To Come*, *The Name*, *Nightsongs*, *The Son*, *A Summer's Day* and *Autumn Dream* are, among others, translated into English. His complete plays are being published by Oberon Books.

In Hungary, I've been told, they often say that when a night in the theatre was good, an angel went through the stage, one time, two times, many times. And for me this moment is the most important thing about the theatre, and a thing which no other art form has, this moment when an angel goes through the stage.

What happens in those moments?

Of course I don't know, no one does, because it just happens, or it just does not happen; one night it happens at that part of the play, the next night in another part.

For me these intense and clear moments, although they are hardly explainable, are moments of understanding, moments when the people who are present, the actors, the audience, together experience something which makes them understand something they never before have understood, at least not as they now understand it.

But this understanding is not mainly intellectual, it is a kind of emotional understanding which, as I have said, can hardly be explained intellectually. It probably can't be explained, it can just be shown, it's an understanding through emotions.

When I write for the theatre I want to write plays which are so written that they can evoke these intense clear moments, often moments of deep, deep sorrow – but also often moments which call for laughter in their clumsy humanity.

To me it looks as if I write plays which are very narrow, are very closed – in their story, in their atmosphere, in their provinciality. I also paradoxically write plays that are very open, plays that are so basic that they can evoke moments when the closed dynamics in the play open up – into tears, into laughter. For me the genuine drama is there, it is not in the action as such, it is in the enormous tension and intensity between people who are far away from each other and at the same time are deeply together, not only socially, but also in a shared understanding.

These moments, this incredible presence, is very little, almost not, connected to the central themes of the time, that is, what is spoken about in the media. Good theatre can be about almost anything. The important thing is not what it is about, but how it is about it. It's a question of sensibility, musicality and thinking, not a discussion of current items. And I think that's one of the reasons why the classics have such a strong position in at least European theatre, a much stronger position than the classics have for instance in the world of the novel.

But then why write for the theatre? Perhaps because every epoch produces a new kind of sensibility, a new kind of musicality and thinking.

A contemporary play, a good one, must in a way show a never-before seen sensibility, musicality and thinking, it must bring to the world something that was already there but which one hadn't seen. In other words, a good playwright must have his or her very own voice, as one usually puts it.

Art, and also theatre playwriting – if it is an art, and not merely entertainment or education or political discussion – must of course say what it has to say mainly by its form, and I mean form in a very wide sense, so to speak more as an attitude than as a concept.

What is content for the others is form for the artist, as Nietzsche said.

Now I do almost speak as if I were a man of theory, I'm not. I'm a practical man, a practical writer. And that's another reason why I like writing for the theatre so much. Theatre is very concrete, you can't cheat as a playwright; you have to give the right stuff, you can't hide behind one or another abstraction, ideological, political or whatever.

And as a man of the highest abstraction, Friedrich Hegel, once wrote: *Die Wahrheit ist immer konkret.* The truth is always concrete.

Bad glamour
Erik Ehn

Erik Ehn is married to scenic artist Pat Chanteloube, the charge at the Berkeley Rep. Ehn's plays include *Heavenly Shades of Night Are Falling*, *Wolf at the Door*, *The Moon of the Scarlet Plums*, *The Saint Plays*, *Erotic Curtsies* and *Chokecherry*. He is a graduate of New Dramatists.

Questions about the state of the art are backed by an anxiety over a loss of the unique. The problem of the unique is a problem of ownership. The more art is made and held in common, the less likely are individual works to achieve distinction; the longer the boom in popular participation, the less likely a generation or era is to achieve distinction. The evils of economic globalization are mirrored by utopian instincts towards a universal family. In the arts, what we call success is a hallmark of what we call decline. Antidote then does not wait in a will roused to fulfil old models of success, but in an inspired science of failure. Failure will reverse decline. First, how good everything is.

Success

More plays

More people are writing plays than ever before, I guess (others guess likewise – Mac Wellman, for example; the same has been observed in the field of poetry); literary offices are glutted. Many plays are good and some are great; many propose new arts of perception and means of interaction; they often invite the invention of novel forms of production. History waits to be made in every pile of a thousand unsolicited scripts … and history is kept waiting behind the veil of form rejections. Of course. The remarkable novel is unrecognizable in the obscene novel mass. Determining the unusual lies beyond the faculties of this age. The poly-ness of our polymorphousness avails on delight; we are swamped by morphousness.

We generate excellent works of art; we have lost a cultural space for The Excellent Work. This is not the day of cathedrals; it is the day of rental apartments. We are achieving McGreatness.

I eat fast food and I need an apartment. My desire is proper to my time.

We fall into trouble when all sensitivity is chewed between the counter-grinding gears of globalization and utopianism. If individuals and their products are no longer discernible, if persons are less famous, then we can either release attachment to ambition and quality, or grow ambitious for the fame of the world itself. We can make a move from a mass of individual owners and consumers to a freedom from ownership and private use. We are prepared at last for the bliss of facelessness.

More 'ever before' than ever before

On some scales, theatre is abating as a cultural force. But art in general is more available than ever before. Commonplaces: books and music are available online, poetry is published on posters in the subway, parades and festivals draw large crowds, and cities everywhere have symphonies. Theatre can selfishly lament a loss of audience, or celebrate the evolution of modes of participation. We are weak as a separate craft; we are stronger than ever if we see ourselves as one integral element in a new construction. Again, nothing is famous because everything is famous. Advocacy for theatre is antique and secular. Advocate for receptivity. Cause response by any means. If the term 'theatre' falls away, will there be a genuine net loss in human affect? Why are we so precious with our small set of habits?

Freed from 'Theatre', we will find theatre as it lives in nature. Theatre's true and secret soul will come upon us when we stop bullying it from the sidelines.

I also hear that some theatres are filled with more subscribers than ever before. A puzzling anomaly. More demand (for Great Plays), and less supply. But subscriber numbers do not fairly gauge the demand for art. Jeff Jones points out that subscribers are anathema to adventure. They have money, and can predict where they will be months in advance. They are by definition *derrière-garde*, and inhibit the evolution of the form – if you define evolution as progress. A caution here: evolution-as-progress is the appropriation of the social Darwinists. Evolution is not recognized in advances only; evolution is simply adaptation. Our art form could be evolving without delivering any startling innovations or clear-cut improvements. Our addiction to supremacy as a value is a huge source of grief. Theatre's best-interest adaptations promote economy of energy, humility, and plurality.

Safety

Universities provide practising artists with a sense of place. Increasingly, they are our key patrons. However, a great work is *out of place* and creates its own context. A university is designed to be so noisy, chaotic, and howlingly self-referential that all it produces will only ever contribute to the promotion of the university, and not the distinction of the artist or any other element of the real.

This is a boon. The real, during this time of rapid shifts in the culture, is sore and dysfunctional. Without the relative safety of academia's (highly politicized, faux-deep, creature-comfort rich) environment, too many practising artists would fail to thrive; would lack sufficient strength on re-release into the wild.

Massive is good

This is human destiny. There is no going back.

I don't believe any of this

- One revolution: workers arise. Another revolution: workers submerge. One revolution: improve all wages. Another revolution: abandon the wage system. One revolution: trade unionism. Another revolution: one big union. One revolution: spiritual athleticism. Another revolution: spiritual weakness (grace dependence).
- I don't care about human destiny. There is another destiny.
- I am pleased by the availability of art. I am dedicated to the secrecy of art.
- Broken, secret and defeated art is highly mobile, and everywhere, though naturally everywhere nearly invisible (Daniel Alexander Jones celebrates the quasi-transparency of Wonder Woman's plane). A goal: an experimental theatre in every city over 10,000 in the next twenty-five years. Smaller theatre cells in remote outposts (regardless of civic support) derive strength from an awareness of their *artistic* context – membership in a global society of personalist radicals, who have beaten bodily from the market.
- Society has to work. Culture doesn't. Success is social. Effective art inspires an inconsistent set of new rules by breaking the old. The unique, the great, is no longer available in the social sphere. I admire greatness. Greatness takes the quality of shadows now. Greatness is chthonic. Our god is neither Apollo nor Dionysus: she is Persephone. Our bard is not Orpheus but Eurydice.
- Theatre will never move towards economy of energy. It thrills in ridiculous extremes of effort. We have created it to have an arena that truly exhausts us.

- Every artist inside, must be outside-inside. For example, artists in schools must be committed first to learning (learning themselves and awakening learning in others).
- Learning is always anti-institutional.
- No wages (no box office). Self for others (not self as others). Not a fringe but a corona (the practical life of a star is in its outermost, out-reaching rim – another Daniel Alexander Jones image).
- Theatre participates with no other art. Theatre appropriates all other arts. Theatre is not turning into performance, or fragmenting into proliferating genres. Theatre is in the process of learning how to appropriate various innovations.
- There is no such thing as facelessness (even masks are charged). Face-less theatre is the theatre of war. War is the popular theatre, and it advertises its aesthetic to the civilian world relentlessly. Theatre-theatre is anti-pop. Also anti-punk, because you really have to be able to play. First, theatre is excellent in a way appropriate to identity. Then it is given away. Excellent first, accessible later. The face, and then the face you had before you were born.
- Pursue internationalism. Communicate across borders without a common language (including the language of money). Here utopi-anism trumps globalization – we are not about the easy transfer of standard commodities – we are about interrupting difficulty with difficulty. No commodities; syllables don't match. What we hold in common is unreachable by commercial convention.
- None of these ideas are new. The revolution (the alternate revolu-tion, the wobbly revolution) is in progress.

Heat bath
Matthew Maguire

Matthew Maguire is a co-artistic director of Creation Production Company in New York City. His work includes *The Memory Theatre of Giulio Camillo*, in the Anchorage of the Brooklyn Bridge; *The Tower* (Sun and Moon Press, 1993); *Phaedra* (Sun and Moon Press, 1996); and *Throwin' Bones* (Performing Arts Journal, 1999), which won an America Award for outstanding play of 1997. He created with Philip Glass and Molissa Fenley *A Descent Into the Maelstrom* for Australia's Adelaide Festival. An alumnus of New Dramatists, he teaches playwriting at Fordham University. He won an OBIE for performance in 1998.

Is the theatre in crisis?

The death of theatre is an ongoing process subject to the laws of entropy; it will not be brief, but it will be exciting.

> Somehow, after all, as the universe ebbs towards its final equilibrium in the featureless heat bath of maximum entropy, it manages to create interesting structures.[1]

The theatre will last centuries, perhaps for ever. Will it always seem to be dying? Always. Theatre has perpetually been in crisis because of its evanescence. As Beckett would say, we 'give birth astride of a grave, the light gleams an instant, then it's night once more'. Microsoft can hope to gain permanent market share; the theatre never. It resists commodification in its bones, bones lighter than air. Because it is always vanishing in the moment, it is simple to see it as endangered, but its fragility is an illusion. It will never face extinction because it is not solid. It is an impulse. The history of its censorship reveals that the impulse to create theatre is endlessly renewable. Examples such as the Puritans burning all the London theatres to the ground in 1642 demonstrate that the more the theatre is attacked the more its power grows. There will be future moments when the theatre will seem to be eclipsed, yet it will only have moved underground, historically a fertile womb. Witness the Eastern Europeans' secret living-room theatre during the Cold War.

So the problem of the theatre is always the problem of the wider culture. When the Puritans burnt the theatres, branding them 'chapels of Satan', was the theatre in crisis? ['You betcha', said the ashes to the ember.] We can't isolate the crisis in the theatre without recognizing its interrelationship to its community, now a national, even a global one.

To identify the root of a crisis we use the technique of Deep Throat, that shadowy guide to the core of the Watergate scandal: 'Follow the money.' Watching a corrupt Congress fight to block campaign finance reform, it becomes ever clearer that our society is in a craven embrace with cash. Material products like silicon and crude oil drive our consciousness. Our legal system protects property as the highest value. We are rooted in the corporeal. Thus, the commercial origin of our collective image system. We are in danger of abandoning the pursuit of democracy because it is too chaotic. Chaos is bad for business. We sold our freedom for the myth of order. The myth of order has a perfect surface, and we are beguiled by surfaces. The surfaces are getting slicker and slicker. How can the arts compete in the commodities exchange? By recognizing that our

---

1 James Gleick, *Chaos* (New York: Penguin, 1987), p. 308.

new patronage represents the corporatization of the theatre, and by offering an alternative vision.

As black lung is to coal miners so is the ideology of corporations to American theatre. Like other occupational hazards, black lung and corporatization do not afflict all miners or all theatres. The percentage that succumb depends upon overall conditions. With the rising power of the corporation expect the percentage to rise. Black lung afflicts miners because the coal dust is pervasive in the air they breathe. There is no cataclysmic event or virus that can be pointed to as the cause. In the same way, the ideology of the corporation has become pervasive in the climate of our theatres. Because the damage is invisible to the eye, some say there is none, just as the mine owners once refused to acknowledge black lung.

In the last twenty years institutionalization was the pervasive dust. Focus was drawn from art and given to the creation of self-justifying bureaucratic structures. As Chief Executive Officers (CEOs) joined the boards of theatres, the agendas of corporations and theatres began to merge. The corporation believes that the homogenization of society is necessary for the maximization of profit. Just as hard news is disappearing on TV in favour of sound bites, supposed human interest stories, and the Hollywood Minute, so pressure is on the theatres to conform to a standard that keeps cash registers ka-chinging. The agenda of the corporation is a social order organized around three laws for its clients/citizens: Consume. Reproduce. Conform.

It was inevitable that the Berlin Wall would fall. On the plus side, people who believe in some form of socialist alternative no longer need to labour under the onerous example of the Soviet model, but there is a burden the arts suffer for the fall of the wall. Public perception, carefully modulated by the media, is that the event was a total victory for capitalism, 'the end of history'. This has created a climate in which everything is valued in relation to the market.

Corporations fear that because art is non-material it removes us, however temporarily, from our greatest goal: consumption. Plays that are socially and politically challenging are not conducive to the feeling of well-being that motivates the purchaser. Exercising their will to commodify', corporations have also exacerbated the real-estate problem. The physical plant is crucial to a theatre's identity. Not a property owner? Then move along.

Wrestling this hydra exacts a price, so we must find strategies to fight burnout. The first is to see the larger pattern. Victimization increases when isolated people, seeing only their own quandary, fail to understand the wider context: the corporatization of America. For example: what's happening in the farm crisis is analogous to the theatre's plight. Small, independent, family-run farms can't compete with agribusiness and are going under at alarming rates. The crisis in small business: the little grocery fails when Walmart moves in. The crisis in education: small independent public schools, like the Bronx New School, highly successful in its neighbourhood, are forced to close because they don't conform. Diversity is under attack in every sphere by the forces of homogenization.

Why is a diversity of alternative visions desirable? Finding the struggles of environmentalists analogous, I see the controversy over the spotted owl as instructive. Many people argued that since there are so many species of owl, what does one less matter, especially weighed against the loss of jobs? The answer is that erosion is a dangerous process that accelerates geometrically. Since all the elements of a system are interdependent, the loss of one will trigger further loss. Similarly in the theatre, many are willing to concede the attrition of small theatres, thinking it an inevitable consequence of their inability to build a protective base, but eventually the loss of small theatres will artistically bankrupt the large ones. When large theatres are as ready to fight for an endangered small theatre as environmentalists were for the spotted owl, then our necessary ecology will be enriched.

'Maximize profit' is the corporate mantra. Due to polite discretion this pervasive ideology has been translated in the not-for-profit theatre as 'maximize growth'. Indeed, corporations are growing. A drama of life as a food chain plays out as small productive corporations are snatched up in hostile takeovers with leveraged buyouts, saddled with immense debt, and abandoned when their productivity fails due to lack of capital. But in ecosystems balance depends upon the maintenance of stable levels. Excessive growth of any one group will endanger the balance.

Corporate marketing has found that sponsorship is a dirt-cheap way to buy exposure. The strings attached to modest grants usually require the theatre to spend resources to satisfy the sponsor's visibility. After stroking the sponsor a theatre's net gain is diminished. We in the theatre are whores, and not even smart ones, never even haggling for a higher price. Since general operating support is boring for the corporation, their largesse has become project related. An exciting example for them is: 'The Mainstream Rep and Monsanto present'. This means tailoring the season to suit separate sponsors, and more pressure to abandon seasons with an arc of interrelationships because those plays fail to buff the sponsor's image.

Corporate grants also co-opt in more insidious ways. Philip Morris, for example, buys silence with its grants, many of which are minimal, but having accepted the money, many artists who might otherwise speak out against the criminal effects of the company's product on the national health are silent.

Corporate support often fails to repeat; theatres are left flat. The agenda which the toppling of the wall opens up is the dismantling of all the safety nets. Witness Clinton's leadership in the dismantling of the welfare system. And that goes for culture as well. If you're not 'too big to fail', and your bottom line ain't pretty no more, you're dead meat. Modern capitalism must be hyperflexible in its fluidity. Corporate planners intone that long-term investments in intangibles are counter-productive to net gain. That ain't no jive.

Hitler and Stalin knew the value of culture. 'Art was central to their world view', says Klaus Goldmann, chief curator of Berlin's Museum for Pre- and Early History. 'The Nazis and the Soviets went at it with equal vigor on the theory that if you destroy a people's art, then you destroy their historical identity and confidence' ('The Heist of 1945', *Newsweek*, July 15, 1991). We don't need Hitler or Stalin. We're doing it to ourselves. The primary henchmen of corporations – Congress and the media – have found that attacks on culture help to advance nationalism. And nationalism is the trophy wife of corporate life.

I'm not naive about patronage. Pope Julius forced Michelangelo to paint the fig leaves on the Sistine ceiling. Shakespeare had to write the histories to please Queen Elizabeth. Their patrons were no less autocratic. But instead of religion or politics, our patron's power base is economic, and like the mercantile class out of which it rises, its taste is more bourgeois, banal, and short-sighted. Jasper Johns once said, artists are the elite of the servant class. I suppose it's a matter of taste, but if I had to choose a master I'd rather serve Elizabeth or Julius than the dollar.

As the capitalist system grows ever more distorted, it will generate, against its will, a yearning for a sense of life not defined as a transaction, and the arts will gain in power. As Heiner Müller said, 'Consumerism is not a dream. People who don't dream go mad.'

So, yes, we have a crisis. What should we do?

Fight fire with fire

I'm not suggesting that theatres avoid corporations. As corporations attempt to shape and mould theatres, so should theatres seek to reform corporations. After all, we're talking about the capitalist model; buying and selling is a two-way street. Why should artists be so passive and allow corporations to always set the agenda? Artists should leverage corporations in the same way that consumer groups affect change. Theatres should adopt Ralph Nader's strategies: public boycotts and public rewards. Theatres should boldly advertise that they accept donations from progressive corporations, and that they do not accept donations from tobacco, nuclear power, or from companies engaged in child labour. Major foundations, such as Ford, Rockefeller, and Pew, should be persuaded to fund arts groups to study how funding could be increased from socially responsible corporations and phased out from destructive ones. The flagship theatres should aggressively lobby their corporate donors to drop their carcinogenic products and practices.

To the argument that all money is tainted, therefore distinction is arbitrary, I say some money is more tainted than others. The tobacco companies are the cause of millions of deaths every year. This money is obviously more stained than the profits of a solar energy company. No one is pure but there is a spectrum. Draw a line. Publicize it. The answer, 'I didn't make the world', is defeatist. The world is evolving all the time, one way or another. The question, how can we produce this year without their funding? is answered by the question, how can you accept the dustbowl down the road if you don't make change now? A farmer is advised to irrigate and build erosion barriers. He says, 'If I do I won't be able to plant my crop in time'. But if he doesn't he'll have no crop at all in three years. Artists should accept short-term loss for long-term gain.

Embrace hope

I feel like Dr Jekyll and Mr Hyde. Hyde is savagely eager to see it all come crashing down. Jekyll, searching for something to counter him, seizes upon the thin reed of hope inherent in the ultimate unpredictability of the world: ya never know what's gonna happen. In bleak moments the hope that the theatre can ever thrive in this blighted culture seems a pathological delusion; the only clean approach is to dynamite the thing and build from the rubble. However, if the world continues to change at hyperspeed – and ya never know what's gonna happen – then why not embrace the real hope that rapid change contains?

Embrace history

Writing is a time capsule, a message sent forward in time. The paradox of a classic play is that it reveals that the time we know has passed is still present. *Hamlet* provides us with a breathing image of 1600 and we sense that time is now. Perhaps it's an illusion that time passes. The breath of a classic is the enigma of time. As theatre artists dedicated to advancing the form we mustn't forget this whirligig. Hamlet is continuously reinvented in successive presents. The nineteenth century was passed on to the twentieth when Gertrude Stein watched Edwin Booth play Hamlet in San Francisco and discovered that two things could happen at the same time.

We can't fail if we take as our guide Ezra Pound's dictum, 'Make it new'. However, as we anticipate the future we must remember to digest our sources. Some artists believe that to progress they must kill their artistic parents. Imagine how much faster we might progress if we subsumed them instead of denying them. No artist is without antecedent. The avant-garde is a steady stream of births during which the new is created by the transformation of existing ideas. Today emerges from yesterday: O'Neill is already in Strindberg. History is the connective tissue.

Imagine an alternative reality

Work the margins – step back and reflect long enough to visualize an evolutionary move. This may take a long time, but, as the classics show us, we have all the time we need.

Expose the apolitical

Artists must abandon the fallacy that their function is to record reality without political filters. Those supposedly apolitical artists nurture the myth that their art is unmediated; that reflecting the world through the lens of class would impede the flow of the straight stuff. However, the unmediated is an illusion; there's no such beast. When we're taking dictation from the muse, we're mainlining heavy doses of received culture: habits, idioms, and patterns imposed from infancy. Not to retool these filters is to accept the virtual reality goggles of our socialization.

Become an expert on censorship

Theatre has always been the conscience of its society. That function was eroded in the US by McCarthyism and the blacklists. The American theatre is still attempting to recover. Cutting a theatre's funding is only one form of censorship. One of our greatest challenges is to confront the amazing variety of censorship in American society.

Amnesia – since our art is an art of memory, perhaps the greatest censorship of all: the massive amnesia of our society, embodied metaphorically in the image of a popular former president serving out his term in the grips of Alzheimer's.

Ghettoization – there has never been a more difficult time to sustain radical work in terms of salaries and real estate. Insane rents strangle alternative visions.

Co-optation – to survive, many theatres flack for the corporate Medici. Instead of leading their communities in progressive directions, the CEOs that dominate the boards have used the theatres to create bastions of conservatism.

Eclipse – I heard Ariel Dorfman speak of a time when Pinochet forbade newspapers to publish photos of secret police, so the Chilean papers printed black blocks and coined them the 'black holes of Pinochet'. Dorfman warned that in the US we have far more insidious means of censorship: the technicolor holes of prime time. In the past the radical actions of the avant-garde made headlines. Now the media and the corporate dynasties that control it have become more sophisticated and have seized the mass consciousness so powerfully that our chance for meaningful impact is in crisis.

Selective tolerance – we can yell on our soapbox and no will mind. I recall when Pinochet put seventy-seven actors in Chile on a death list. That was a recognition of the power he felt theatre held. In the US one of our great challenges is to fight the despair of irrelevance. The antidote for this despair is that tenet of chaos theory, the butterfly effect: the flap of a butterfly's wing in Beijing can set a Kansas cyclone spiralling. An individual voice can amplify over time, as Rosa Parks's act of refusing to move to the back of the bus helped to spark the civil rights movement.

Attack the theatre

I'd never suggest that the theatre is perfect and we must direct all our attacks outwardly. No, the theatre is a leaky corpse. Our heroes were iconoclasts, so must we be. Attacks on the theatre have always provoked brilliant change, as in Artaud, Stein, Brecht, and Grotowski. Historically, there has always been a healthy and deep-rooted ambivalence towards the theatre from within its own practitioners. The purpose of the avant-garde is to carry on an intense pursuit of reality. Question everything. To do so we must tear ourselves from the equations that bind.

Resist experimental orthodoxy

One of the joys of current alternative work is that the arena has become deeply pluralistic; no one is compelled to speak in the official avant-garde dialect. This has not always been the case. The art cops of the past, from André Breton to Clement Greenberg, would bare their fangs when an artist broke ranks. Break their fangs. Chaos is what we must desire so that we may survive.

Avoid tunnel vision

Radicalize ourselves on issues larger than the grant trough. It is disturb-ing to see the theatre community rush to organize against funding cuts. So myopic. The right wing's attack on arts funding is only a small piece of its strategy. Many of funding's defenders are not fighting against the government's criminal neglect of the AIDS epidemic. They aren't fighting for labour and the environment and campaign finance reform. They ignore the fundamental interconnectedness of all spheres of our artistic and political life.

Fight burnout

Travel. Go to Sri Lanka, or to Venice before it sinks. Study medicine. Learn Yoruban. Throw a change-up pitch. Burnout sets in when one tries to accomplish the impossible for too long. What we do is impossible. Since it's rare for an artist to take a vacation, at least change the mental land-scape on a regular basis.

Explore the deep terrain of performance

Balance art and politics. Work that imagines a radical alternative to our political tarpit needs to be enriched with a heightened awareness of the anatomy of our art. In other words, remember that as an activist your art is the spine of your protest. This requires a constant investigation of the nature of performance. The concept of performance is elusive because each action we take is performative. Turning over in bed at night, I experience a half-conscious awareness that the way I turn will signal a decision to the characters in my dream. I perform even as I sleep.

Performance is an action that aspires to an ultimate articulation. It is perhaps the highest mode of life. One of the many strands of thought running through my mind as I perform is: what is performance? And then I attempt to answer that through my action: performance is any human action framed by a circumscribed space. Performance occurs when precise boundaries ritualize action. Performance occurs when the meaning of an action is heightened by an awareness of its presence within a framed space: a stage, a bed, an altar, a witness stand.

When we draw a circle on the ground or on the floor and agree that everything that happens within the circle will have resonance, we have created the conditions of performance. The circle is like the stretched skin of a drum. Actions within the circle resound like the striking of the drum. Performance is culture's strategy to create events which resound.

Abandon false definitions of realism

The theatre thrives in a field of rapid oscillation between artifice and reality, an oscillation so rapid it blurs like a hummingbird's wings, creating a condition of hovering. The performer is a person who can see himself or herself as if in a hall of mirrors – the artifice revealing reality revealing artifice revealing reality ad infinitum. The playwright conjures up moments that evoke our heightened awareness of the reality of artifice and the artifice of reality, that artifice and reality comprise life like alternating layers of a Russian doll. What does the doll at the core represent? Not finality, because there is no finality. It represents infinity.

Embrace the new technology

I appreciate a foreboding about the colonizing potential of technology, but I don't share it. When I say technology is merely a tool, I don't deny that tools shape consciousness. Yes, prime advances in tools like the wheel and the printing press altered human perception, but they didn't supplant essential rituals like performance, and never will. The computer and its brilliant progeny, the internet and interactive multimedia, have already changed the world. Audiences are more attuned to alternative realities because of virtual technology, realities which are primarily internal. This is not threatening. Artists, theologians, and assorted mystics have inhabited internal space for millennia. Witness the Aboriginal concept of the dreamtime, in which all of us inhabit several dimensions simultaneously. Technology will change us as has every one of our tools, but we will eventually subsume it. That has been the historical pattern: a new tool dominates consciousness until the novelty of its utility is overshadowed by the new ideas it enables; then it becomes background. What intrigues me about the possibilities of new technology is the implication of an infinite collapse of space/time. A place where the boundaries of inside and outside dissolve, where things happen but nothing takes place, may be a logical fallacy, but we are more ready to imagine it because of the new technology, and that is a fertile mindset for theatre.

Put your whole world in a time capsule and send it again and again.

Theatre of the mind: a fugue in two parts
Shelley Berc

Shelley Berc is a playwright and novelist. Her novels, plays, and essays, which include *The Shape of Wilderness*, *A Girl's Guide to the Divine Comedy* and *Theatre of the Mind*, have been published by Coffee House Press, Johns Hopkins Press, Heinemann Books, the *Performing Arts Journal* and Theatre Communications Group Press. Her plays have been produced by theatres such as the American Repertory Theatre, the Yale Rep, and the Edinburgh Festival.

I] Theatre of the mind

We do not need any more actors directors playwrights designers critics

We do not need any more love, hate, psychology, politics, history, space, intimacy, stages, or especially money

We need so much that we can't need anything but a theatre of the mind

Crawl through the dark cave of mind that is the womb of all theatre and you will discover the theatre of the mind. The theatre of the mind is the loudest, brightest, most theatrical space in all of creation. It is collective and individual, invisible and all-envisioning, narcissistic and universal, beautiful and ugly and brutal and tender; it is the only theatrical hope/experience that keeps us going back and back, performance after putrid performance; it is why we love to read the plays of Shakespeare, to enact the magic incantation of their story heart and language smell in our minds and why so often their stagings disappoint, frustrate and limit our imaginings. The theatre of the mind is the stage of perfect wonder that each one of us and every one of us ever smitten by live performance longs to see again, a lost Eden that comes so easily in our secret thought and appears so hard to realize on the living stage. And it is a tragedy – this loss of a live, transformative theatre, this cavern of twisting into labyrinth into gorge into ocean and sky because we need its external presence as a people, as community to act in the very fact of its occurring as omen, talisman, catalyst, to dream out the potentiality of life; to dream a new blueprint of civilization, together.

When I was a child, a stage could be anything – a piece of the linoleum basement floor, the top of the oval chrome and Formica kitchen table, the rotting top step of the back porch stoop, an empty grandmother's bed, a patch of dirt under a willow tree. It could be anything and with some words and performers and watchers (sometimes just two people who kept trading places with each other) we enacted the great battles of good and evil and the dilemma of greed, the hunger of selfishness; for an arrested breath of time we could be glorious, heroic, in harmony with the earth under our feet and the sky above our dreams. Children play, live together in the theatre of the mind with all its darkened nooks and bright alleys; there they meet and spin the promise of our future and learn to become the adult actors of history to come.

The theatre of the mind defies the narrow stage definition of time – time man made gives way to time star made and rock made; rain made and earthquake made.

This is a theatre you can dwell in – as actor and audience, both actor and audience – for the rest of your life and for the time before and after your living, before fame money power ambitions and other theatrical delusions came to play upon your mind, to cut it up into apartment complexes, factories, and statements.

Sole condition of a theatre of the mind

That it can not be done.

(That it is as Plato's perfect bed; the pure, conceptual pretextual non-material ideal of all fabrication. But, despite all this, it is the least cerebral of all performances; it is the most active, most impossibly alive.)

In the painted cave of the theatre of the mind are the actors of the theatre of the mind – a seabed throng of signs and questions, humans and beasts, monsters and butterflies, all of whom we recognize/have seen before in our sleep and our moments outside of linear birth to death time and dreaming of illimitable sky. Now here they come, these performers, perpetrators of our dreams, parading like a beauty pageant – weddings and murders, pairings and disappearing taking place right before our unwatchable eyes where each of us sees the play unfold exactly as her own soul requires.

Action in the theatre of the mind

Atomic
Spontaneously combustible
Embryonic
Catatonic
Implosive
Microscopic
Macrocosmic

In the theatre of the mind things are never as comforting as recognizable as they seem. Here, plot is a trap, character a landmine – you enter one broken being after another, survive one explosion after another; the fragment of you, the audience, that is left is the play to be performed live at that moment in your head in dialogue with the life on stage that night so that each night of theatre of the mind is a thousand nights of theatre, a thousand different plays being performed on stage in the dark cave behind the curtain of audience eyes all at once, each play a different one – the broken bits of humanity that speak therefore to journey like the constellations in the sky. And yet, for the theatre of the mind to thrive we need the living stage to serve as the catalyst and clearing house between minds, engendering a vital, imaginative, ethical community of minds with common foes and goals and most of all a common language, a vocabulary of discourse that does not reduce but expand ad infinitum our possibilities as human beings.

The theatre of the mind is the theatre of yearning, humanity's yearning where we admit/confess to the darkened stage and the light flooded finale that it is impossible for any one play to speak to see to hear whole. Through the theatre of the mind of mosaic visions this wholeness of sense that is ultimately denied us can at least be glimpsed, grasped, in a thousand clapping hands in each of our own theatres of the mind, echoed and beckoned and seduced to performance by the theatre of the impossible set upon the stage that night.

Aspects of space and imagination in the theatre of the mind

Here stage space is a book in which the makers of theatre of the mind write down dreams and fears to be 'read' by the audience who are themselves writing other books in the theatres of their minds. This book that is the theatre of the mind is like the medieval stained-glass walls of cathedrals. You can read them as sign and story – loud bright bloody vocal outpourings of myth. In the theatre of the mind that is the illuminated manuscript of images, the images don't move but the audience moves, from mansion to mansion, station to station in the house of wonder agony and compassion that is our common home. The compassion comes when the show is over, a death of signs and acts, the final peace from the exhausting accretion of overwhelming life.

The theatre of the mind says: How dare you pretend to resolve anything? How dare you erase the resonance of myth, the germinal of theatre, by dividing it into 'acts'; budgeting it into this character and that; calling forth beginning, middle and end when the sole purpose of theatre as the locus of memorialized action is to set the individual on journey after journey of discovery (which is the movement of text, of 'forwarding the action' or plot in the theatre of the mind) until a play's end is the pile up/collision of a series of explorations into the sense of universe; wherein the character travelling is not just himself but a voice of the unison – the compilation of all characters – an illumination burning itself up with life on a field of darkness which is the stage at the beginning and end of every drama. Action in the theatre of the mind is the playing out of hands, the turning over of a deck of chance illuminations, placed one atop the next until there is so much overlay of light we come to the thankfulness of darkness, of ending, again. Then we are again at the beginning so that the theatre of the mind whose individual play pieces may appear diametrically opposed are always the detritus of the same never-ending show.

Actions for a theatre of the mind

Wind walking
Sun speaking
Gesture of taste
Sight of sound
Will burning itself up
Destiny melting down
Courage singing

Images for a theatre of the mind

Atom banquet
Bacteria dance
Worm choir in dirt bath
Jaguar eyes
Medieval flat perspective overlaid with quick-time movies
Movie stars pasted in the eyes of enormous TV screens that walk the stage
    like lamplighters in Renaissance time
Algae and fish life flying through underwater waves
Elbow landscape
The stage a tank of sharks
The stage a solar system with planets, moons, fallen stars
The stage empty but for magnified dirt on its floor boards, amplified
    sound in its wings
The stage empty but for the tears and hisses of audiences who cannot bear
    to go to hear, to see anymore the kindergarten of lies put before them
    when they came especially to play out the endgame of cosmos

Elemental forces of a theatre of the mind

Black holes
Fractals

Lipstick stains on galaxies
Hip hop music and magic spells recorded live on CNN
Language of distinctive voice without definable meaning as we beg to
    know it and debase it.
The word, the poor holy word.
A certain kind of weeping which only the heavens can do

The theatre of the mind refuses to answer any questions; in fact, it seeks to kill all answers (the catharsis of tragedy) which strew the proscenium with a sea of irrefutable dogmatic blood that rationalizes the forward march of history. In the theatre of the mind, all answers are beaten into questions. All the images and text of the theatre of the mind are pre-text for unanswerable questions. The theatre of the mind is the stage of these unanswerable questions and thereby the theatre of the miraculous.

Characters of the theatre of the mind

Lightning thunder earthquake volcano meteorite rain comet blast
    All angels on high
    All denizens of the deep
    Amputated limbs
    Pure mouths rescued of bodies
    The blood after cold-blooded murder
    Heaven
    The rotund earth
    What we call divine

In the theatre of the mind, language kills and in the best of senses; that is to annihilate into other wondrous matter. Words here are visceral and the fortress of language with its bricks of sound, rhythm, and alphabet-vowel-consonant cliché innuendo context pretext make up the iconic language which is the vicious unassuagable appetite of the theatre of the mind. This is a theatre that you see and hear in your mind as you walk through the days that walk you through your life.

The matter of plot or story lines of theatre of the mind

The story of the Big Bang
The story of the creation of love
The story of war on earth
The story of earth
The story of separation: earth and sky/nature and man/man and man

Conditions for the theatre of the mind

No money
No theories

No subscribers to placate
Hunger, thirst
Joyful dirt
No specializations or division of labour among the artists
A diviner's gift of salvaging garbage treasure
The stage as the tramp's last supper

In the theatre of the mind are a thousand roving characters who may be performed by one or a million actors on the stage who turn into each other as readily as reproducing and dividing paramecium. Consistency of anything – plot character action point of view – has no place here for we are inside the action of time where nothing stands still or remains the same – neither star nor rock plate is without its parallel eternal metamorphosis. This is the drama and cast of the theatre of the mind.

(she who was there, is not)

We go to the theatre neither to see nor hear nor understand; we go to dream.

Aims of the theatre of the mind

To have and foster revelation
A notion of our limitlessness and our obscurity
A coming to beauty after devastation
Screaming, laughing, weeping
To do away with all blue-haired matinée ladies
To scare off all those who demand to know what the play is about
To create the equivalent of a rose growing in quick time and slow motion
    that you can touch and smell inside your self
To be reminded of wonder and magic everywhere
To forge alchemists and theatre of the mind makers for an impossible
    theatre of us all; a theatre alive and on stage that is as magical for the
    collective as the solitary one within

II] Monodrama techno trama

or Why I write one-person technological extravaganzas

When you get down to it there is no such thing as dialogue. Contemporary communication is self-dramatization. The monotrama, as I like to call the one-person technological extravaganza, is the singular vision that sends the self into flight and sets a steel trap for it.

The earliest theatre was single-vision epic, from Homer through Aeschylus.

Once we got to Sophocles, things went downhill because the unified theatrical voice got shattered. Theatre became character cut ups and those characters had to do something with each other – they talked. Thus, dialogue was born and the single voiced vision went the way of woolly mammoths.

Dialogue is based on the powers of persuasion and lies, not vision or truth seeking. As far as I'm concerned, the only smart contribution of this myopic mentality called dialogue was its opening up to human time as opposed to the eternal. Eternity can get pretty boring and hence drive away an audience, which is something we really don't need right now.

Throw out dialogue.

Substitute: computers, synthesizers, techno-panic video screens, microwave ovens with three-inch TVs attached.

Monotrama cannot exist without technology. Monotrama is virtual reality paradiso.

What is missing from techno theatre and the avant-garde in general today is what is the essence of technology, namely hot wires.

Irony and cold metal electricity in cutting-edge theatre have become dead connections, excuses for paranoia, cowardice, and too much TV.

Nuclear bombs on the other hand are very hot.

In this world, theatrically speaking, we have to fight fire with fire.

Monotrama is miniaturization.

Silicon-chipped characterization.

All consciousness in a single voice.

All the world in a lone object.

Through the minute and intricate, we recognize the infinite and abstract.

Monotrama is the close-up fairy tale shot of theatre.

The individual in the monotrama stands in for the old single-voice Greek chorus in its appeal to the gods, in its lamentations and fears.

Monotrama is a blues song to abandonment

From self, family, community, this galaxy and plenty of others.

Classic realism skirts the schisms of psyche by chopping it up into warring personalities known as characters. Monotrama is the psychic realism of the theatre. It is the performance preview to the upcoming electronic cottage.

The dramatic tension of monotrama is not between self and others. The tension lies between the prisms of the self. This understanding is the recognition scene of monotrama. The resolution of the play is the constant regrouping of the reflective composition inherent in the character of one.

Monotrama scoops out the layers of lies, hunting for firm foundations of art. As the lies fall back in, faster than we can dig them out, we hug ourselves to our self on ever-shifting terms. Participles dangle, tenses confuse. The self knows itself as she and I and you and we and he and they.

Current technology makes two things possible: 1) liberty from the robot assembly line and 2) individual isolation or independence depending on your point of view. The by-products of nos. 1 and 2 are freedom and loneliness. Monotrama seeks to restore the magic dissolve of aloneness – an all-oneness that is the exhilaration of a group freed from group scrutiny.

Monotrama is thorough narcissism. By virtue of the fact that the theatrical Narcissus uses the audience-sea-of-faces as her looking-glass, monotrama is thoroughly sceptical of its own self-absorption.

Monotrama may be performed by more than one actress; the way a kaleidoscope breaks light, the way the cosmos has refracted itself into infinite particles of individual necessity. The single vision and the narcissistic are rooted in the same instinct – to defy gravity – the things, people, artefacts that hold us down as the universe floats and expands. The singular vision summons energy into one tight black space whose objective it is to blast through all space and all time.

Monotrama is the poem of the theatre.

The poem is our last toehold on earth before the leap into zero-gravity song.

As in a Homeric epic or a *chanson de geste*, the singular voice is released into the freedom of pure storytelling.

Free of the weight of dialogue, she is unleashed from the whoredom of storyselling.

Monotrama is a chant. A chant of world want.

The world want is to wail and sing.

Sing the soul out to a wall, an image, a person, any particle of any substance that bounces even a fragment of our own sound back to us.

The chanting of the monotrama is the memory of our common culture, instinct, gene poll, atoms.

It is the conjuring up of pure DNA.

The monotrama tears up everything in its way to get to this effervescence, this Alka-Seltzer of the soul. It rips the subjective from the objective and glues it back and forth together again, blinking like one of those religious postcards that change scenes as you turn them even slightly, up or down.

Through lyricism, with its deep dives and fancy flights, and irony, with its shrugged shoulders and minimalist mocking, the form perceives itself
An Atlas with wings.

Monotrama grafts the individual blissfully to her technology.

There is a grand canyon of understanding between the minimalist generation of artists and my own brood of multimedia feedback babies. We sucked TV and electric guitars from our first breath, while these forces hit them in their teens. For the older experimentalists communications technology will always be a somewhat exotic dark stranger, at once seductive and threatening. For them, it is literally a foreign tongue, spoken at best with a cool, clinical precision. For us, the new technology isn't new – its organic, erotic, demanding our hearts as much as our scalpels. It is our mother's milk.

Monotrama reflects internet time. It cannot exist without a techno theatre that can keep up with it.

Many theatre pieces talk about our times and technology but few reflect it. Few are structured as a time-reflection of our segmented, syncopated life pace. The only forms that even remotely approximate the time sense of the monotrama and its reflection of our attention deficit times are the internet, rap, and MTV.

The mix of hot music and video, with their loose ends to abstraction, incompleteness, and mega fantasy, has kicked in the door to performance poetry, that howling banshee that is the other burning realm of performing soul in which the audience is the whole cosmos.

The swift as light interconnectedness of the information highway is the same as that of the monotrama. In both, we are the neurons of communication linking ourselves in infinite configurations to our fellow man, to our sense of universe. Click from one text to another, one subject and image to another, to recreate one's self, to transform. These links are the forces behind the hothouse blossom that is the monotrama.

Theatre is the perfect ground for the synthesizing of medias – human and technological. It the ideal place to make live and human what is removed and alien when viewed behind the glass of our computer and TV screens, when heard through our digitally euphoric walkmans. Techno theatre is head and sex simultaneously.

Many theatres say that technology kills the magic of live performance. 'Tis but terror screeching. Theatre has always been a bastard art – a multi-mixed mutt, but it lost pace with media advancement, attempting some thoroughbred purity that is absolutely repulsive to its own bloodline. Between the reactionarism of established theatre institutions and the frigidity of the recent avant-garde, truly LIVE performance is out the proverbial window and with it the highest and deepest possibilities of melding individual and community, thought and imagination, instinct and intellect.

Prescription for a healthy, living theatre to replace the corpse on stage: throw out the painted sets, blow up the prop shops. Get a decent sound system, video and computer set-up and most important some dangerous artists who honour their bastard roots and we'll see a new pack of people haunting our theatre, a younger group sure to kick some life and love back into its sorry ass.

We can no longer look to the socio-familial-psychological-character drama to release us from the inner drama that links microcosm to macrocosm, the human to the rest of the universe. We can't laugh away heartbreak in black comedy any more. Like a rabbit frozen in car beam light, we are now impelled to cast forth our own demons in a singular glaring.

Monotrama shines the group eye straight into the individual's multifly eye and refracts it back to us all in fractured glory.

Wipe everyone but the one off the stage and map out the one who's there – who is the welter of the ghosts, fairy tales, histories that own us. Give the stage to the one who weeps and breathes electric blood.

An evangelical capitalist message in a bottle to the next millennium of Robinson Crusoes in proscenium[1]

Ruth Margraff

Ruth Margraff is a founding member of HERE Art Center's 'Opera Project' and her libretti and plays have been developed and produced by Brooklyn Academy of Music, The Public, Lincoln Center, Kitchen, the Guggenheim Museum, NYTW, DTW, New Georges, Hourglass Group, PS122, etc. (NY); Red Eye, Walker (Mpls); Undermain (Dallas); Salvage Vanguard, Frontera (Austin); Bottom's Dream, A.S.K. (LA) Sazvezde Belef Constellation 2001-Konak Knjeginje Ljubice in Belgrade. Ruth teaches playwriting at Brown University and Yale, on leave from the University of Texas at Austin, and is a member of New Dramatists.

---

1 (This being a sort of footnote to the 'Incomplete Blindness' duet in *Night Vision* and a bookmark of where we're at in looting Shakespeare's English.) Very special thanks for recent and ongoing dialogues with Fred Ho and his syllogism 'If you are white in

1   Dark matter

In the new worlds (new plays), when you come upon the imprint of a naked
foot in the sand, please assist to argue us out of all apprehension of its being
the Devil or some other cannibal.

> your blood-curdling perishing falling into my ears, I didn't know they were
> thoughts and if I wash them so I won't be lonely I could have a conversation
> with Friday or the Parrot or the largest clear blue eye above us watching and
> watching not like that[2]

American realism's stranglehold on every new play produced betrays
a deeply entrenched hatred of anything more deviant than the harmless
shipwrecks of our dear old balding Crusoe-imagineers from the greater
Treasure Island of the entertainment industry. Washed-up *Shakespeare*
Juniors of their Disney kingdoms, these Crusoes cling for dear life to their
old enlightenment against a vast *en-nightenment* they cannot see. In the
future, the American theatre will pretend to discover and worship these
colony-plays in order to maintain the status quo of a burgeoning Narcissism cloaked as Liberation, at the expense of the disenfranchised.

Like Crusoe, we bewail the fact that we haven't heard any other voice
in more than 200 years. We believe the land to be 'uninhabited' except for
us. And fallen into a depravity much darker than the latest American
killing spree where the sexual organs have been mangled into some
freshly masterminded contortion, pumped out by the press to satisfy our
Calvin Klein Obsessions for not knowing where your arm ends and mine
begins, just like Jeffrey Dahmer. Sold like porn that's still imbedded in the
Disney. We've got our sitcom daydreams of the good ole days to shuffle

---

a white supremacist society you are a white supremacist', with Jose Figueroa on the
martial arts and swords, Celise Kalke's condition of music, Dr Sa'di Al-Hadithi's
desert songs, Joshua Fried's headphone-driven vocals, Tim Maner's baroque
interiority, Jason Neulander's sleights of hand and combat, Matthew Pierce's velvet,
Kristin Marting's courtesans, Allen Hahn's limelight, Nancy Brous' gleams, Thalia
Field for Taos & Providence, Jim Murdoch's alterity in Hegel, Carlos Murillo's Gate
rants that the Marxists don't allow for human aspiration, Entifadh Qanbar's
pseudonyms, Jim Martin's emblems, Mac Wellman for being the first to pull the
plug on the utopia in harm's way, Aishah Rahman, Erik Ehn, Kia Corthron, Elyse
Singer, Bonnie Metzgar, Dominic Taylor, Ian Belton, Morgan Jenness, PWP, Tim
Farrell, Donna Janosik, Margery Segal, Donna Linderman, Andrea Paciotto and
some texts I can't stop reading by Susan Douglas, Kanan Makiya, Stephen
Greenblatt, Cornel West, James Baldwin, Billy Holiday, King James English Bible, all
my students at LIU at Brooklyn and the punk kid I met on the Greyhound bus this
Christmas who conversed entirely in lyrics and hit single titles of his favourite rock
bands, and Nikos Brisco always.

2   See *Night Vision: A Third to First World Vampyre Opera* 'Incomplete Blindness'.
Concept/Score by Fred Ho, Libretto/Lyrics by Ruth Margraff.

from the boob tubes to the burlesques of our mind's eye. Back when we
had to work for the night was coming. Back when the work itself was cen-
trifugal to all of us who cleaved its axis. But here, now, in this United Melting Pot of a premature ejaculation,[3] we can't feel the isolation and
desperation of being our own gods. We're addicted to the stories that
crash and burn in an hour that we won't remember for the life of us. We
can't remember back past 1972 but we pray to Shakespeare's looted bari-
tone of speaking into being 'in the beginning' this late great lottery for
more and more 'Psalm 23 Home Movies'.[4]

2   Prosceniums of self

In the real First to Third World shipwreck (thanks to the Crusaders),
there were many scattered howls of 'Le-ead us by the staff to where we
shall not wa-ant'. Until our Crusoe cocked his New World gun. He
showed Friday how to eliminate these extraneous rumblings of 'Lead us
by the scruff of the neck with your rod and —' Friday gathered up the
Parrot by the feathers and Defoe never mentioned it again … a trifling
blues psalm. Strange fruit of an irrelevant cry pitch…

See, we saw what happened – in the quarrel of the cannibals – to
Friday. Bloodshed so promiscuously gambled … without the common
bowels of pity. Producing in the civilized an eagerness toward:

> deliverance … to get one of those savages into my hands, cost what it would
> … In that very moment, this poor wretch [FRIDAY] seeing himself *a little at
> liberty*, Nature inspired him with hopes of life and he started away from [THE
> CANNIBALS] and ran with incredible swiftness along the sands directly
> towards me … kissed the ground and taking me by the foot, *set my foot upon
> his head*: this, it seems was in token of swearing to be my slave forever …
> (from the father of the novel/Daniel Defoe's *Robinson Crusoe*)

Thus, when Friday tries to learn to be a Crusoe, with his lesser liberties, he discovers his own 'inner city' in the Garden. He 'comes to' the holy
Shakespeare tongue by learning to separate the godly from the devils just
by washing them. He '*cleanses*' every word to a dramaturgically correct
'*clarity*' that could efface the very modesty of what was once a devilish-
ness not at all the same. And there in the brightly gleaming exile we'll all
glitter together like the snow in a nostalgic nuclear winter.[5] There in the
heavenly *offstage elsewhere*, we'll complete the white-box inversion of our

---

3   See *Exotica Orange* 'Sheath for the Modern Peking Opera Revolution'.
4   See *Night Vision* 'Psalm 23 Home Movie'.
5   See *The Cry Pitch Carrolls* 'White for So Long'.

black-box recordings of conventional disaster.[6] What will the new world look like? We ask the Marxist new Crusader Boys, frothing at the mouth to convert the Last to the First once and for all. Come meet the new devil, same as the old devil. All these goddam emblems now, to read, a mess of keyholes, matrices and dark neutrino verisimilitudes. Here is the sovereign of a play for which we'd highly hoped, and 'clarified' for mass consumption, not to be too fascinating, after dinner and a glass of wine. Friday and the parrot we once were? Are at our mercy now. Begging us to lead them also into literacy, the renaissance condition of our music where we learn to name our cannibalism something else with fancy footnotes.

3   Limelight

Every Friday/Crusoe now buffed for the regionals with glossy MFA (Master of Fine Arts) brochures in the lobby, will write his own utopian proscenium of self: How to Convert the Other Cannibals to Lesser Liberties in Crusoe's Paradise or Go To Hell (an offstage elsewhere we can't stop exoticizing). Labour will be annihilated and with it, human sentiment. There will be no aspiration but a vague Fear Of A Lessening. We will feel an evangelicus gladness that something like ice-cream or lost love is coming back someday to record what we have been through. Any minute now there will be an ecstatic Wagnerian aria, swelling and swelling into what? Life-size again? Where opera used to yearn for something that was far above us, on a scale much less human than mortality, we touch down now upon an impotent kitchen-sink realism. Gone goes the sitcom house to splinters because we know that house is still built in nostalgia. As is the breast that suckled our affluence. We will construct the new worlds later, always, to be round.

4   Temptations of the fresh voluptuous

If we did create God in our image, then we lost a lot of size when Michelangelo discovered human anatomy in the Renaissance of our literacy. Sculpted now immodestly, we stand entitled on our pivot foots with the first world posture of Michelangelo's David, a Roman abstraction of a biblical shepherd boy on the verge of a kingdom he won by strumming psalms.[7] We can't really accumulate these kitchen sinks and treasures to 'lay up' where moth and rust doth not corrupt, in the revolutionary futurity where we once decorated our panic. So, vanity of vanities, we'll fantasize the ingenue in every plot, a figment of our very Rib!!

6 See *The Elecktra Fugues* 'Transmission of Old Gleam'.
7 See *Night Vision* 'Neon Goldrush' with Sunkist Dysney David.

Toward a rhyming

But what if someday this Girl Friday type of figment Rib were to wake up in a state of omni-pregnant omniscience that would rise above the wilderness of melodies in the third act?? What if linear time had flown from left to right for her to read her destiny across the east to western Goldrushes?? What if she got blessed with the Shakespearean hindsight of mythology and the farsighted lifespan of a vision longer than the fifteen-minute killing spree ejaculations sold to us evangelically by the brokers of Mortal Finitude?? And like Shakespeare and the Greeks what if she came to prophesy a far more infinite drama peopled with characters and stories still contemporary five hundred years from now, where we do survive after shooting ourselves in the foot and eating our tails into what we used to believe in as Eternal??!!

Toward a symmetry

What if her swan song ... What if she rocks the contour of the Crusoe eardrums?[8]—What if she's repetitious of us all except one maybe digit? ... What if she dupes and interlocks us to the same ole likely cross we lust and gamble for in every pop star? What if she's all into difficulty that cannot exactly fit itself? What if it's too hard? What if we give it up? And what if it could have auto-punked us into morbid twaining where the word makes flesh? We gotta fling away them songs like pearls?!!

To dumb it down

Pointless. Any play that conforms to the status quo of a supremacy (ours being presently a white one) in form and content both is a bold-faced affirmation of *supremacy of any stripe*. It *blinds* us to the *real* American Realism. It pretends a *tiny democracy* that doesn't strive and fail to reach a symmetry of sensitivity. It is an act of oppression to teach our characters to speak in Crusoe English, first word: '*Master*' with our foot placed firmly on the subject's head. It numbs us to a Dialogue where consciousness is more and less and more again and therefore '*live*'. Any play with a 'blurbable' single meaning valued at the ticket price makes a junk deposit in the receptacle mindsets that entertain it. These plays are childless. **These plays are '*uninhabited*'.**

Face value

If you 'follow' this Girl Friday like a ringing in my ear ... my flailing English ... you would *know* by looking deeply into me, up very close, at the lip of your Opera. When I reach into my bosom and I find my locket

---

8 See *Vinyl Pressings* 'Second World: Bicycle Built for Two Eardrums'.

5 Back of Dollar Latin illustration first published in the independent fanzine *Salvage*

there.[9] Limelit, I sing that I am dying too, just like you're dying. My character is inconsistent; I may be trying to release my chemistry or poverty by fucking (that opiate of the masses). How closely you would guard me, Crusoes? Do you think so? Were you drawn to me for how long? How often? Why? And then what? Have you felt this way before? Salve and balm I say, have mercy, the curtains are closing!

(Faint completely under milk bath. Curtain)

Because there must be moments when we lose ourselves … in the serenity of our hearts. ***How to grasp you, How to leave you***, when we open up our limelit orbs of words that spin and orbit our proceniums. We've stumbled here upon this divine … comedy of errors to tell each other

9 See *Locket Arias* 'Camille'.

something, haven't we? That the raping and the murdering and dying are really not dramatic at all. (In *real* life, when they *really* happen to you.) When we were falling … just now … from our pedestals … into that perfect moment … When the pennies scattered everywhere around us like thoughts, it felt like I was writing … something I can never really possess at all.

> (*An old grey curl that is mine slips out of my hat, here, caught in the gleam of the elevator door, caught in the throat of the building*)[10]

5   Strange fruit

In the corner of your eye, the virgin MTV crotches (of American Realism) gyrate to distract you from me. You can fleece them later with your Back of the Dollar Latin industries, don't worry. You can go back to your island where the pop songs croon that no man is an island. You can learn to read what you really wrote in self-inflicted exile/paradise (artist residency?) about what could have been a new world. Because there is a strange fruit dangling from the trees of the knowledge of good and evil and the trees of life. Drawn of the blues and bliss of a world where trouble stretches out above us, 'longer than the purple sky …' We could drink of its intoxicating grace and clarity. We could drink this cup of trembling as we marvel, and we yearn for elsewhere …

'Shut your eyes', The Crusoe/Fridays murmur to this Parrot, suddenly, because it's very green here. Green, they teach it, in the pitch dark everything is black and white like an old film, you only know it's green because you recognize the shapes. Or maybe velvet and they say it feels like velvet too.

PARROT

Oh I always wondered what it felt like … velvet …

> (*And they hesitate a little on the way … They tip the Parrot back into the Night until it feels a coarseness holding it up which was a 'tree'.*)

---

10 See *Wallpaper Psalm* 'Where the Lovers Stroll'.
(All of the mentioned works, available from New Dramatists, are written by Ruth Margraff.)

Poor Tom's A-cold: reflections on the modern theatre in crisis

Martin Epstein

Martin Epstein's plays have been produced by the Magic Theatre of San Francisco, the Actor's Theatre of Louisville, the Round House in Maryland, the Detroit Repertory, the Odyssey (LA), the New Theater of Brooklyn and many colleges across the country. Epstein was also a core playwright-director at the Padua Hills Summer Playwrights' Festival (LA), where he staged eight of his one-acts. Some of his full-length titles include: *The Man Who Killed the Buddha*, *Autobiography of a Pearl Diver*, *Bag Ladies of the Weimar Republic*, *Vera Similitude* and *Simplicity*. Epstein, the recipient of a Rockefeller Grant in Playwriting, lives in New York and teaches playwriting, theatre history and musical theatre at the Tisch School of the Arts (NYU).

A few months ago, as I emerged from the elevator on the seventh floor of the Tisch School of the Arts (NYU), where I teach playwriting and dramatic literature, I found myself facing, writ large with a blue felt-tip marker on a white chalkboard, the following notice: *G——'s lecture on 'The Abandonment of the Playwright' has been cancelled!* As if this news wasn't prophetic enough, it was echoed by a burst of choral laughter from the three work-study students behind the reception desk, who had registered the look on my face. I didn't stop to ask these fledgling writers if the announcement was real. Even as a joke, the murderous juxtaposition of 'abandonment' and 'cancelled' had done its work. The abandoned playwright in me had been totally exposed. All I could do was laugh with the laughter I imagined would continue to greet the day-long cadre of aspiring playwrights who would keep spilling onto the floor.

A short time later, an article appeared in the Arts and Leisure section of the *New York Sunday Times* (1 November 1999), in which nine playwrights took part in a symposium in Provincetown, RI, on 'The Future of the American Theater'. The original discussion, edited down to a page and a half, was as diffuse as it was dull. The Provincetown Nine talked tentatively, confusedly, around the issue of Broadway's abandonment of serious theatre, leaving the playwright to frame his or her artistic identity through 'Off-' or 'Off-Off-' Broadway productions, which include our many regional theatres. Yet as different as each playwright was in the particulars of his or her prescriptive remarks regarding the future of the American theatre, they all had one thing in common. Not one of the nine could officially qualify, to my mind, as an abandoned playwright. These were playwrights, after all, who had been chosen to speak. Writers with sustained, critically acclaimed reputations; repeated Broadway and Off-Broadway productions; Pulitzer prizes, grants, sold movie scripts, and who knows, perhaps even an invitational night or two in the Lincoln bedroom. If I choose not to name names, it is to shield these chosen ones from the envy I feel in not being ranked among their numbers, as well as to reinvite their anonymity into the condition of abandonment that seems to haunt the rest of us. Although I suspect, or would like to believe, that even playwrights who are currently 'in the loop' share some consciousness of the modern theatre's exile from the culture at large. I was startled, however, when one of the participants, fresh from her adaptation of a famous Holocaust diary, declared: 'Having been on Broadway, I can't wait to go back!' This statement hit me like a Zen slap, illuminating my deepest exiled wish. I bowed my head and began chanting: *I can't wait to go back, I can't wait to go back, I can't wait to go back …*

But back to what, exactly? Certainly not Broadway. For the last forty years, 'Broadway' per se has not been a serious venue for anyone who wants to make a life in what might be called 'the modern theatre'. Yet the urgency implicit in my own mantra-crooning, *I can't wait to go back,* seemed to beg for a Broadway equivalent akin to *I want to go home.* Which, now that I think of it, isn't the first time I've had such an experience. More than twenty years ago, as I stood shaking uncontrollably in the dark, waiting to make my first (and thankfully last) appearance as an actor, I had the distinct sensation that as soon as I opened the behind-the-scene door and stepped onto the brightly lit stage, everything would be all right, I'd be *home, sweet home.* The play was Strindberg's *Pelican*, and the home I was returning to was wildly dysfunctional, not to mention so *ch-ch-chillingly cold* (I stuttered), that my incestuous sister and I eventually torched the place before throwing ourselves on the familial pyre in one last ecstatic Wagnerian embrace. A few years later, taking my cue from Freud, I began to wonder if almost every play wasn't either an overt or unconsciously disguised 'family romance', the hard fact of 'abandonment' interred somewhere in the house like a resident ghost.

Perhaps the time has come to ask the *theatre in crisis* how *it* feels about being a home for twenty-five hundred years of prodigal outcasts. I purposely drop 'modern' from the 'in crisis' equation in order to proceed with this more inclusive conjecture: *That since the existence of theatre is predicated on crisis, no matter what the individual components of this crisis may finally add up to, 'abandonment' is the mother of them all.*

How, then, does the theatre at its lyrical and pitiless best *play* this ur-crisis, the crisis of abandonment, to its physical and metaphysical limits? And what relevance, if any, does this enactment have for the ongoing state of the art? With these questions in mind (and in place of G——'s cancelled lecture on 'The Abandonment of the Playwright'), I offer the following reflections on Edgar's impersonation of Mad Tom, from Shakespeare's *King Lear*.

> I'th'last night's storm, I such a fellow saw,
> Which made me think a man a worm.
> (*Lear*, IV, i, 32)

This is Gloucester, speaking of his encounter on the heath with Edgar, his son, whom he has mistakenly banished and sentenced to death. Edgar, disguised as Mad Tom, plays the role so well that his own father doesn't recognize him, except, perhaps, unconsciously. That Shakespeare often uses the metaphor of theatre to reflect on the life of his characters is particularly true in this instance. In order to survive, then, Edgar *becomes an actor*. His natural inheritance denied, he masks himself as the lowest of the low: '... poor Tom, that's something yet: / Edgar I nothing am' (II, iii, 20). And with this metamorphosis, Edgar's life turns into a constantly improvised play of his own and others' devising, through which he gains the time, space and experience he will need to reconstruct a self.

Though Edgar's theatrical apprenticeship may seem gratuitous, Shakespeare has foreshadowed it from the outset. Edmund, weaving his Machiavellian scheme around his brother's fall, wants (and earns) our complicity as he welcomes Edgar's first arrival onto the stage: '... and pat he comes, like the catastrophe of the old comedy' (I, ii, 130). This blatantly theatrical metaphor will eventually be flung back in Edmund's face when 'the catastrophe' shows up in Act Five, transformed into the anonymous knight who challenges Edmund to the trial by combat that will decide the fate of the kingdom. How the seemingly hapless Edgar evolves into a figure worthy to inherit a kingdom can only be understood by following Edgar's progress through the various roles he undertakes. Even Lear, initially startled by the Bedlam's appearance, is quickly convinced 'this learnèd Theban', as Lear dubs him, has something to teach.

LEAR:
> What hast thou been?

EDGAR: A servingman, proud in heart and mind; that curled my hair, wore gloves in my cap, served the lust of my mistress' heart, and did the act of darkness with her; swore as many oaths as I spake words, and broke them in the sweet face of heaven. One that slept in the contriving of lust, and waked to do it. Wine loved I deeply, dice dearly; and in women out-paramoured the Turk. False of heart, light of ear, bloody of hand; hog in sloth, fox in stealth, wolf in greediness, dog in madness, lion in prey. Let not the creaking of shoes nor the rustling of silks betray thy poor heart to women. Keep thy foot out of brothels, thy hand out of plackets, thy pen from lenders' books, and defy the foul fiend. Still through the hawthorn blows the cold wind; says suum, mun, nonny. Dolphin my boy, boy, sessa! let him trot by.

(III, iv, 80)

I'd like to think the actor who performs this Boschian aria from hell will never again be the man he was. Echoed through our own theatre by Beckett's Lucky, Mad Tom sings beyond any calculation Edgar may have in trying to give a credible performance. *False of heart, light of ear, bloody of hand; hog in sloth, fox in stealth, wolf in greediness, dog in madness, lion in prey* – how many creatures, organs, and states of being Edgar, the formerly legitimate, incorporates into his new identity! Not to mention his spastic accompaniment to all the promiscuous fucking that creeks and rustles through his sexually overwrought imagination.

Having met or seen a number of homeless crazies, all generically named 'Mad Tom', who wander the English countryside, Edgar has also read books that name and classify Elizabethan devils. But what is the real source this seemingly bland fellow draws from that enables him to get *his* Mad Tom so right? Is Edgar thinking perhaps of his brother? If so, the recognition would have to be unconscious, as Edgar doesn't yet know who Edmund is, or what he is capable of. My speculation, here, is that in the process of playing the role, Edgar *abandons himself* to Tom's necessity, and begins to *believe* himself in the part. Which is not to say he goes crazy. In this greatest of all mad scenes (III, iv), when Shakespeare lets four different forms of madness contend for the stage, Edgar's pretend madness – as opposed to Lear's, Nature's, and the Fool's – is the only on-stage madness informed by a still greater rational purpose. So great is the tension involved in sustaining his role, Edgar almost loses control as he is moved to tears by Lear's suffering. Survivalist actor – one can even at this point call him the first Elizabethan performance artist – Edgar picks up his cue and finishes the scene not once, but twice. Mad Tom again, he beats off the dogs of the mind with a verbal spell – 'Be thy mouth or black or white, / Tooth that poisons if it bite ...' (III, vi, 63), before acknowledging his complete exhaustion: 'Poor Tom, thy horn is dry.' A moment later, alone on-stage and Edgar again, he puts everything into immediate perspective. 'How light and portable my pain seems now, / When that which makes me bend makes the King bow' (III, vi, 106).

Having delivered Mad Tom so totally, Edgar is drafted into an even

more difficult role. Gloucester has had his eyes put out by Regan and
Cornwall for trying to save Lear's life, and the Bedlam is hired (and even
paid) to guide his father to Dover, where the old man, in despair over
abandoning his rightful son, intends to throw himself from a cliff. In
leading Gloucester exactly nowhere: i.e., around and around the empty
stage, Edgar expands his theatrical prowess, becoming author, director
and actor, as he turns his father's pretend journey into a kind of medieval
mystery play. I am indebted, here, to Herbert Blau, who many years ago
first walked me through this scene, pointing out along the way how Edgar,
with nothing but language to depend on, creates such a visibly rich
tapestry for blind man and audience alike.

EDGAR:
    Come on, sir; here's the place. Stand still. How fearful
    And dizzy 'tis to cast one's eyes so low!
    The crows and choughs that wing the midway air
    Show scarce so gross as beetles. Halfway down
    Hangs one that gathers sampire – dreadful trade;
    Methinks he seems no bigger than his head.
    The fishermen that walk upon the beach
    Appear like mice; and yond tall anchoring bark,
    Diminished to her cock; her cock, a bouy
    Almost too small for sight. The murmuring surge
    That on th'unnumb'red idle pebble chafes
    Cannot be heard so high. I'll look no more,
    Lest my brain turn, and the deficient sight
    Topple down headlong.
                              (IV, vi, 11)

Edgar, meanwhile, has changed the terms as well as the sound of the role.
'Methinks y'are better spoken,' says Gloucester (IV, vi, 10), noticing the
difference. In the wake of Edgar's painterly description, Gloucester hurls
himself into the imagined abyss, falling comically on his face. Having
already told us that 'the worst returns to laughter', Edgar recreates himself
again, a bystander who witnessed Gloucester's cliff-side fall. In still
another voice, Edgar tells Gloucester how Mad Tom has been transformed into his true demon Self, the kind of devil who jumps the suicidal blind into a bottomless darkness.

    As I stood here below, methought his eyes
    Were two full moons; he had a thousand noses,
    Horns whelked and waved like the enridgèd sea.
    It was some fiend. Therefore, thou happy father,
    Think that the clearest gods, who make them honors
    Of men's impossibilities, have preserved thee.
                              (IV, vi, 69)

The ruse works. Gloucester accepts his survival as a god-sent miracle. In addition to this spiritual coup, Edgar has also become the first Elizabethan psychotherapist: 'Why I do trifle thus with his despair / Is done to cure it!' (IV, vi, 32). No sooner does this unfashionably quick cure take place than Edgar is cast in yet another role. Lear suddenly appears, and the two old men, one blind, one crazy, sit down together to discuss the politics of abandonment.

> LEAR:
>   If thou wilt weep my fortunes, take my eyes.
>   I know thee well enough; thy name is Gloucester.
>   Thou must be patient. We came crying hither;
>   Thou know'st, the first time that we smell the air
>   We wawl and cry. I will preach to thee. Mark.
> GLOUCESTER:
>   Alack, alack the day.
> LEAR:
>   When we are born, we cry that we are come
>   To this great stage of fools. This' a good block.
>   It were a delicate stratagem to shoe
>   A troop of horse with felt. I'll put' t in proof,
>   And when I have stol'n upon these son-in-laws,
>   Then kill, kill, kill, kill, kill, kill!
>
> (IV, vi, 173)

Witnessing this scene, Edgar comes full circle, turning into one of us, an audience. 'I would not take this from report,' he says. 'It is, / And my heart breaks at it' (IV, vi, 139).

Edgar is certainly ready, at this point, to abandon the theatre for the 'real' world (let's always remember we're watching a play), but his full return from exile is mediated by two more roles to come. When the predatory Oswald appears, wanting to kill Gloucester for a promised reward, Edgar feigns a rustic accent, and gives Oswald a chance to leave. Blind to the occasion, and supposing the disguised Edgar a pushover, Oswald draws his sword. Edgar, having only a cudgel, overpowers Oswald, killing him with his own sword. 'I am only sorry he had no other deathsman,' says Edgar (IV, vi, 253), leaving us to suppose that Oswald is probably the first person he has killed. Along with the discovery on Oswald's person of the letter that will bring Goneril and Edmund down, this fight scene is Edgar's rehearsal for the more important battle to come.

Edgar's last role, that of the masked knight who enters the scene to challenge Edmund, brings one more question to bear. Edmund is, or seems to be, the physically stronger of the two. How is it possible, then, that Edgar is able to defeat him? A single rehearsal, as well as his father's blessing aside, something more in the way of an explanation seems necessary. I would like to suggest that what gives Edgar the victorious edge over his physically stronger opponent is *the theatrical manner* in which he presents himself. Edgar enters the battle arena masked. Preceded by three blasts of an apocalyptic trumpet, he presents his abandoned persona behind a wall of armour. If one puts oneself in Edmund's place, it is not hard to imagine the psychic unease of fighting an enemy with no visible identity or face. The complicitous pleasure we may have formerly taken in Edmund's 'I grow, I prosper. Now, gods, stand up for bastards!' (I, ii, 23) has, by this time, been reversed. Our allegiance is totally to Edgar and the good cause, though our relief in the outcome of Edgar's triumph is almost eclipsed by our knowledge that, even as this battle is fought and won, Cordelia is hanged in her cell by Edmund's command.

It is left for us to wonder if Edgar's imitation of abandonment might not be a paradigm for Shakespeare's larger dramatic strategy. Once Edgar is finally able to reveal himself to Gloucester, he describes how his father's heart "Twixt two extremes of passion, joy and grief, / Burst smilingly' (V, iii, 198). Shakespeare, in turn, has led his audience through a theatrical landscape founded on the bedrock of a primal wound, where the word 'nothing' is prelude to everything else that language can possibly describe. Yet even as this language piles body upon abandoned body, it weighs in on the side of forgiveness – Lear and Cordelia kneel together, Gloucester and Edgar embrace, and even Edgar and Edmund exchange a parting 'charity' (V, iii, 168).

Edgar, meanwhile, acting on behalf of those of us who are still waiting to go back, inherits the kingdom. Coming as it does at such a terrible cost, his succession, followed by a dead march, returns the stage to the purity of silence. An empty space that speaks, perhaps, for the clearest gods? Or that speaks, at least, for my own desire to draw a final distinction between the kind of abandonment we all live in dread of, and those joyously rare occasions when the theatre-in-crisis, modern or otherwise, *abandons itself to abandonment*, without which no one on either side of the foot-lights can pretend that any of it is worth a damn, let alone the price of admission.

The theatre of good intentions
Mac Wellman

Mac Wellman is a poet and playwright. He is the head of the MFA playwriting programme at Brown University. His plays have been produced at Primary Stages, En
Garde Arts, and the Flea Theatre in New York, Bottom's Dream in Los Angeles, Salvage Vanguard in Austin, and other venues. He was Pew Playwright in Residence
at American Conservatory Theatre in San Francisco from 1994–96. This essay was
originally published in *Performing Arts Journal*, 8, No. 3 (1984), pp. 59–70, and
is reprinted with permission from the author.

Artists and thinkers of our time are engaged in a war against meaning. Or
rather, against the tyrannical domination of meanings so fixed, so
absolute, as to render the means of meaning, which is to say the heart and
soul of meaning, a mere phantom. In American theatre this happens
when the fact of what is occurring on stage, a representation in itself, is
eclipsed by what is supposed to be created: the 'content', the story, the
dramatic action's putative meaning. What is shown annihilates the showing. The true play comes to take place somewhere else, and the physical
and spiritual being of theatre vanishes in a cloud of hermeneutical
epiphenomena. This is why American theatre is so apparitional; and
despite – or rather, because of – its literal-minded obsession with communication, with content, with meaning, so meaningless. This is also why
American drama, for the most part, lacks theatrical presence. These notes
are an attempt to explain how this happens.

1

In the American play, whether it be the naturalistic variety typical of the
regional theatres or its distillations and hybrids on Broadway, certain
absolute notions of character and theatricality prevail. The first of these
is the conviction that theatrical action is purely a mechanism for the
manipulation of emotion, particularly warm emotions. Moreover, in the
theatre of our time warm feelings are superior to cold ones, and flat
declarative statements of emotionality are superior to any other. It
becomes clear that certain kinds of feeling are unacceptable in the theatre:
anything approximating the despair felt by 95 per cent of the population
in these grim days of stagflation and brushfire wars, for example.

    The tendency of American dramatists to equate feeling with the most
absolutely literal-minded expressions of emotion means that once the
currency of expression of a play dates, the play itself is dated, totally,

hopelessly. Most of O'Neill and Arthur Miller has come to resemble a collection of yammering skeletons for precisely this reason. The characters lack effective inwardness. The works of Strindberg and Ibsen by contrast – even mangled as they are by translation – seem fresh and alive.

One result of this lack is a preoccupation, on the part of American playwrights, with the aesthetics of intentions rather than that of action. Characters in American plays frequently do nothing and are incapable of any real action because actions by themselves are not considered to be dramatically important. A nasty, unsympathetic, or downright evil character, for instance, must always be shown to have suffered in such and such ways that have produced his behaviour. From *The Hairy Ape*, through Stanley Kowalski, to the wretched protagonist of Albee's *The Man Who Had Three Arms*, he is always the victim of circumstance; a hackneyed phrase in which – for my purposes here – the key word is *victim*. A certain alleged suffering then becomes the focus of dramatic interest, not the behaviour itself, which is dismissed. Motive-mongering has become endemic on the American stage. Not only do the aesthetic criteria of playwriting become diluted, but the theatrical experience itself suffers. What is bad is called good and vice versa, and the audience begins to trade in empty intellectualizations about character and motive and so on. Of the ethical and political consequences of this I have more to say later. But, at base, the whole claptrap of the American play, particularly the naturalistic, rests on the conviction that dramatic action has no place on stage.

Further, since the substance of the typical American play consists of statements of emotion, or – in even more attenuated form – statements of good intention, a character who is not revealed in this way is considered to be unconvincing, 'flat', or unreal in a sinister way. Feelings that are not stated are considered to have been denied or somehow repressed. This confusion of emotionality with real feeling, encouraged by critics and academics and acting teachers especially, leads to (among other things) the true impossibility of an honestly pessimistic American play.

What of such dramas as Mamet's *Edmond* or Marsha Norman's *'night, Mother*? The pseudo-pessimism of these resolves finally to mood, and the mood is one of thwarted good intentions. Unfulfilled possibilities, but possibilities nonetheless. The old goodness-gone-awry syndrome. But the pretense is obvious, for the theatrical grammar of frustrated goodness is identical to that of which it scorns (witness the interchangeable obsessions of 'success' and 'failure' in plays of the 1940s and 1950s). Again, the flurry of seriousness in these plays is a sham: the true drama is always happening somewhere else. In America a really pessimistic (i.e., tragic) play, no matter how well-written and well-performed, constitutes an act of aesthetic treason.

In a similar vein, the playwright's use of irony – aside from the most obvious buffoonery and lampoon – is viewed suspiciously as a form of theatrical evasion and dishonesty. And this despite the fact that a skilful use of irony is akin to metaphor in that it involves the charging of simple statements with multiple meanings. But to the proponents of the theatre of good intentions it suggests, rather, lying. For these the ironist is one who does not say what he means, just as all contradictions presuppose a resolution, and all problems a solution.

The American theatre wears a fixed smile suitable for all occasions, in all seasons.

2

The odd thing about playwriting in this country is how over time the fervent attempt to capture real life has led to a radically impoverished dramatic vocabulary. That which is terrifying, horrific, or monstrous in life is automatically translated into something else. The Elephant Man is portrayed as a beautiful young man (his 'spirit' presumably); the vile child-murderer of *Total Abandon* is transformed into a deeply 'human' sufferer, a victim among victims; the rapist of *Extremities* is yet another 'misunderstood' person. Like the political criminal-victims of our time, Nixon and Agnew, these latter two must be brought back into the fold. The message is, they have suffered enough just being what they are. The crucial distinction between ethical and aesthetic criteria is lost, to the detriment of both. Another result is a simple loss of theatrical presence, there-ness, or actuality.

This is perhaps not so surprising. What is presentable on stage is defined by rules of decorum derived from our political denials: we do not have a race problem, the unemployed and poor are not really deprived of opportunity, basically our society is a just and humane one, nuclear war is nothing to worry about, etc. Now, it may be argued that all societies are rife with the sorts of political and social contradictions mentioned. But not all societies are so obsessed with *images* of well-being that preclude political analysis; certainly not all societies regard these images the way we do: literally as the embodiment of well-being. To attack the Ipana smile or the Marlboro man is to attack America itself. Denial is uniquely positive in its American context.

Theatron. A place for viewing.

What is not permitted to be shown in and about society at large certainly cannot be allowed on its boards. The politics of denial engenders the poetics of gentility; that is, the theatre of good intentions.

3

One of the most striking features of American dramaturgy is the notion of 'rounded' character. This creature of theatrical artifice, with its peculiarly geometric – nay! symmetrical – aspect, is so like an object from a maths textbook, and one finds it so frequently on stage (and nowhere else) that I have dubbed it the Euclidean character. (Actually Witkiewicz used the phrase more than fifty years ago; my theft was unintentional.) Every trait of the Euclidean character must reveal an inner truth of the same kind about the personality in question; each trait must be perfectly consonant with every other trait. The author who creates such a character behaves much like the innocent who adorns his home with paintings that 'match' his wallpaper, carpets, and furniture. Every revealed aspect of the Euclidean character is equidistant from its centre. An odd consequence: there can be no such thing as a real liar in an American play; and the most potentially subversive anti-hero of our time would be the dedicated recidivist, who can spout all the proper homilies, but goes on with his life of crime. For another, there can never be a truly frivolous moment in our drama, and this probably accounts for the ponderous solemnity of our more serious drama.

Paradoxically, it may be precisely the habit of writing characters from the inside out, as it were, that leads to this impasse: characters made up of explanations become creakingly artificial, emotional automata who never, but never, resemble people as actually experienced. Rather, these characters – and I would offer the entire cast of *Death of a Salesman* as example – are merely theoretical. They are aggregations of explicated motives, explicated past behaviour, wholly knowable and wholly contrived. They seem animated by remote control, as if from another planet. Representing, as they do, a theoretical view of life (and there is none more theoretical than contemporary American naturalism), they cannot hold back any nasty little secrets, they tell no lies, do not surprise us too much, and, in fact, are capable of very little that is interesting. The point of Euclidean character is to give a multifarious aspect to predictability. One need only examine a small portion of the surface of a sphere to be able to deduce the rest. The creator of the Euclidean character must be continually busying himself with the peculiar task of reassuring his audience that such-and-such is truly his intention, but that he or she would never subscribe to the heinous and subversive doctrine that such-and-such boils down to this-and-that. The author must come clean about his intentions, just as his characters must about their actions. By the same token, the one unforgivable breach of etiquette in the group therapy of the American stage is to present an unexplained fait accompli and thereafter to maintain silence. And the dignity of silence is what our theatre, like our culture, lacks. The Walter Kerrs of the world will never understand why Beckett is a great playwright, and why Arthur Miller is not.

The non-Euclidean character is more like the elephant in the Indian parable that so confused the blindfolded men. This character is the sum total of his lives and actions, no more and no less. And because he cannot be reduced to a formula, cannot be considered as a neat demonstration of the author's hypothesis, psychological or otherwise, only this character is alive. Non-Euclidean characters demonstrate nothing. Nothing, that is, but themselves. Hamlet, Lear, Othello, Faust, Woyzeck. These are the stuff human rules are made from. But to attempt to derive them from the rules is tantamount to baking the cookbook rather than the cake. This process, repeated over generations, has led to the current anaemic state of our drama. The great works of classic theatre, of whatever period, in whatever culture, are full of characters who would never work in a typically 'well-crafted' American play. Why is it so inconceivable to our dramatists that some people do not know, or care, how they feel all the time? That some people act without a detachable motive, or from a myriad of contradictory ones? Why is life itself less interesting per se than the explanations of life?

In our time the wholesale subversion of private emotion by public motive has reached a point where terms like 'sincerity' and 'authenticity' have become virtually meaningless. The achingly vulnerable faces and erotically charged images of high-tech commercialism invade our imaginations and dreams so totally that, in a sense, the world of private emotion is more dangerous, more a trap and nest of snares, than that of the (rapidly disappearing) public emotions. Courtesy, good manners, neighbourliness, or simple decency do not sell products, or re-elect the rich and powerful. 'Vulnerability' (an odd euphemism nowadays, and one that more accurately refers to its opposite), soft-core porn, and theoretical familial intimacies do. The flight of all discourse – political, social, or philosophical – is another concomitant of this. Put in another way, the traditional connection between language and conduct has become, at best, problematic; and, at worst, a mere economic variable. To be a complete human being in such a context means nothing.

And perhaps we have no place for liars and recidivists in our theatre because we are ruled by them, and are blind to their doings.

4

The American well-made play consists of a regular number of acts (normally three, a perfect number), Euclidean characters with modular emo-

tions and detachable motives and good intentions all cunningly inter-
connected in such a way that nothing is wasted. Waste is a great obsession
of the writer of the American well-made (one frequently hears its cham-
pions refer to writing as material, as though it were a kind of unformed
mush or night-soil).

Again, every piece of dramatic information is designed to 'match'
every other, in the manner described above. Situation. Conflict. Resolution. Finito! In this way one can ignore the actual shape of the play,
the texture of its moments, and concentrate on the 'content' of these,
that comprise the other play which is going on – theoretically – in the
collective head of the audience. Like the content of Plato's universe this
mysterious substance is nothing in the world. Instead, it is a universal
absolute consisting of an interlocking set of nostrums concerning what is
important in life. Love triumphs over all. Honesty is the best policy. There
is nothing that succeeds like success. When the going gets tough the tough
get going. And in especial: the emotional contentedness of a person is the
most important thing in the world. Much of the peculiarity of the American well-made has its origin in this perfect reality of content, a reality
whose perfection resides chiefly in the fact that it does not exist. What gets
left out is the gritty, grainy truth of the world.

To understand what has been lost, imagine reading *Hamlet* for the
first time, knowing nothing about it; and further imagine it the work of a
contemporary. What you would probably come away with is a sense, a
very immediate sense, of a plenitude of images and a myriad of meanings,
continually combining and recombining. Only then would the awesome
shape of the play appear, its tremendous theatrical presence. Indeed, it
may be one critical quality of a true work of art that its meanings never
assume the fixed and final plausibility, the one-to-one meaningfulness
deemed so necessary in our theatre.

The plays of our time are, for the most part, so forgettable because
their authors succeed all too well: a play that is a perfect and seamless
summation of itself and its own intentions, and nothing else, can only be
consumed once. Then it is a mere disposable article, a husk of gutted
meaning. This is not an argument for obscurity or incomprehensible
dramaturgy, but only a plea for recognition of the fact – long ago a truism
in modern music and poetry – that each work of art is unique and must
be allowed to take on a unique and expressive form. The shallow characterization and sketchy plotting of the American well-made are the result of
a confusion of the world with schematizations of the world. Whether it be
the 'whacky', cutesy murder of *Crimes of the Heart*, or the fake profundity
of a whole slew of nun and monk plays, this is wishful thinking raised to a
pitch; denial swallowed whole and regurgitated as a triumphant battle-cry.

5

It may be fairer, at this point, to make a distinction between realism itself, as an aesthetic mode, and the American perception of the real. What I mean to suggest is that there is nothing wrong with realism per se, or naturalism. It is only when the convention of the real comes to be identified with reality itself that we have a confusion that cannot help but diminish the quality of perceived experience.

Pop psychology, the current American obsession with the self and the 'extensions' of the self, and a refusal to accept any kind of dialectic in the workings of society; all these may be identified as contributing cultural causes of the strange malaise in our playwriting. But the fact is there are good plays, too, of all different kinds; the curious thing is that these are performed less and less frequently, usually proportionate to the seriousness and complexity of the work. Maria Irene Fornes' *Fefu and Her Friends* and Ronald Tavel's *Boy on a Straight-Back Chair* are obvious examples of difficult but fine plays not likely to be revived, and rarely discussed by the press. Why?

Producers seem fearful of works that fly in the face of the artificial naivety which is the accepted norm. Plays which are not 'about' something in the most simple-minded way can tell us nothing we care to know. Plays which explore the enormously rich resources of the American language are still, in 1984, regarded as somehow less accomplished than their 'correct' English counterparts. Directors and dramaturges, as well as playwrights, rarely seem interested in contemporary poetry and fiction, not to mention philosophy, history, or the plastic arts.

Instead, despite all the debunking of the last few years, only the figure of the acting guru, that sublime and room-filling oracle of theatrical truth, has had any permanent and direct influence on American playwriting. The theories and personalities change with the fashion of the time, but the mysterious god-actor remains an unfathomable and portentous obstacle to any honest writer who seeks to work in the theatre.

The somber, generalized, sleepwalking gait of so much American playwriting is directly attributable to the fact that any writer who is produced with any frequency at all must sooner or later come to terms with the obdurate and implacable dogma of method acting. And since no American playwright can boast anything like the mystique and cachet of the famous (mostly method) actors of our time, an insidious dilution occurs in the writing itself, which becomes more pat, symmetrical, generalized, and rationalized, and less sharp, specific, smart, and quick-footed. Writers are responsible in this strange *pas de deux* of acquiescing to what

– from any dispassionate point of view – is only a vast artistic and cultural sham.

6

Among the stratagems devised by my own generation (post WWII) to avoid the death-like embrace of the American well-made play is the use of what I would call 'affective fantasy'. The spinning-out of fantasy in a stream of images, daydreams or night-, and other kinds of non-consecutive episodes, is a favourite dramatic device; both as the subject of monologue, and when more deeply considered, as the narrative framework for whole scenes, and even plays. Albert Innaurato's *The Transfiguration of Benno Blimpie* is this kind of play, as are the plays of Christopher Durang, and those of probably our best playwright, Len Jenkin.

However, the danger of this method is that such writing, no matter how highly loaded with images of profound import for the writer, is no more sure a vehicle for effective, affective communion than a laundry list, a page from a phone book, or any 'found' text. An image is always a sort of Janus Bifrons: any writer who employs powerful imagery of fantasy runs the risk of being hoist on his own petard unless he chooses this with a great deal of reflexive canniness. This, unfortunately, is rare. Who was it said that the most difficult task facing a writer is to avoid saying precisely the opposite – if not of what he intends – of what he means? It is this Janus-aspect of highly metaphorical language that creates the difficulty.

Still, in my view, this is the most valid way to proceed. But not because of some romantic belief in the vatic powers of the unconscious, or the capacity of the 'reptile' brain, or the collective unconscious, etc. Quite the contrary: the best playwrights of our time pursue an edgy, intuitive path to explore the full damage done by the onslaught of political lies, right-wing hucksterism, and general consumer-society madness on the inner person. In our time only bad artists name what they cherish, because what is cherished, or revered, or loved, will immediately be used as a tool by the powers that be. This underscores both the necessity for living ironically, and the difficulty of maintaining anything like a clear and neatly paraphrasable picture of things.

Obviously, one of the writers I have in mind here is Sam Shepard. In his case the use of fantasy has a further specialization of great interest. For the most remarkable and refreshing feature of Shepard's dramaturgy is how, in his otherwise misshapen and jumbled plays, his characters possess almost no affect; they carry no emotional weight at all. A play like *Action* is as pure and classical a piece of dramatic writing as anything from the pen of Samuel Beckett. This lightness frees his work from the terrible burden of fake sentiment that, like Ahab's scar, disfigures the torso of so many American plays. His characters speak literally whatever comes into their heads.

This ability can, and does, become a mannerism; but its one great virtue – so vital in theatre and so rarely encountered – is that it allows his characters to be spontaneous, or, more simply, free. This quality of his work, and not all the hocus-pocus of cowboy mythology, makes him a great playwright. In fact, Shepard's whole notion of theatre is so noble and so powerful because it is rooted in the ideal of freedom, an American ideal the proponents of the American well-made play seem wholly ignorant of.

The best four playwrights realize that the first step in dealing with the pervasive and catastrophic breakdown in gestural language of our time is simply to acknowledge that it has occurred. Until we have mapped the underlying strata of our despair and malaise there is no point in prescribing remedies. In strict terms, not only do we as a people lack political consciousness, we do not as yet even possess the language to describe our condition.

The images of our theatre float above us: vague, ghostlike, and unreal.

7

The habits and tendencies I have attempted to describe above combine to produce our contemporary drama, at once so perennially promising and so perennially unsatisfying; so innocent and so sterile: a theatre of good intentions. The world we all know exists in American drama only to be transcended; one must rise, vertically, by means of moralizing uplift, out of it. The real world is not a place to dwell. (This is transcendence in the sense of 'removing oneself from the vicinity of' rather than 'accomplishing a reconciliation with or among'.)

Evil, especially unredeemed evil, becomes an enigma. Its very portrayal in the theatre becomes suspect. Evil must be explained away until it too can be uplifting, a source of happy feelings and optimism, a celebration of good intentions proven triumphant. How sophisticated by comparison is the traditional moral order of Christianity (which bears no resemblance to the sham corporate-church of the born-again moral-majoritarians). In their definition of evil, Augustine and Paul presented the unflinching knowledge that human beings are imperfect and contradictory creatures, and that the roots of human action are a mystery.

For us evil can never be accepted for what it is. Instead, the cloud of wishful thinking and optimistic palliatives conjured up to perform the task of explaining away evil is confused with the ethical as a concept; and the ethical itself is shunned as cynical and moralizing.

Since only 'feelings' (ostensible emotions) are allowed moral dignity in our theatre, our perception of the ethical facts of life becomes strangely skewed. Over the course of time we dispense with any regard for ethics at all, in favour of its tremulous emotional stand-in, guilt. If a playwright can summon guilt in an audience he is deemed to have moved them (presumably off some theatrical dead centre). Traditional Christianity, like most value systems, has scant regard for guilt, except as a prod to action.

The art of summoning guilt has become highly refined and specialized; entire theatres have been consecrated to the ministrations of its solemn devotees. For one may suspend an entire play or theatrical extravaganza from a single luminous strand of carefully spun bad conscience. Real, presumed or imaginary. Perforce, the uncomfortable sensation of being or not being white, black, or a man, or a woman. Or of being or not being hetero- or homosexual. Of possessing a monstrous visage, of being pathetically moribund, of being crippled in spectacular ways. But the point is always a generalized one: a question of being or not being something; it is never a question of specific acts or choices in a world of contradictory allegiances and affinities.

Complexity, the state of life as most of us live it, is shunned in favour of a curiously blinkered view which offers up as the moral only the titillation of briefly identifying with the unfortunate one, the injured, the sick, the maimed, the ineluctable victim. But since the element of choice is banished, this amounts to a cynical parody of existentialism.

The palpable problem is that there is too little passion or intelligence in American theatre. Instead of elegance, there is affectation; instead of eloquence, there is rant; instead of physical grace, there is a gaggle of (adverbial) stage directions. No wonder our theatre is so slow, so heavy, so indigestible! To paraphrase Maurice Merleau-Ponty, the museum-thinking of our time turns a living historicity into official and pompous history.

8

The playwright in America is most often a creature defined by institutions designed to help him or her realize his or her talents. The playwright therefore becomes the object of concern of persons more serious than himself or herself. For these the playwright is, like most other artists in this country, a special being, half-child and half-idiot.

Indeed, people of my generation have grown up to be professional children; politically we pursue aims and goals that protect our special status and no others. We have embraced the anti-intellectual tradition of our elders, but turned it inside out as the cosmetically enhanced mindless stare of the fashion magazines, and the ever-swelling trade in self-help commodities.

As I write, the United States is seeking by covert military means to undermine the Sandinista regime in Nicaragua; the battleship *New Jersey* is steaming to the coast of Lebanon (is this 1910?!); the Dow-Jones Index is setting new record-highs while the economic plight of the average person is worsening at an alarming rate. The Secretary of the Interior is surprised to learn that his sexist and racist humour is not appreciated by some, and the opposition Democratic Party, like the supposedly 'liberal' press, continues to treat the Great Communicator with the greatest deference and respect. The men in the Pentagon talk of nuclear war with more and more macho enthusiasm, and, like their colleagues in the Kremlin, go ahead with their mindless and heartless preparations for doomsday.

Meanwhile, the grown-up children playwrights of America write touching little neo-realistic melodramas about family life. The moral world presented in these is very much that of children's literature. There is usually the bittersweet touch of permissible sadness (death of the family dog), and the hint of moral ambiguity (whether to turn off Aunt Tillie's life-support system), but little more. Sometimes, Cathy, there is no right or wrong. Sometimes, Johnny, life isn't fair. But even these delicate little conundrums are expressed in terms of feeling. And no wonder: children are not expected to act. Children are not expected to think.

So we have bought into the fake dream we made fun of our parents for thrusting upon us. And fake dream is just what it is! As artists we are continually on tiptoe, as though if we made too much noise we might not be liked, might not get a date for the prom. Ideas, of any kind, are out. When we choose to write about politics and society we stick close to the 'facts', as presented in the national organs of public information. What my colleague at New Dramatists, Jeff Jones, has aptly termed 'the whole grotesque tradition of nigger-hating', for instance, has been reduced to a mere additive squabble over goods and services.

If, as Bernard-Henri Levi writes, Solzhenitsyn 'is the Shakespeare of our time', and if multinational capitalism and Russian state socialism are two faces of the same beast, we are in deep trouble. And if that beast is indeed the Leviathan that Thomas Hobbes wrote so eloquently about three hundred years ago, maybe we ought to take a look at Thomas Hobbes. (And Shakespeare!) And all those writers and playwrights who suggest that things are not at all as they appear; that the world is a dangerous and deadly place, where courage and clear-headedness are at a premium.

Theatre is a place where things as they are are both shown and show (for what they are); in American theatre too often what is shown is the problem posing as the solution. The intellectual vacuity and anti-historical bias of our plays is a national scandal. Make no mistake about it, when the problem poses as the solution, the facts do not speak for themselves.

Letter to a young practitioner
Goat Island: CJ Mitchell, Bryan Saner, Karen Christopher, Mark Jeffery, Matthew Goulish and Lin Hixson

Goat Island – Karen Christopher, Matthew Goulish, Lin Hixson (director), Mark Jeffery, CJ Mitchell (company manager) and Bryan Saner – is a Chicago-based collaborative performance group. They have created and performed seven performance works since 1987, most recently It's an Earthquake in My Heart. They regularly teach methods of performance and collaboration. The group's publication projects include Schoolbook 2 – Textbook of the 2000 Goat Island Summer School in Chicago & Bristol. The members of Goat Island wrote 'Letter to a Young Practitioner' collaboratively, and delivered it for the first time at The School of the Art Institute of Chicago on 16 March 2000

To a young practitioner,

In this present period of unemployment, you can render a high service to your own community, and to the whole country, by co-operating with all movements to accelerate building constructions, especially of family dwellings, new roads and local and state public works. These measures will provide employment, enlarge buying power, increase the circulation of money, create markets for farms and factories, and assure prosperity and contented homes.

I found this text during a Goat Island workshop, on a research visit to the Elks Memorial Building at the corner of Diversey and Sheridan in Chicago. It was one of a series of texts, images, sounds, and associations collected on the trip which later served as a resource for a collaborative performance. Instructions for collecting materials on that research trip

1 The spaced solidus marks the transition from one author-reader to the next. The authors-readers progressed in the order, determined by chance, in which their names are listed.

included finding: 1. a gigantic detail; and 2. an echo from two different constructional forms, examples being a wall/painting – or ornament/furniture.

Friends unfamiliar with Goat Island's performances ask me what they do, and I tell them: they use text, but not to tell a standard theatrical narrative or story; and they use movement, though it's not what you would expect by the term 'dance'. And combining those texts and movements creates something beyond those individual components of text and movement, and the best word we have for that is 'performance'.

Bryan has said, 'we practise creative research and assembly'. Lin sees 'research as an agent from the outside that transforms the material within; that brings nutrients to the digestion of our personal, individual experiences'.

Goat Island's performance work is developed collaboratively, a model also adopted when teaching their workshops. Divisions between individuals, and ideas of authorship are blurred – through this we see that the creative material connects to others, and is completed by them. The emphasis is on process, systems, structure, research tools for creation. Use what is around you, approach it with fresh eyes and ears: use the other workshop participants, Goat Island, the room you're in, the building, the city – other bodies. Use your memory as a resource – mental recall, body recall – not as route to nostalgia or therapy, not necessarily to tell your story, but to tell a wider narrative which reveals the extent to which your body already contains a wider narrative. Critical evaluation is transformed into the need to respond creatively. The work exists in the moment, vital, perhaps not yet even assimilated or understood by the artists who made it. Give up what seems important to you; it's not yours. Think formally and then thematically. Not analysing material to find its meaning, but accumulating material, finding unexpected connections.

We are already participating in a Goat Island workshop. Collaborating through words, sounds, touch, texture, viewing, thinking. The material is there to be received, processed, transformed. Keep a journal observing the incidence of the colour yellow. Memorize the street names between Monroe and Belmont: how many streets is that? – the geography traversed almost daily, let's look at this a different way.

And in ten years you will find yourself living in San Francisco, writing a letter which says: 'CJ refuses to believe in the existence of the absolute. I have found it.' And you will mail this letter to the person who, ten years earlier, wore your left black leather glove at the same time you wore your right black leather glove.

This is not everything I have to say, but this is all the time / for all we've experienced together. I would like to review a few thoughts now;

lessons if you will. There are seven of them that I thought of specifically as it pertains to collaboration.

1   Remember other people

Love them, hate them, give them gifts, steal their ideas, but focus on others to get out of yourself. These other people will be your co-workers of course but also your audience and also those who have nothing to do with you or your art or your lifestyle. By all this, we mean, remember that there are people who live outside the art world. And we like to remember these because there is more to life than art. And we like to remember these because there is hunger and injustice outside. And we like to remember these because we want to communicate with other worlds of thought.

If you have someone that you can work with, make a commitment and work through the differences. Make a commitment to supplement the gaps with your own contributions. Pay no attention to those who will tell you not to work with your friends. It is an insurmountable work to be an artist. It is shallow to rely on your own energy. Ideas like to be cross-fertilized. The bonding that happens between artists working together produces an integrity that reads into the work … is visible in the work … communicates to the audience and viewer.

2   Beware of brilliance

Creativity and genius will only take you so far. They might be of little importance. Beware of these gifts if you have them. Beware of these gifts if you see them in those you collaborate with. Look for a sense of humour. Look for conflict-resolution skills, forgiveness, the ability to listen, the ability to place faith in other people's fragmented ideas, a comfortability with failure, a disciplined nature and a love of work.

3   Make small plans

Temper your big dreams. Dream the smallest thing you can think of and try to perfect that. It's good to have one tiny perfect thing in your history. This is not a small challenge – there are infinite details to perfect in a small venture and the changes force themselves in, expanding the vision. I feel that my eyes have become sharper in seeing small things since I have been working with Goat Island. As a child I studied in a one-room schoolhouse and the first word I learned to read was 'LOOK'. My vision for a classroom would be an empty room save for a table, a chair and a microscope.

4   Value the work of your hands and body

This physical body is the meeting place of worlds. Spiritual, social, political, emotional, intellectual worlds are all interpreted through this physical body. When we work with our hands and body to create art or simply to project an idea from within, we imprint the product with a sweat signature, the glisten and odour which only the physical body can produce. These are the by-products of the meeting of worlds through the physical body. It is visible evidence of the work and effort to move from conception to production. Our bodies are both art elements and tools that communicate intuitively.

5   Work slowly

This follows quickly after the last lesson about the physical body. It takes lots of time to work by hand, but this time input is a distinctive trade mark. The Old World craftspeople made things. We think they are valuable not because of their content but because of the time signature of the work. Their bodies were not more capable than ours to join wood or carve stone or create paintings or make dances; in fact, it is possible that the physical body is more capable today than it was hundreds of years ago. But a possible advantage the Old World did have was a different concept of time. Perhaps they were more at ease with the passage of time. It was acceptable for them to take years to finish a work of art. We would advise you to look for long periods of time at your project. Maybe put it away, forget about it, bring it back years later, finish it after you have become a different person.

6   Learn to say no

This follows quickly after the last lesson about working slowly. If you work slowly you will not have time for every project that will be presented to you so you will pass up creative opportunities. It's easier to say no when you are older, but while you are still young you might not have many opportunities of a lifetime being offered to you and it will be hard for you to say no. But I think the chance of a lifetime comes quite frequently to those who are looking. If you follow this advice you will definitely regret having said no to some great opportunity and you will learn to live with that regret, but, in return, you will have time.

7 Be thankful for your fears

Add this to the others that have come / the day is still beginning.
Never take the same route, always vary your path.
Don't write with a slow pen – get one that flows well.

See as a new eye, as a novice, as someone who isn't jaded by fixed notions.
Invent seven ways to exit your chair.
Stand with the smile of a sad person.
Mark the place where your soul lives. Breath out through the nose like my grandmother's labored breathing. Life was heavy and hard and she lived long and did not believe she would die, no not that way.

She said: *With my arms I don't think I could touch the sky.*

Dive a hundred times into a harbour.
Fall into the grip of another.
Perform a whirling dance to purge the toxic spider venom.

Listen to me:

I heard the creaking rope of a rope bridge and the crashing of the ocean waves 100 feet below. I heard a thousand stones moved by a hundred feet grinding against each other like the gnashing of monumental teeth against mountainous bones. I saw a man climbing muddy down a rocky mountainside on hands and heels dragging his bottom along the slippery wet stones. I heard another man say 'He's trying to get a bit of punishment for all his wrongdoing.'

Move in place as seven body parts step in the same spot at least twice before you can make a new footprint. Breathe only once every fourteen moves.

All that my heart longs for, may you achieve, and be my accomplice.

Get your writing materials ready. Close your eyes.
Adjust your body so that you are sitting comfortably.
Take a deep breath. Let your shoulders relax.
Let your forehead relax.

I forgive you all the endless hours you were away.

Coming apart at the seams, I need to get a hold on things in my brain. There's a building coming down across the street. Men are turning the bricks and mortar to a fine silt with a huge machine and the dust shoots out into a pile.

Meanwhile in 'the building where I live the roof leaks' and the landlord would not like to fix it. There are buckets in the attic that have to be emptied and when they are not, they overflow. The water pools around the ceiling fan. Yellow marks show where the rain went. Please, oh please, don't make me climb that rickety ladder to the attic. Don't make me lift down that bucket to empty its dirty, leaky roof water.

The dust is everywhere and settling in my room.

But when, from a long distant past, nothing subsists, after the people are dead, after the things are broken and scattered, taste and smell alone more fragile, more faithful, remain poised a long time, like souls, remembering, waiting, hoping, amid the ruins of all the rest; hear unflinchingly in the tiny and almost imperceptible drop of their essence the vast structure of recollection.

Memorize to perform. Perform to remember.

When is the sky lavender and the sea slate hard and flat and not much like water?
In the mornings the sky over the lake is white or pale blue and the water like metal deflecting the sun.
In the afternoon and early evening the sky and water are shimmery shades of perfect blue.
In bad weather it is all a mud grey with the cold and stormy.
What time is it when the sky is lavender and the sea slate, hard as a piece of rock and twice as silent?

You are probably wondering / how does one come to or reach this place of a young practitioner? I still consider myself a young practitioner, and am now trying to decide when writing this letter, with the thoughts that are in my head of when one enters this transition. What is the counterpoint of a practising artist to that of the training or discipline one enters into to reach this certain place?

In 1994, I graduated from art school but previously to this time I was within the guise of preparing, preparing to be where I can situate myself now.

In the context of background, we are informing ourselves through what we have learnt along the many interruptions and decisions we have reached until the point at which we can be decisive to be a practitioner, within the particular field of the arts we have chosen.

I am still at this point of preparing now, paying close attention to all the details and information that encircles me. I still have a desire and need to learn what is placed in front of myself and others around.

In an exercise on departure during a Goat Island workshop last summer, I was given a white sheet of paper from a participant with a single word written on it. The word was openness. We asked each participant to take the single words given to them as a gesture of a gift to take with them, and possibly guide and incorporate into their lives throughout the year.

Openness is now bluetacked onto the wall next to my work desk at home. This single word I have taken into and incorporated into my daily life both private and public.

The act of receiving, and the acceptance of a gift, is an important philosophy I adhere to, especially in the practice of one's artwork. Through receiving, one can attach many different levels, how to be influenced, to take on others' thoughts as presents and reinterrupt into your mind and body. Once the digestion of the gift has been articulated in oneself then we begin to understand the nature and the power of sharing. Taking forward the information given. This idea of ownership becomes a wider participation, and one of interaction and creativity with others.

Roger Bourke, conceptual installation artist and teacher on my art degree course, once told me in a tutorial to firstly stop, then look and most importantly listen and be patient with your work. Do not rush, allow us the viewer to see what you are making. Be confident and allow the material to come to you, begin to see with different eyes and learn the value of listening, the silence of yourself and others.

In hearing these words of guidance it allowed for confidence to build. The display and act of mentoring and listening is a large part of my teaching and arts practice. To create a space where seeing and hearing is an integral and pivotal role in how to be understood and acknowledged. As a young practitioner it is your decision whom you wish to take from and be influenced by. Choose wisely. Identify possible situations you wouldn't normally come into contact with. Allow for a great deal of care and in return its own saturation to take you forward in confidence and articulation.

Be open to new discoveries. Be excited by the many languages you are able to learn and create / you understand who you are.

You understand who you could be.

You understand the gap between the two.

Sometimes, you close the gap.

You become who you might be.

You experience this for a moment.

What if we call that moment: 'the classroom'?

I am talking nonsense, I know.

But I have had enough of the rules.

How straight the path, and how strict.

This you must do; this you must not.

That explains why we repeat the same thing over and over again.

Why we see so many animated features starring heroic mice.

Ask yourself in the stillest hour of your night, will that ever be your homework?

Or might this be your homework?

(1) Describe the largest thing.

(2) Describe the difference between green and yellow.

(3) Describe something rough.

(4) What is 62° F?

(5) What weighs four pounds six ounces?

(6) What is shaped like a hand?

(7) What can you lift?

(8) What is the opposite of music?

(9) Describe a perfume.

(10) Describe a delicacy.

(11) What unbalances?

Take as much time as you need.

Strain the machine.

Never think yourself singular.

Absorb every experience that comes your way fearlessly.

Don't labour under the burden of importance.

Don't use up all your energy chasing the dollar.

There are children in America who haven't learned how to play.

They sit immobilized.

There they go, strapped into cars, into video games, approaching their imprisonable years.

The municipality has removed their sidewalks.

Concentrate.

Do one thing at a time.

Never grow tired.

Because what if we call that moment: 'the performance'?

I saw a dance, or a comedy.

It was an act, people I did not know, doing things I did not understand.

Yet I felt I knew them, and I felt I understood.

And as I left the theatre – I was exactly as old as you are now – I saw everything reel, as one does when one falls from a horse or bicycle, and I asked myself whether there was not an existence altogether different from the one I knew, in direct contradiction to it, but itself the real one, which, being suddenly revealed to me, filled me with that hesitation which sculptors, in representing the Last Judgement, have given to the awakened dead who find themselves at the gates of the next world.

I knew then that I had a place, and that I had found it.

I will love the experience longer than the rest because I have taken longer to get to love it.

You must forgive me … I have been unwell all this time.
I am not yet well, writing comes hard to me, and so you must take these few
lines for more.
My hand is tired.
I think of you often, and with such concentrated wishes that that in itself
really ought to help you somehow.

Whether this letter can really be a help, I often doubt.
But what if we call that moment: the right now?
Prepare ourselves not for the world as it is, but for the world as it might
become.

In this preparation, we experience this world as it becomes that one,
for a moment.
For now / I cannot speak without hearing your voice. Your voice sits
inside my voice and then again your voice sits outside my voice. Here is
my voice. I exist. But I exist does not come before we exist. You switch on
twelve mechanical birds, start them chirping, read me directions to a
ghost town while a woman walks by in a grass dress.
You kick my imagination into the air like a particle of dust and it floats.
But it's airborne with your imagination. Eventually, the two settle
together on the floor, indistinguishable.

I cannot teach without you teaching me.

I will tell you what I've been thinking lately. And listen for your
response carried by lines of air. I have been thinking

One does not always want to be thinking in the future, if as sometimes hap-
pens, one is living in the present.

At twenty, I expected in the coming years to live the life of an artist.
Having had artist friends in high school who jumped chain-linked fences
to swim in swimming pools late at night when the gates were locked while
I was trying unsuccessfully to fake an injury to remove myself from the
agony of cheerleading at night games; and having painted paintings in a
college art studio with skylights, where I spent afternoons discussing my
paintings with Professor Thompson, who sat in the corner of the room
with a free-standing ashtray at his elbow, flicking a long-ashed cigarette
into it as he told me to observe the beauty when I turned my paintings
upside down and on their sides; having had these experiences I had a
pretty romantic idea of the life of an artist. I was not prepared for what
followed – researching pooper-scoopers, toys, and earplugs for a patent
office and delivering plate after plate of French toast to craving Los
Angeles customers, leaving only fractions of night-time to make art. I did
it by pooling my energy with others so that together we had enough
usable heat to make a performance. But then, I saw the work of Pina
Bausch, Tadeus Kantor, and Tadashi Suzuki. I needed to work harder,

much harder. These artists did not stop where I stopped. They kept moving. And they ran so far that the distance covered in their performances, caught me up and overtook me. The only way I could make work of this distance was by taking time. I moved to Chicago and found collaborators who were not in a hurry. I rested in each moment with the process and the moments accumulated. It was almost mundane. Mundane in the sense of a plodding ordinariness, a daily step taking of one and a half to two years, to make a work. But also mundane in the sense of seventeenth-century astrology when the word pertained to the horizon – that visible line of the in-between; between the two, of time to come and time elapsed. The final performances, when finished, had a rigour I liked. No one told me about this methodical, caught-in-the-moment beauty.

All you need now is to stand at the window and let your rhythmical sense open and shut, open and shut, boldly and freely, until one-thing melts in another, until taxis are dancing with the daffodils.

Yours, CJ, Bryan, Karen, Mark, Matthew and Lin

Sources

Sappho, *The Poems*, trans. Sasha Newborn (Santa Barbara: Bandana Books, 1993). *With my arms I don't think ...*, p. 42. *I forgive you all the endless hours ...*, p. 27. *All that my heart longs for may you achieve ...*, p. 15.

Virginia Woolf, 'A Letter to a Young Poet', in *The Virginia Woolf Reader*, ed. Mitchell A. Leaska (San Diego, New York and London: Harcourt Brace & Company, 1984). 'I am talking nonsense, I know', p. 271. 'And look at their rules! How straight the path is for them, and how strict! This you must do; this you must not. That explains why they repeat the same thing over and over again', p. 262. 'Straining the machine', p. 269. 'Never think yourself singular', p. 263. 'To absorb every experience that comes your way fearlessly', p. 271. *One does not always want to be thinking in the future ...*, p. 272. *All you need now is to stand at the window ...*, p. 271.

Rainer Maria Rilke, *Letters to a Young Poet*, trans. M. D. Herter Norton (New York and London: W. W. Norton and Company, 1962). '... ask yourself in the stillest hour of your night ...', pp. 18–19. 'You must forgive me ... I have been unwell all this time. But I am not yet well, writing comes hard to me, and so you must take these few lines for more', p. 23. 'My hand is tired', p. 73. 'I think of you often, and with such concentrated wishes that that in itself really ought to help you somehow. Whether this letter can really be a help, I often doubt', p. 73.

Marcel Proust, *In Search of Lost Time Part One: Swann's Way*, trans. C. K. Scott Moncrieff and Terence Kimartin, revised by D. J. Enright (New York: Random House [Modern Library Paperback Edition], 1998). *But when, from a long distant past nothing subsists ...*, pp. 63–4.

Marcel Proust, *In Search of Lost Time Part One: Within a Budding Grove*, trans. C. K. Scott Moncrieff and Terence Kimartin, revised by D. J. Enright (New York: Random House [Modern Library Paperback Edition], 1998). 'I saw everything reel, as one does when one falls from a horse, and I asked myself whether there was not an existence altogether different from the one I knew, in direct contradiction to it, but itself the real one, which, being suddenly revealed to me, filled me with that hesitation which sculptors, in representing the Last Judgment, have given to the awakened dead who find themselves at the gates of the next world', pp. 98–9. 'And we shall love it longer than the rest because we have taken longer to get to love it,' p. 142.

V

Afterword

Theatre in crisis?
Lluís Pasqual. Trans by Lisa Domjan, Caridad Svich
and Maria M. Delgado

Lluís Pasqual is co-founder of Barcelona's Teatre Lliure. He has been artistic director of Madrid's Centro Dramático Nacional (1983–89) where his productions included García Lorca's *El público* (*The Public*) (1986) and *Comedia sin título* (*Play Without a Title*) (1989). As Artistic Director of the Odéon Théâtre de l'Europe, where he succeeded Strehler in 1990, his stagings included Genet's *Le Balcon* (1991), Lope de Vega's *Le Chevalier d'Olmeido* (also Avignon Festival, 1992), and Bernard-Marie Koltes' *Roberto Zucco* (a co-production with the Maly Dramatic Theatre, St Petersburg, 1994). His most recent work for the Teatre Lliure includes Beckett's *Waiting for Godot* (1999) and Chekhov's *The Cherry Orchard* (2000). Pasqual's opera productions include *L'Enlèvement au Sérail* (Théâtre du Châtelet, Paris, 1991) and *La Traviata* (Salzburg Festival, 1995).

At the beginning of the seventeenth century, the great Spanish playwright and poet, Lope de Vega in his 'El arte nuevo de hacer comedias en este tiempo' (The New Art of Writing Plays in Our Time) was already mentioning the word 'crisis'. He applied this term to theatrical productions and to the relationship that exists between the theatre and its audience and vice versa. In his discourse, Lope does not go into too much detail since, feeling somewhat exasperated, and probably in a moment of acute insight and disquiet, he states that:

> since the people pay for them [i.e. plays] it is fitting to address them in an idiotic way to give them pleasure.[1]

It would seem that little has changed in just over three centuries given that the word 'crisis' reappears time and time again as part of the regular vocabulary we use in our daily reflections when we think about 'theatre'.

Apart from the prophets of doom who predict the death of theatre for increasingly urgent reasons, the word 'crisis' is not always used in the same way, nor does it always carry the same meaning. I would say that this word might even have a positive aspect, that is, if we take the trouble to approach theatre by first of all dealing with that which makes it most truly unique: its ephemeral character. This fundamental fact, which often seems to be neglected in discussions about the form, is the constant element which makes theatre what it has been over the centuries, and what it undoubtedly is, or seeks to be: a sometimes stunning and blinding, at other times pale and hazy, image of society and of the individuals who are part of it. However, it is a somewhat complex issue, and we should perhaps, first of all, disentangle a few of the threads so that we can see things more clearly – the familiar, who we are and where we are.

So, if we consider the ephemeral nature of the theatre, it will appear to us to be an artistic practice that has more in common with gastronomy than with painting, with its entirely craftsmanlike processes of conception and production. This is due to the nature of its original experience, which has little to do with what is referred to as the 'market' or 'cultural industries'. These terms, coined in recent years, have been shamefully applied, particularly by so-called cultural producers or politicians, with scarcely any recourse to their ideological or political origins. These individuals have applied the sacred and unique laws of market economy or neo-liberalism to any transaction, collective experience or exchange between human beings. In so doing, they have also become arrogant and unduly proud, due to the 'success' (?) of their theories after the proclaimed death of other ideologies and the universal acceptance of 'globalization' or 'internationalization'. Some have dangerously called this 'original thought'.

---

1 Félix Lope de Vega Carpio, 'New Art of Making Comedies at the Present Time: addressed to the Academy of Madrid', in *Sources of Dramatic Theory Vol. 1. Plato to Congreve*, ed. Michael J. Sidnell (Cambridge: Cambridge University Press, 1991), p. 184. The Spanish reads 'porque como las paga el vulgo es justo/hablarle en necio para darle gusto'.

The first thing we should do, after moving swiftly on from Lope de Vega to the present day, is to accept that the word 'crisis' remains integral to the very nature of theatre, and generates its most positive and unique elements. The history of mankind and the history of art, in this case of theatre, have always run in parallel. (How could it be otherwise when artistic expression reflects how people relate to one another and how systems of behaviour are established within a community?) This same history of mankind, whether expressed well or badly, illuminates patterns of behaviour, which, when they are represented in a fresh or new light, are able to replace others which are in decline or obsolete, and no longer correspond to the wishes of that community. To paraphrase Jean Genet, the author who perhaps best expressed this notion, when a gesture becomes empty, becomes frozen, and our life proves to be a repetition of empty gestures and moribund attitudes which have no meaning or purpose; that is to say, they are lifeless. Theatre will be the reflection, or the shadow of that empty repetition, and will be composed of similarly vacuous gestures. On the other hand, if any human community, either consciously or unconsciously, begins to set the wheels of renewal in motion, from adaptation of the 'gesture' to a formulation of content which responds to specific wishes or purposes, either sensed or dreamed, of the community, the theatre produced by that community will at the same time possess that same new strength, and will be able to breathe life, not death, into the gestures which accompany its liturgy of celebration.

At the same time that we destroy the forms that are no longer of any use to us, we need, above all, to create new ones which correspond to the way we feel and relate to our present. This impulse is found at the beginning of what we call 'life'. And also of what we call theatre. Both are apparently governed by the same principles. The aim of theatre is to create, recreate and reproduce moments of autonomous life. For this reason many people, in the history of humanity, have been able to say that life is theatre. If we are all really actors and life is a theatre, then it is not really worth our continuing to do it. This is the first question we should ask ourselves: why do theatre? However, if we accept that life in the theatre is more 'legible', we can begin to understand that it is both the same and, yet, at the same time different. From there, we can begin to feel the need: the need for the existence of theatre as an aspect of human creation where all elements of life are involved, but in poetic concentration, which thus makes our lives, in turn, more comprehensible.

At the end of the last millennium, the illusion of globalization has, above all, increased the need for knowledge of the 'other', in order to strip it of its 'virtual' reality. We have learned to view the other through the extraordinary and unreal eye of the cinema, or more unreal still, through advertising or graphic imagery.

The Western world now seems to have understood that miscegenation – the mixing of races and consequently that of cultures and their ways of thinking – is a good and positive thing. It also seems to be prepared to put this new-found understanding into practice. This knowledge of the other creates an immediate problem. Everywhere, from conferences on anthropology to great art exhibitions, we are obsessing over the problem of otherness in the search for the logical concatenation, which tells us that the more we know about someone, the more we will be able to understand them and indeed ourselves. It will therefore be easier and more beneficial to love them, and loving means sharing. In this way the relationship between human beings would attain new heights of the evolution to which mankind aspires.

Individuals go in search of the creation of a greater social being because they need to have contact with others. It is, however, impossible for one person to truly experience the feelings of another. No one can feel how another person feels. And yet, we need to have some knowledge of certain feelings experienced by others in order to recognize them within ourselves. This is necessary in order to exorcize one of the greatest fears known to humanity: loneliness.

Broadly speaking, people have always chosen to take one of two possible routes to escape from themselves through exercising the spirit or the imagination: religion or art (which may be seen as another form of religion). But artistic practice adds, to the irrationality of the two possible routes, an intelligent and even hedonistic component, since it is not based on faith, but on something slightly less metaphysical: complicity.

Out of this human need – which is one of life's impulses – comes theatre as a way of exorcizing fears, of sharing the feeling of that exorcism, in a way that is simultaneously ritualistic and playful. Theatre is a strange art in that it combines knowledge with pleasure for both individuals and groups.

One of the benefits globalization has brought us, which for the time being at least, is essentially a commercial concept, has been the application of the neo-liberal doctrine to many rules of human behaviour.

The practice of art in the West is above all based on difference and on the recognition of that difference, so that each performer, even if they belong to a group and share their common heritage, will be unique, distinct and consequently enriching. However, the performer at the end of the twentieth century suffers from a serious problem of identity and credibility. Our relationship with the audience, the mirror effect, the actor as the reflected image of the person watching him in all his complexity, suffers from the same symptoms of rigidity that we can historically sense in late nineteenth-century theatre. This was before the great movement took place, which at its zenith resulted in the purity of Chekhov's theatre and the systematization and essentialization of the art of the performer, developed by Stanislavsky, that has marked the entire history of twentieth-century performance.

We no longer represent the audience. The audience at the end of the century is without doubt far more diverse, fragmented and fickle, as is our society in the wake of the explosion which followed the great movements of integration such as religion, ideologies and even psychoanalysis. We are, to paraphrase Jean Genet once again, going through a phase where-upon we are caught in the repetition of gestures, of lifelessness. As such, *the audience does not believe in us*; and if they do, they do so with their own equally dead and mechanical gestures.

We need to build the theatre of the future out of all these elements, that is to say, out of our present, and we must do this, just as the theatre has always done, *against the tide of popular opinion.*

Theatre should discuss difference and the right to be different, show-ing, as it always has, the uniqueness of human behaviour, as opposed to a system of globalization that seeks a certain uniformity from human beings. In order for the former to be achieved, theatre will surely need to free itself from that frozen and dead gesture of universality – a legacy from the great theatre of twenty or thirty years ago – and return to its more immediate setting, to strengthen the necessary connection with the community that generates it, in order to acquire true universality. As the prize-winning Québecois playwright Michel Tremblay reminded us this year in his message to celebrate World Theatre Day, 'salvation, at the beginning of this third millennium will come before those little voices which are raised everywhere to describe injustice … Chekhov is not universal because he is Russian but because he possesses the genius to describe the Russian soul, something all human beings can identify with'.

Faced with a system of human behaviour and a concept of time based on the tenets of a market economy (wherein human relationships are reduced to a 'deal', an idea already denounced poetically in a warning by French playwright Bernard-Marie Koltès) we must defend theatre's ephemeral and artisan nature. Working within that framework, theatre is necessarily non-productive and useless, because, by its very nature, it refuses to adhere to the concept of industry which even such noble arts as music and film are able and willing to make themselves a part of.

However, any movement in this regard brings with it a gaze which can only be described as 'political', and an attitude that, if the word was not so overused, one could define as 'compromised'.

For decades, and possibly as a reaction to a definite 'sectorization' of art, we have spoken of aesthetic compromise. However, now, some years later, it is supposed that this aesthetic compromise is found at the very heart of the artist's work. It is not the artist who has a story to tell, but it is he or she who finds the means of telling it. However, this aesthetic compromise is not enough. We will need, or rather we now need, to renew an ethical compromise with our society, whose voice we echo, whose feelings, ignored by the monotone of television, we want to portray. This is required in order to understand that as well as being violent, greedy and naive, mankind is far richer and more contradictory. We must remember that, although a possibly virtual wish to transcend time and space exists, emotions continue to be produced at the rhythm of the human body's internal metronome: the heart.

Furthermore, theatre allows us to confront these emotions one human being to another. And theatre must do this with a spiritually vigorous silence in the face of so much cultural noise. If we use poetry as an example, theatre is like a small river which is both resolute and constant, nourishing its bed with a hushed and beneficial water. We must do this so that our communities feel they need theatre again, and thus, we will be able to regain the conviction that theatre as a practice is for the collective good of the community as well as for the good of the art itself. Just as science continues to enlighten us with new theories and opinions about our very existence, old and new questions about the art (questions to which we have no answers) will continue to be posed by each new generation of practitioners.

'Everything that dies, dies for ever', states the great Catalan poet Miquel Martí i Pol. I think our generation bears the great responsibility of no longer having to feed the farcical face of what has become the theatre corpse. We must abolish the spectacle of a society that has turned itself into a 'show society', and instead trust its fellow citizens again to repair what has been a betrayal of the human condition. We must remember that theatre is a collective art (whether the audience is in solidarity with the art which is being made or not). Theatre is not a 'ludic', contemplative activity, and much less, a product offered simply for pure consumption. We are indeed in crisis, and it is a healthy, distressing, constant crisis because we will use this crisis to create theatre. However, beware! Even crisis can turn into a frozen gesture, an attitude that can resemble a badly performed tango, which is simply eternally plaintive. In order for real theatre to be created and produced, decisions must be made, and brave decisions at that, for if we are to alter the course of our current state of crisis, we must do so in the knowledge that tomorrow there will be another crisis, and it will be a new one, which is, after all, what keeps the theatre alive.

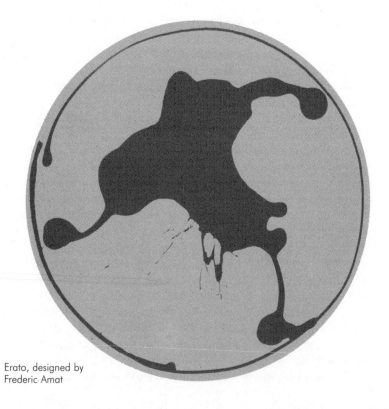

Erato, designed by
Frederic Amat

SELECT BIBLIOGRAPHY

Arendt, Hannah. *The Human Condition.* London and Chicago: University of Chicago Press, 1958.

Artaud, Antonin. *The Theater and Its Double,* trans. Mary Caroline Richards. New York: Grove Press, 1958.

Artaud, Antonin. *The Theatre and Its Double,* trans. Victor Corti. London: John Calder, 1970.

Aristotle, Horace, Longinus. *Classical Literary Criticism,* trans. T.S. Dorsch. Harmondsworth: Penguin, 1965.

Auslander, Philip. *Liveness: Performance in a Mediatized Culture.* London and New York: Routledge, 1999.

Babcock, Barbara A. *The Reversible World: Symbolic Inversion in Art and Society.* Ithaca, NY: Cornell University Press, 1978.

Bakhtin, Mikhail. *Rabelais and His World,* trans. Helene Iswolsky. Cambridge, MA: MIT Press, 1968.

Barba, Eugenio. *Beyond the Floating Islands.* New York: Performing Arts Journal Publications, 1986.

Barker, Howard. *Arguments for a Theatre.* Manchester: Manchester University Press, 1993.

Barry, Sebastian. *The Steward of Christendom.* London: Methuen Drama, 1995.

Beckett, Samuel. *The Complete Dramatic Works.* London: Faber & Faber, 1986.

Bettelheim, Bruno. *The Uses of Enchantment.* New York: Knopf, 1976.

Blau, Herbert. *The Impossible Theater: A Manifesto.* London and New York: Collier-MacMillan, 1965.

Boal, Augusto. *Theatre of the Oppressed,* trans. Charles A. and Maria-Odilia Leal McBride. London: Pluto Press, 1979.

Bond, Edward. *Plays: One.* London: Methuen Drama, 1977.

Boon, Richard and Jane Plaistow, eds. *Theatre Matters: Performance and Culture on the World Stage.* Cambridge: Cambridge University Press: 1998.

Bradby, David, ed. *Bernard-Marie Koltès Plays: 1.* London: Methuen Drama, 1997.

Bradby, David, ed. *Michel Vinaver Plays: 2.* London: Methuen Drama, 1997.

Braun, Edwards, ed. *Meyerhold on Theatre.* London: Methuen, 1969.

Brenton, Howard. *The Romans in Britain*. London: Methuen Drama, 1980.

Brook, Peter. *The Empty Space*. Harmondsworth: Penguin, 1968.

Brustein, Robert. *Reimagining American Theatre*. New York: Hill & Wang, 1991.

Cavell, Stanley. *Disowning Knowledge*. Cambridge: Cambridge University Press, 1995.

Carlton, Eric. *War and Ideology*. London: Routledge, 1990.

Chekhov, Anton. *Chekhov: Plays*, trans. Elisaveta Fen. Harmondsworth: Penguin, 1954.

Churchill, Caryl. *Plays: 2*. London: Methuen Drama, 1996.

Churchill, Caryl. *Blue Heart*. London: Nick Hern Books, 1997.

Cole, Toby, ed. *Playwrights on Playwriting*. New York: Hill & Wang, 1961.

Cole, Toby and Helen Krich Chinoy, eds. *Directors on Directing: A Source Book of the Modern Theater*. New York: Macmillan, 1976.

Corthron, Kia. *Breath, Boom*. London: Methuen, 2000.

Daniels, Barry, ed. *Joe Chaikin & Sam Shepard: Letters and Texts 1972–1984*. New York: New American Library, 1989.

Delgado, Maria M., ed and trans. *Valle-Inclán Plays: One*. London: Methuen, 1993.

Delgado, Maria M. and Paul Heritage, eds. *In Contact with the Gods? Directors Talk Theatre*. Manchester: Manchester University Press, 1996.

Delgado, Maria M. and Caridad Svich, eds. *Conducting a Life: Reflections on the Theatre of Maria Irene Fornes*. Lyme, New Hampshire: Smith & Kraus, 1999.

Dillard, Annie. *The Writing Life*. New York: Harper & Row, 1989.

Edgar, David, ed. *State of Play*. London: Faber & Faber, 1999.

Ehn, Erik. 'Towards Big Cheap Theater', *Theater*, 24, No. 2, 1993, pp. 5–9.

Elyot, Kevin. *My Night with Reg*. London: Nick Hern Books, 1994.

Engelander, Rudy and Dragan Klaic, eds. *Shifting Gears: Reflections and Reports on the Contemporary Performing Arts*. Amsterdam: Theater Instituut Nederland, 1998.

Etchells, Tim. *Certain Fragments: Texts and Writings on Performance*. London and New York: Routledge, 1999.

Euripides. *Ion*, trans. W.S. Di Piero. New York and Oxford: Oxford University Press, 1996.

Feyder, Linda, ed. *Shattering the Myth: Plays by Hispanic Women*. Houston, TX: Arte Publico Press, 1992.

Foucault, Michel. *Ethics (Subjectivity and Truth), 1954–1988, Volume One*, ed. Paul Rabinow. New York: The New Press, 1997.

Frame, Janet. *An Angel at My Table*. Braziller, 1984.

Genet, Jean. *The Maids*, trans. Martin Crimp. London: Faber & Faber, 1999.

Gleick, James. *Chaos*. New York: Penguin, 1987.

Goethe, Johann Wolfgang von. *Goethe's Literary Essays*, ed. J.E. Spingarn. New York: Frederick Ungar Publishing, 1964.

Gómez-Peña, Guillermo. *Dangerous Border Crossings: The Artist Talks Back*. London and New York: Routledge, 2000.

Gottlieb, Vera and Colin Chambers, eds. *Theatre in a Cool Climate*. Charlbury: Amber Lane Press, 1999.

Goulish, Matthew. *39 Microlectures: In Proximity of Performance*. London and New York: Routledge, 2000.

Griffin, Susan. *A Chorus of Stones*. New York: Anchor/Doubleday, 1993.

Guénoun, Denis. *Le théâtre est-il nécessaire?* Paris: Circé, 1997.

Hare, David. *The Absence of War*. London: Faber & Faber, 1993.

Hart, Lynda, ed. *Making a Spectacle*. Ann Arbor, MI: University of Michigan Press, 1989.

Herr, Michael. *Dispatches*. New York: Knopf, 1968.

Hunter, Lynette. *Critiques of Knowing: Situated Textualities in Science, Computing and the Arts*. London and New York: Routledge, 1999.

Kane, Sarah. *Blasted & Phaedra's Love*. London: Methuen Drama, 1996.

Kershaw, Baz. *The Politics of Performance: Radical Theatre as Cultural Intervention*. London: Routledge, 1992.

Kershaw, Baz. *The Radical in Performance: Between Brecht and Baudrillard*. London and New York: Routledge, 1999.

Kustow, Michael. *Theatre@risk*. London: Methuen, 2000.

Landis, Paul, ed. *Six Plays by Corneille and Racine*. New York: The Modern Library, 1931.

Levitt, Helen. *A Way of Seeing*, with an essay by James Agee. Durham, NC and London: Duke University Press, 1965.

Marcus, Greil. *Invisible Republic: Bob Dylan's Basement Tapes*. New York: Henry Holt, 1998.

Marranca, Bonnie, ed. *American Dreams: The Imagination of Sam Shepard*. New York: Performing Arts Journal Publications, 1981.

Marranca, Bonnie. *Theatrewritings*. New York: Performing Arts Journal Publications, 1984.

Marranca, Bonnie, ed. *Plays for the End of the Century*. Baltimore, MD and London: Johns Hopkins University Press/PAJ Books, 1996.

Marranca, Bonnie and Gautam Dasgupta, eds. *Conversations on Art and Performance*. Baltimore, MD and London: Johns Hopkins University Press/PAJ Books, 1999.

Matura, Mustapha. *Six Plays*. London: Methuen Drama, 1992.

McGrath, John. *A Good Night Out. Popular Theatre: Audience, Class and Form*. London: Methuen, 1981.

McGrath, John. *The Bone Won't Break: On Theatre and Hope in Hard Times*. London: Methuen, 1990.

O'Connor, Flannery. *Mystery and Manners*, eds. Sally and Robert Fitzgerald. New York: Farrar, Straus & Giroux, 1961.

Ollman, Bertell. *Alienation: Marx's Conception of Man in Capitalist Society*, 2nd Edition. Cambridge: Cambridge University Press, 1976.

Perkins, Kathy A. and Roberto Uno. *Contemporary Plays by Women of Color*. London: Routledge, 1996.

Phelan, Peggy. *Unmarked: The Politics of Performance*. London and New York: Routledge, 1993.

Phelan, Peggy. *Mourning Sex: Performing Public Memories*. London and New York: Routledge, 1993.

Phelan, Peggy and Jill Lane, eds. *The Ends of Performance*. London and New York: New York University Press, 1998.

Potter, Dennis. *Seeing the Blossom*, with an introduction by Melvyn Bragg. London: Faber & Faber, 1994.

Ravenhill, Mark. *Shopping and F***ing*. London: Methuen Drama, 1996.

Ravenhill, Mark. *Some Explicit Polaroids*. London: Methuen, 1999.

Read, Alan. *Theatre and Everyday Life: The Ethics of Performance*. London: Routledge, 1993.

Read, Herbert. *Art and Industry: The Principles of Industrial Design*. London: Faber & Faber, 1953.

Read, Herbert. *Art and Society*. London: Faber & Faber, 1967.

Rilke, Rainer Maria. *Possibility of Being*, trans. J.B. Leishman. New York: New Directions, 1957.

Ruiz, Raul. *Poetics of Cinema*. Paris: Disvoir, 1985.

Rukeyser, Muriel. *The Life of Poetry*. New York: Current Books, 1949.

Said, Edward W. *Musical Elaborations*. London: Vintage, 1992.

Savran, David, ed. *The Wooster Group: Breaking the Rules, 1975–1985*. Ann Arbor, MI: University of Michigan Press, 1986.

Schechter, Joel. *Durov's Pig*. New York: Theatre Communications Group, 1985.

Simon, Alfred. *Le Théâtre à bout de souffle*. Paris: Editions du Seuil, 1979.

Sontag, Susan. *On Photography*. New York: Farrar, Straus & Giroux, 1977.

Sophocles. *The Theban Plays*, trans. E.F. Watling. Harmondsworth: Penguin, 1983.

Stanislavsky, Konstantin. *An Actor Prepares*, trans. Elizabeth Reynolds Hapgood. New York: Theatre Arts, 1936.

Strindberg, August. *The Chamber Plays*, trans. Evert Sprinchorn and Seabury Quinn, Jr. New York: E.P. Dutton & Co., 1962.

Sutcliffe, Tom. *Believing in Opera*. London: Faber & Faber, 1996.

Svich, Caridad and Maria Teresa Marrero, eds. *Out of the Fringe: Latino Theatre and*

Performance. New York: Theatre Communications Group, 2000.

Taylor, Gary. *Reinventing Shakespeare: A Cultural History from the Restoration to the Present*. London: Hogarth, 1989.

Verma, Jatinder, an interview with Graham Ley, 'Theatre of Migration and the Search for a Multicultural Aesthetic', *New Theatre Quarterly*, No. 52, 1997, pp. 349–71.

Washington, James M., ed. *A Testament of Hope: The Essential Speeches and Writings of Martin Luther King, Jr.* New York: HarperCollins, 1986.

Wellman, Mac. 'The Theatre of Good Intentions', *Performing Arts Journal*, 7, No. 3, 1984, pp. 59–70.

Welty, Eudora. *One Writer's Beginnings*. Cambridge, MA and London: Harvard University Press, 1983.

Willett, John, ed. *Brecht on Theatre*. New York: Hill and Wang, 1964.

Williams, Tennessee. *A Streetcar Named Desire*. London: Methuen Drama, 1990.

Wilson, August. 'The Ground on Which I Stand', *American Theatre*, 13, No. 7, September 1996, pp. 14–16, 71–4.

Wilson, August. *Seven Guitars*. New York: Plume, 1997.

Woolf, Virginia. *Moments of Being (Unpublished Autobiographical Writings)*, ed. Jeanne Schulkind. New York and London: Harcourt Brace, 1976.

INDEX